Mastering Microsoft Dynamics NAV 2016

The compilation of best skillset to harness Microsoft Dynamics NAV for Administrators, Consultants, and Developers

abindra Sah

BIRMINGHAM - MUMBAI

Mastering Microsoft Dynamics NAV 2016

First published: March 2017

Production reference: 1170317

Published by Packt Publishing Ltd.
Livery Place
35 Livery Street
Birmingham
B3 2PB, UK.
ISBN 978-1-78646-430-9

www.packtpub.com

Credits

Author

Rabindra Sah

Reviewer

Danilo Capuano

Commissioning Editor

Aaron Lazar

Acquisition Editor

Denim Pinto

Content Development Editor

Priyanka Mehta

Technical Editor

Dhiraj Chandanshive

Copy Editor

Stuti Srivastava

Project Coordinator

Vaidehi Sawant

Proofreader

Safis Editing

Indexer

Tejal Daruwale Soni

Graphics

Abhinash Sahu

Production Coordinator

Nilesh Mohite

About the Author

Rabindra Sah is a Microsoft Dynamics NAV technology specialist. He started his career as a Dynamics NAV consultant in the year 2011 with a Microsoft gold partner company in Nepal, where he fortified his functional skillset and evolved as a versatile Dynamics NAV professional. His hunger to solve problems and positive communication skills helped him flourish as an all-round consultant. His deep understanding of the Dynamics NAV system allowed him to successfully implement the company's first international project, which was funded by International Red Cross and Red Crescent Society. He has been a part of more than 12 full-phase Dynamics NAV projects and has earned several appraisal certificates from the clients and donor organizations for his extraordinary dedication and co-ordination.

Rabindra is a technology enthusiast and quick learner of new technologies, which has allowed him get along with the latest Microsoft releases and related technologies. In addition to Dynamics NAV expertise, Rabindra also has a deep understanding of .NET technologies. Besides .NET, he also possesses a deep-level understanding of programming languages such as C and Java, which broadens his domain of competence. He believes that learning and sharing should go hand in hand, so, he is also an active member of online Microsoft communities, where he loves spending his time resolving the issues posted by other developers and end users. He is also an active blogger and loves to post problems and solutions that he comes across in his daily professional life.

To further improve his skills and better understand the evolving Dynamics NAV system, he recently took several on-campus courses, such as algorithms, design patterns, software engineering, and enterprise architecture, during his Masters in Computer Science at Maharishi University of Management in United States.

He is also an active volunteer item writer for Association of Dynamics Professionals for Microsoft Dynamics NAV Certification, where he participates in online meetings and contributes to the design of the certification examinations. He also creates materials for the examinations. Recently, he also got involved in the Microsoft Dynamics NAV courseware project lead by some of the best brains in the field.

He is currently working as a Senior Associate for Microsoft Dynamics NAV in RAND Group, a Microsoft gold partner company, in Texas, USA.

You can find him on LinkedIn at https://www.linkedin.com/in/rabindrasah.

I am very grateful to God and to everyone who kept me motivated and encouraged me throughout the process of this book.

First of all, a special thanks to my parents--my mom, Pramila Sah, and my papa, Shatrughan Sah; my grandpa, Sri Narayan Sah; my family, Om Shankar Sah, Govind Sah, Umida, and Shaanvi; other family members, Bipin, Navin, Meena, Uday Shankar, Hari Shankar, and Punita; my special friend Anjani, and my close friends Rohit, Navin, Shamid, and Pavan, who always stood behind me and allowed me to spend a lot of time apart from them.

A big thanks to Robert Sherlock, Donnita Bass, Thu Tran, and Anatoly Sinyavin for helping me grow as a better professional these past years.

I would also like to thank my university, Maharishi University of Management, and all the professors there who helped me fortify my technical skills and gain enough confidence to aim for higher goals.

I would like to extend my thanks to the editors and all the members at Packt who directly or indirectly helped me on this book, especially, Priyanka, Denim, and, last but not least, Danilo Capuano.

About the Reviewer

Danilo Capuano is a senior Software Engineer with over 10 years industry experience. He lives in Naples, Italy, where he earned a degree in Computer Science. He currently works as a Solution Architect on Microsoft Dynamics 365 NAV in an IT company.

You can contact him on his official website, http://www.capuanodanilo.com/, or find him on Twitter at @capuanodanilo.

He has reviewed the books, *Microsoft Dynamics NAV 7 Programming Cookbook*, *Microsoft Dynamics NAV 2013 Application Design*, and *Programming Microsoft Dynamics NAV 2015*, all by Packt.

www.PacktPub.com

For support files and downloads related to your book, please visit `www.PacktPub.com`.

Did you know that Packt offers eBook versions of every book published, with PDF and ePub files available? You can upgrade to the eBook version at `www.PacktPub.com` and as a print book customer, you are entitled to a discount on the eBook copy. Get in touch with us at `service@packtpub.com` for more details.

At `www.PacktPub.com`, you can also read a collection of free technical articles, sign up for a range of free newsletters and receive exclusive discounts and offers on Packt books and eBooks.

`https://www.packtpub.com/mapt`

Get the most in-demand software skills with Mapt. Mapt gives you full access to all Packt books and video courses, as well as industry-leading tools to help you plan your personal development and advance your career.

Why subscribe?

- Fully searchable across every book published by Packt
- Copy and paste, print, and bookmark content
- On demand and accessible via a web browser

Customer Feedback

Thanks for purchasing this Packt book. At Packt, quality is at the heart of our editorial process. To help us improve, please leave us an honest review on this book's Amazon page at https://www.amazon.com/dp/1786464306.

If you'd like to join our team of regular reviewers, you can e-mail us at customerreviews@packtpub.com. We award our regular reviewers with free eBooks and videos in exchange for their valuable feedback. Help us be relentless in improving our products!

Table of Contents

Preface

The goal of this book is to explain Microsoft Dynamics NAV 2016 from the root level and understand the different capabilities of the system. The book will give you a deep understanding of the system, which will help you to improve your activities such as development, implementation, testing, version control, and maintenance. The book heavily focuses on the methods for improving the performance of the system so as to minimize the cost on one hand and improve the productivity and user experience on the other. The book mostly covers real-life scenarios and presents solution in simplified manner to engage all kind of readers.

After reading this book, you will understand the different features, techniques, and technologies that directly impact on the implementation of the system. The book focuses on reducing the time and increasing the productivity of developers, consultants, and administrators and provides the ways to handle the process in a standard fashion.

What this book covers

Chapter 1, *Microsoft Dynamics NAV Installation*, explains about the installation process of Microsoft Dynamics NAV 2016 in detail. It mostly covers the cloud technologies and how NAV can be deployed on cloud. The chapter also explains in detail how PowerShell can be better utilized to make life easier

Chapter 2, *Upgraded Features and Configurations in Dynamics NAV 2016*, helps you understand the different components that take part in configuration processes. The chapter covers most of the latest features and their implications in Microsoft Dynamics NAV 2016. You will get an overview on design pattern and their significance to the system.

Chapter 3, *The C/AL and VB Programming*, explains the core concept of coding with the C/AL programming language and the compilation details. You will get some hands-on practice with VB programming if you follow the contents carefully. The main intention of this chapter is not to provide the details about the functions and features, but provide the core concept which will boost the concept of computer programming with respect to C/Side Development Environment. This chapter is highly recommended, not only for technical professionals, but also for non-technical readers.

Chapter 4, *Testing and Debugging*, shows you how to find out the testing technique in Microsoft Dynamics NAV 2016. Here you will also learn how to write your own test code and test it yourself. In addition to the self-generated unit test, we will examine the test codeunit provided by Microsoft which is more than 600 in count. You will learn how they can be used to test the standard process. This chapter will discuss the core concept of testing with respect to the Dynamics NAV system.

Chapter 5, *Design and Development Considerations*, explains the design and development considerations of Microsoft Dynamics NAV. Most consultants do not understand the importance of design considerations and they end up generating a weak design, and eventually an inefficient system. This chapter is intended to provide a broad perspective on how to approach any design or design operation, and how to convert that design to the actual development. The chapter will also clarify the difference between customization and development. It also explains how you can understand the dataflow using a special feature called test posting.

Chapter 6, *Version Control and Code Management*, covers totally new concept of version control, which is somewhat new to the Dynamics NAV world. For most experienced consultants and developers who have strong C# and other programming experience, this concept might not be that new, but those who have always worked with the NAV system might perceive this as being new. You will learn the most basic ways to harness some of the functionality of version control in Dynamics NAV. For some, it might look like a lengthy process to actually implement, but once you understand the core concepts, you will love it and implement it in team projects in particular. In this chapter, you will also understand the pattern that can be used while branching and how it can be of great importance while using version control.

Chapter 7, *Tuning Up the NAV System*, shows how you can avoid designing a low performing system in the first place, and secondly you will observe how you can better optimize low performing system. It is essential to understand the core of the system and its performance in standard given condition so that we can easily sense any slowdown in the system.

Chapter 8, *Security in Dynamics NAV 2016*, explains all about security aspects of the Microsoft Dynamics NAV system. You will be able to consider some of the important contents of security system. You will also understand how to prevent your system from different malicious logics and how to reduce the risk of security failures. It is highly recommended for everyone, especially administrators, to understand the concepts in this chapter in order to provide a robust defensive environment to the Microsoft Dynamics NAV.

Chapter 9, *Upgrade and Migration*, explains about the modern upgrade process. You will also get an overview of the most optimal and efficient ways of upgrading process, which involve automating the processes, analyzing the time and effort, and understanding the core concept behind the upgrade project. You will also perceive the difference between the upgrade processes if carried out on different versions and how that might affect the project duration.

Chapter 10, *Interfacing NAV with Other Applications*, helps you understand the most important concept of integration with external systems. An interface is like a trade route through which the outside world can help your system grow. The best software has the most secure and powerful integration system so that it can be extended as per your requirements. Here you can learn all the concepts that can be used in Microsoft Dynamics NAV to make it an even better and stronger solution.

Chapter 11, *Extending Dynamics NAV 2016*, helps you understand the different integration concepts of the Dynamics NAV 2016 system with other Microsoft and related technologies. You will learn how you can better utilize the power of other languages and technologies in the Dynamics NAV system. You will also get a glimpse of different reporting tools, some NAV based extensions, and how they can be implemented along with Dynamics NAV system.

Chapter 12, *The Future of NAV*, covers an overview of major future products from the perspective of Microsoft Dynamics NAV 2016. In addition to the future releases of Microsoft Dynamics NAV, you will also see an overview of closely related technologies such as Dynamics 365, which is one of the most talked about and most confusing technologies in terms of future of Dynamics technology. You will also find out about the new development environment, which can be used to develop vertical solutions such as extensions, with a simple interface.

What you need for this book

The following software is required for this book:

- Microsoft Dynamics NAV 2016
- Visual Studio Community Edition
- Visual Studio Data Tool
- Online subscription to Azure and Office 365
- Online subscription for PowerBI, Dynamics 365
- SQL Server 2014 Management Studio
- Microsoft Office 2016

- Internet Explorer 11
- Notepad

Who this book is for

This book is ideal for administrators, developers, and consultants who are looking to take their knowledge of Dynamics NAV to new heights. You're expected to have a basic knowledge of Dynamics NAV workflows and C/AL, C/SIDE development.

Conventions

In this book, you will find a number of text styles that distinguish between different kinds of information. Here are some examples of these styles and an explanation of their meaning.

Code words in text, database table names, folder names, filenames, file extensions, pathnames, dummy URLs, user input, and Twitter handles are shown as follows: "Also call this local function, AddItem, into the OnRun trigger."

A block of code is set as follows:

```
LOCAL AddItem()
CLEARLASTERROR;
IF ExceptionHandle.Try('12345','MyTestItem') THEN
  MESSAGE('Item added Successfully')
ELSE
  MESSAGE('Error Returned Error : %1 - %2',
  GETLASTERRORCODE,GETLASTERRORTEXT);
```

When we wish to draw your attention to a particular part of a code block, the relevant lines or items are set in bold:

```
LOCAL AddItem()
CLEARLASTERROR;
IF ExceptionHandle.Try('12345','MyTestItem') THEN
  MESSAGE('Item added Successfully')
ELSE
  MESSAGE('Error Returned Error : %1 - %2',
  GETLASTERRORCODE,GETLASTERRORTEXT);
```

Any command-line input or output is written as follows:

```
C:\Python34\Scripts> pip install -upgrade pip
C:\Python34\Scripts> pip install pandas
```

New terms and **important words** are shown in bold. Words that you see on the screen, for example, in menus or dialog boxes, appear in the text like this: "In the **Report Properties** window, click on the code option in the left pane."

Warnings or important notes appear in a box like this.

Tips and tricks appear like this.

Reader feedback

Feedback from our readers is always welcome. Let us know what you think about this book-what you liked or disliked. Reader feedback is important for us as it helps us develop titles that you will really get the most out of. To send us general feedback, simply e-mail feedback@packtpub.com, and mention the book's title in the subject of your message. If there is a topic that you have expertise in and you are interested in either writing or contributing to a book, see our author guide at www.packtpub.com/authors.

Customer support

Now that you are the proud owner of a Packt book, we have a number of things to help you to get the most from your purchase.

Downloading the example code

You can download the example code files for this book from your account at http://www.packtpub.com. If you purchased this book elsewhere, you can visit http://www.packtpub.com/support and register to have the files e-mailed directly to you.

You can download the code files by following these steps:

1. Log in or register to our website using your e-mail address and password.
2. Hover the mouse pointer on the **SUPPORT** tab at the top.
3. Click on **Code Downloads & Errata**.
4. Enter the name of the book in the **Search** box.
5. Select the book for which you're looking to download the code files.
6. Choose from the drop-down menu where you purchased this book from.
7. Click on **Code Download**.

Once the file is downloaded, please make sure that you unzip or extract the folder using the latest version of:

- WinRAR / 7-Zip for Windows
- Zipeg / iZip / UnRarX for Mac
- 7-Zip / PeaZip for Linux

The code bundle for the book is also hosted on GitHub at `https://github.com/PacktPubl ishing/Mastering-Microsoft-Dynamics-NAV-2016`. We also have other code bundles from our rich catalog of books and videos available at `https://github.com/PacktPublish ing/`. Check them out!

Errata

Although we have taken every care to ensure the accuracy of our content, mistakes do happen. If you find a mistake in one of our books-maybe a mistake in the text or the code-we would be grateful if you could report this to us. By doing so, you can save other readers from frustration and help us improve subsequent versions of this book. If you find any errata, please report them by visiting `http://www.packtpub.com/submit-errata`, selecting your book, clicking on the **Errata Submission Form** link, and entering the details of your errata. Once your errata are verified, your submission will be accepted and the errata will be uploaded to our website or added to any list of existing errata under the Errata section of that title.

To view the previously submitted errata, go to `https://www.packtpub.com/books/conten t/support` and enter the name of the book in the search field. The required information will appear under the **Errata** section.

Piracy

Piracy of copyrighted material on the Internet is an ongoing problem across all media. At Packt, we take the protection of our copyright and licenses very seriously. If you come across any illegal copies of our works in any form on the Internet, please provide us with the location address or website name immediately so that we can pursue a remedy.

Please contact us at copyright@packtpub.com with a link to the suspected pirated material.

We appreciate your help in protecting our authors and our ability to bring you valuable content.

Questions

If you have a problem with any aspect of this book, you can contact us at questions@packtpub.com, and we will do our best to address the problem.

1

Microsoft Dynamics NAV Installation

Have you ever had the chance to spend a night at a sea-side cottage, where you can appreciate the vast endlessness of nature from a window? It captivates our imaginations and instills a desire to understand the vastness of this creation.

Let's change the perspective and visualize the same sea from a height (let's say, from a space station), and you can see all its boundaries, its size, and its color and understand its significance. Similarly, if you want to understand a software, then you have to see it within a broader context. It allows us to intake the most out of it in an optimum way.

Now, returning to the ground, instead of the sea-side, here we will discuss C/SIDE, and instead of an ocean, we will discuss the vastness of Microsoft Dynamics NAV 2016.

Here, in this chapter, we will learn about the different new technologies that have been implemented in the installation process of Microsoft Dynamics NAV 2016. The chapter will also guide you through the step-wise installation process with detailed diagrams and screenshots.

The chapter intends to clear the confusion about PowerShell, which is an essential component of the Administration section in the Microsoft Dynamics NAV world. Microsoft has made PowerShell compulsory in some sections. The chapter requires a basic-to-medium level knowledge of the installation process. We will not include the basic installation steps so as to save time and space, and will focus more on the current hot topics in the field of NAV Installation.

At the end of this chapter, we will explain the different terminologies and techniques used by expert NAV Administrators. This chapter is intended for those whose systems are on-premise, and who are looking to better manage it on-premise, or are planning to opt for cloud technologies.

In this chapter, will cover the following points:

- Architecture of the different models that are used while installing the system
- Details on the cloud technology and how it is useful
- Differences between installation environments
- Walkthrough of installation and deployment scenarios on different platforms
- Details on PowerShell and its usage

The background- before we start

Microsoft Dynamics NAV 2016 is a Microsoft Product, which delivers a complete ERP Business solution for small- and medium-sized organizations. You might want to know why this software package is not suitable for large industries; let's investigate this.

First, let's understand the difference between a large customer (Enterprise-level industry) and a smaller customer (Small and Medium business) from the ERP perspective. The ERP software sees a customer as a large enterprise if the number of employees is over 5,000. A company with lesser number of employees but a greater turnover can also be taken as an Enterprise-level customer. Another key factor in determining the size of a company is the size of data, whether it is high or low.

There are cases where Microsoft Dynamics NAV has been implemented in companies with 500, 1000, and even a couple of thousand users. But the main idea behind choosing the right ERP Software depends on many factors such as the following:

- Functionality
- Performance
- Interface and integration
- Out-of-the-box features
- Future customization requirement
- Cost
- Maintenance

As a consultant, our duty is to determine the best solution, and convince the customer on that. We must make sure that the system covers all the functionalities, or most of it. The performance should be within the acceptance limit. Their system should be equipped with sufficient interfacing API and services so as to integrate the updates and third-party integration, as the customer might like to integrate some in the future. It should provide out-of-the box customization features so that the client does not have to rely heavily on the developers for small changes. This, in turn, can be one of the most decisive factors, as modern users want some level of control with themselves. The system should guarantee easy and cost-effective customization if requested by the user. It should not be rigid. The cost of the system should be within an acceptable range, since clients have a budget for the product implementation. Last but not least is the maintenance cost; if the cost of maintaining the software is too high, then it is less likely that the customer is going to choose the product. Most of the customers also want to know the maintenance time requirement of the system.

Here we can conclude that there is a very thin line when we want to select the right product, since some of the products have a stronghold in some of the aforementioned points, while others have advantages regarding other points. We should spend an ample amount of time determining the right product for our client. Thankfully, Microsoft Dynamics NAV fulfills most of the criteria mentioned here, and so, it is the leader in the Dynamics family when it comes to the number of satisfied customers and number of implementations.

Architectural components

Microsoft Dynamics NAV can be installed on-premise, as well as on cloud. It is the most flexible and robust product of the Microsoft Dynamics family. Microsoft Developers have worked a lot on installation and configuration, which allows the product to have multidimensional installation options. It can be easily deployed to a multitenant environment. It supports PowerShell, which is like a magician, and provides added power when it comes to administering and installing the system. Installation of Microsoft Dynamics NAV 2016 on Azure is one of the key points to look for. We will be more focused around these points in this book.

I have tried to show the easiest and most efficient ways to accomplish the installation process in this chapter. There might be other ways, but I have tried to stick with the simplest one.

We should always install three core components of Microsoft Dynamics NAV 2016, which are the three tiers that comprise the core of NAV Architecture.

Three-tiered architecture

Like previous RTC versions, the Microsoft Dynamics NAV 2016 architecture is a three-tiered architecture, which uses three core components as follows:

Tier 1	Tier 2	Tier 3
Client Tier	Middle Tier	Data Tier
RTC (Windows Client/ Web client, web-service clients (SOAP Web Services and OData Web Services), and an NAS services client for programmatic access)	Microsoft Dynamics NAV Server	SQL Database Server (Application Database, Tenant Database)
Client User Interface For example: Frontend Application-RTC	Multitenant server, which manages business logic and all kinds of communication. For example: Multitenant Server-Development Environment	Database Server of Data layer For example: SQL Database server-Database

Here in the following diagram, you can clearly understand the different tiers in the Microsoft Dynamics system:

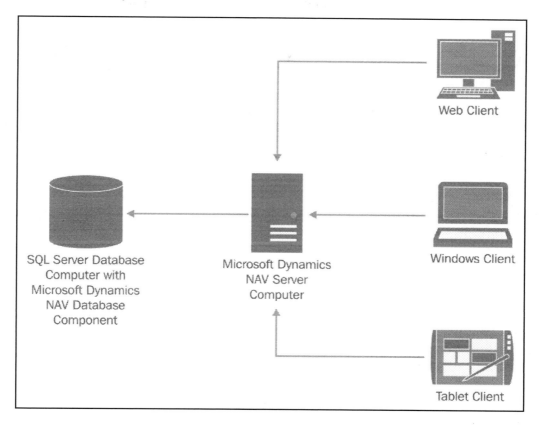

NAV Application Server

NAV Application Server, or **NAS**, is a middle-tier server component, which can be utilized without a user interface for task scheduling, client offloading, and specialized integration scenarios. Since, it executes business logic without any user interaction, they are managed completely from the Microsoft Dynamics NAV server administration tools in the **NAS Services** tab:

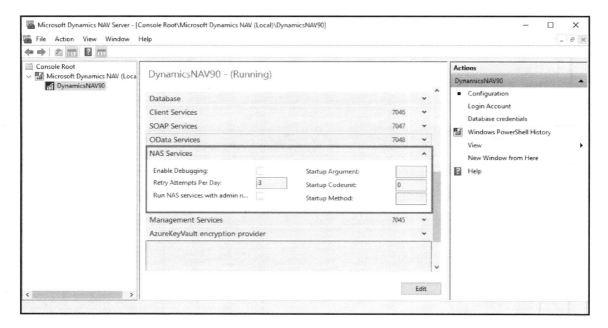

It is always better to create a Microsoft Dynamics NAV server instance for each NAS services application. The following are the two main reasons:

- Convenience
- Performance

Whenever you use NAS services for Microsoft Office Outlook integration, managing job queues, create a separate Microsoft Dynamics NAV server instance for each NAS service application, then modifying the setting for one of these services will not affect other services. On the other hand, configuring NAS services applications to use separate server instances makes better use of the server resources. This lets you run more applications with less degradation.

Multiple configurations

We can implement multiple configurations for the three-tier architecture in Microsoft Dynamics NAV.

The core components that comprises the tiers must be installed. We can choose a single machine for all the three tiers, or a separate machine for each tier.

Multitenant environment

There are various architectures that can be implemented for the Microsoft Dynamics NAV installation process. It all depends on the requirements. If there is a need of a single database system for a single group of users, then multi-tenancy has not much significance. But when we are trying to implement Dynamics NAV as a SaaS, keeping the system constant for multiple clients, then the significance of multi-tenancy comes into play.

 Multi-tenancy is a software architecture where a single instance of the software runs on a server and supports multiple customers or tenants.

In a multi-Tenant environment, we keep the business data of each tenant (client) in different databases while keeping all the SQL Server application objects in a different database.

Because of the level of separation between the three layers, now we can use the same shared NAV objects with more databases.

Each tenant can hold one or more companies, as depicted in the following diagram:

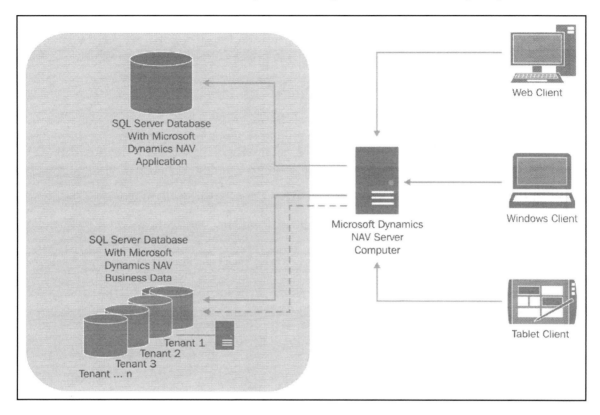

Azure (cloud service)

Microsoft Azure is an infrastructure and cloud-computing platform, which helps us solve problems such as building, deploying, and managing different applications. They are implemented by huge datacenters managed by Microsoft Corporation. It initially started with the IaaS service, but later also started providing PaaS.

Differences between on-premise and cloud

This quick public cloud adoption can be explained by several factors such as the following:

- Minimal up-front investments or commitments are required
- You pay for what you use
- Users can test any of the services prior to purchase
- Less human resources are required for infrastructure maintenance
- Service offerings are easy to compare
- Software upgrades can be automated

The latest member of the Dynamics Family, Dynamics 365, is not hosted on Azure, since Azure does not provide SaaS.

The difference between on-premise and the different cloud services can be better understood by the following diagram. As you can see, in on-premise setup you have different levels of control whereas in the cloud services the controls and access are limited:

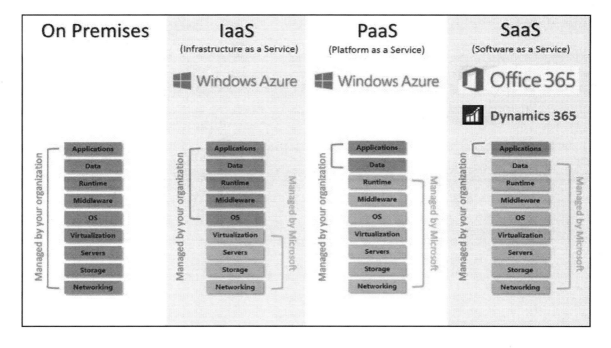

Microsoft Azure – relevant services

There are a number of relevant services that play an important role during the deployment process. They are as follows:

- **Virtual machines** (Dynamics NAV SQL Server)

  Virtual machines services are similar to the on-premise environment and the installation is also pretty much the same.

- **Cloud services** (Ports load balancer scale fail over)

  A cloud service has one public IP-address. It is located in a region or affinity group. It is possible to link to the owned domain. It can contain multiple VMs with local IP addresses.

  All the VMs can be accessed via endpoints on the cloud service. Endpoints can be loaded-balanced or port-forwarding.

- **Storage** (Hard disks backups)

  Storage in Azure contains hard disk space where we can put backup, PowerShell commands, and other files.

- **Network VPN** (VM network)

  Network VPN helps extend the private network space in the public domain where you can define other virtual machines, or VM. Each VM has a unique IP address in the same subnet so that they can see each other and communicate as per the command.

- **Active Directory** (User directory synchronized from AD Office 365 users)

  Azure Active Directory provides identity and access monument. It can be integrated with the on-premise Active Directory. It can also be used to Integrate with Dynamics NAV.

Microsoft Azure Management Portal

Use the link, `https://manage.windowsazure.com/`, in order to access the management portal of Windows Azure. It manages all Azure Services. Also, PowerShell is available for more options (this topic is covered in detail in a later part of this chapter).

 To access the link `https://manage.windowsazure.com/`, make sure you have a subscription for Windows Azure.

Three-service model

Cloud computing offers its services in three different models: **Infrastructure as a Service (IaaS)**, **Platform as a Service (PaaS)**, and **Software as a Service (SaaS)**. These models offer increasing abstraction. The following diagram shows how services provided using the same channel have been categorized so as to keep it easy to understand:

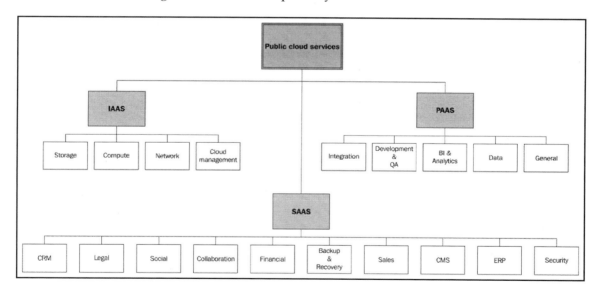

Infrastructure as a Service

Infrastructure as a Service helps companies to move their physical infrastructure to the cloud with a level of control similar to what they would have in a traditional on-premise data center. Core data center infrastructure components are storage, servers (computing units), the network itself, and management tools for infrastructure maintenance and monitoring. These are depicted in the following diagram:

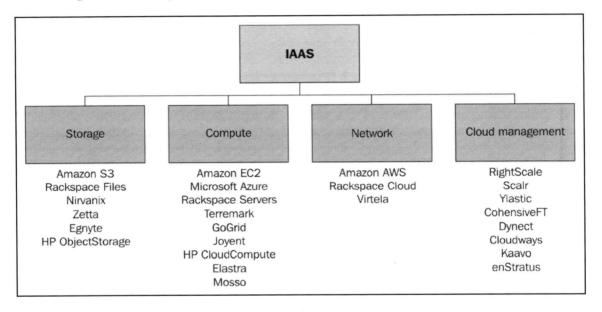

Infrastructure as a Service taxonomy

 IaaS includes virtual machines, servers, storage, network gear, and any other hardware/OS.

Platform as a Service

Platform as a Service provides the user with a configurable application platform including a preinstalled software stack. PaaS can be understood as another abstraction layer above the hardware, OS, and virtualization stack:

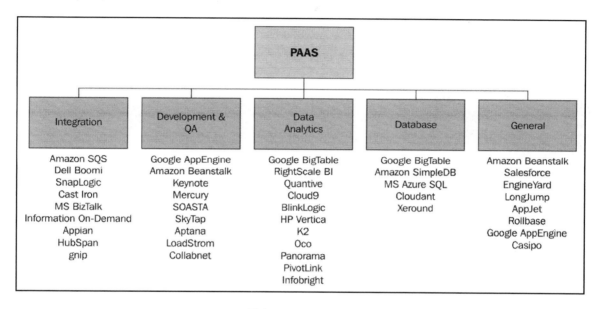

Platform as a Service taxonomy

Software as a Service

PaaS provides execution runtimes service without direct access to the OS (databases, development platforms, and application servers).

Software as a Service is a cloud services delivery model, which offers an on-demand online software subscription.

The latest SaaS release of Microsoft is Dynamics 365 (previously known as Project Madeira). The following diagram illustrates the SaaS taxonomy. Here you can clearly understand different services such as Sales force, NetSuite, and QuickBooks which are distributed as SaaS:

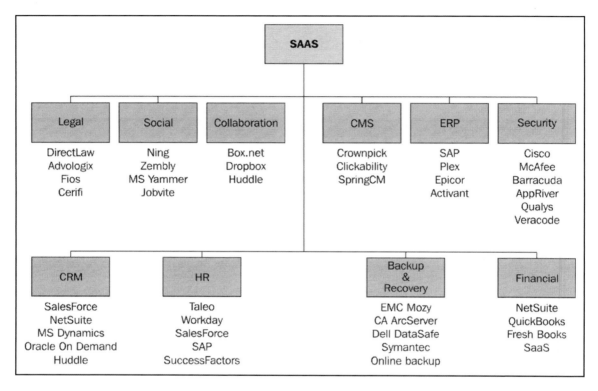

Software as a Service taxonomy

 SaaS includes software services such as Microsoft Office 365, Microsoft Dynamics 365, and so on.

Difference between on-premise, SaaS, PaaS, and IaaS services

In an on-premise architecture, one needs to take care of all the services and layers of the software system starting from the network layer up to the application layer (client). Here, the cost of maintenance is high, and it is a redundant service.

In IaaS, Microsoft provides a virtual abstraction of the operating system, which can be used as any on-premise operating system, and hence it lowers the cost of maintaining low-level systems.

In PaaS, a specific platform is exposed to the user so as to make the service even more precise and the user is concerned only up to the platform he/she is using; all the layers below it are managed by Microsoft.

SaaS is the latest of all services, where specific software can be isolated from all those complex layers. The user just needs to worry about the software layer, and everything beyond that is handled by the cloud factory. It is the easiest and most efficient model in cloud technology.

Introduction to the NAV Universal application

Nav Universal is an application designed for phones and tablets to run Microsoft Dynamics NAV. It is the client-side part, which offers portability and flexibility of usage. It is basically targeted at small- and medium-sized businesses which want to access data from a hand-held device, on the go.

In general day-to-day use, these apps are used for functions such as the following:

- Approving invoices
- Getting an overview of business
- Viewing the progress report
- Lightweight data entry
- Checking the status of documents

The following diagram illustrates the architecture of the NAV Universal application in details:

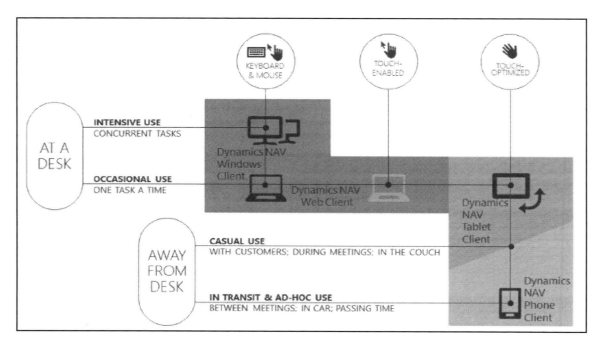

The Microsoft Dynamics NAV Tablet client and Microsoft Dynamics NAV Phone client support the same credential types as the Microsoft Dynamics NAV Windows client and Microsoft Dynamics NAV Web client.

Out-of-the-box tools in the Installation DVD

We do not always need to search for treasure in the ocean, sometimes we can find it in our backyard pond as well. The Microsoft Dynamics NAV Installation DVD is no less than a treasure for an NAV professional. It includes almost all of the installation tools, upgrade tools, PowerShell scripts, Test tools, and much more. Most of the times, this resource remains unnoticed, which is why I would like to go into detail for some of these important tools:

Folder with numbers such as 1029-4105

There are almost 15 folders in this category. These are folders that contain agreement terms in different languages. They also contain the developers' help file, which is an extremely valuable asset for NAV Developers and consultants. Let us understand its components in brief.

License.rtf

This license agreement (*Agreement*) is an agreement between Microsoft corporation (or one of its affiliates based on where you are) and the user of the system. The main intention of this multilingual license agreement is to inform all non-English speaking users about the terms and conditions in their local language.

setupres.dll

These files are the **dynamic-link library** (DLL) files, which represent implementations for the shared library concept in the Microsoft world, and are generally used by the operating system and various other programs.

devitpro.chm

Microsoft has compiled a documentation file, which contains the **Help** section in the .chm format; which consists of a collection of navigational HTML pages. The files are compressed and deployed in a binary format for the compiled HTML. This is a very important file for consultants and developers as well as for administrators and implementers. The contents of this file are considered as treasure for most developers, since this contains all the syntax of all the functions that can be used in the C/AL code. It also gives a detailed walkthrough for system deployment. In addition, this file contains the business logic flow, which can be extremely valuable for consultants.

ADCS

ADCS stands for **Automated Data Capture System**. The pattern implemented by ADCS helps Microsoft Dynamics NAV to communicate with different handheld devices through web services.

For example, if we want to test any handheld device that transmits a radio frequency, then we can use a radio receiver to capture those radio frequencies, and then a VT100 plug-in can be used to test that connection. The plugin helps Microsoft Dynamics NAV to receive the data transmitted from the device. The data is fetched in the form of an XML file, and can be used for further processing.

ClickOnce Installer tools

This folder contains the tools used for the ClickOnce installation process. The details of the ClickOnce process is explained in a later part of this chapter.

CRM customization

This folder contains a zip folder called DynamicsNAVIntegrationSolution.ZIP, which contains customization settings, content type, solution code, and other web-related resource files. It also contains a JavaScript file, which contains functions such as ConnectToNavClient, which is used by the NAV system to connect to the CRM and vice versa. It can be used by developers to make changes in the connection.

Outlook

It contains the `.msi` file, which can be used to install the outlook add-ins. This is a useful tool if you, by any chance, miss the installation of Outlook components during the Dynamics NAV installation process. It can also be used if the outlook component is corrupted.

Prerequisite components

This is a very important folder, which should be properly understood before we start the installation process. It gives the details of all the prerequisite components that are required for the installation process. It is extremely important that one must fulfil all the prerequisites in order to guarantee a successful installation process:

Name	Date modified	Type	
IIS URL Rewrite Module	9/2/2016 11:06 AM	File folder	
Microsoft .NET Framework 4.5.2	9/2/2016 11:06 AM	File folder	
Microsoft Report Viewer 2015	9/2/2016 11:06 AM	File folder	
Microsoft SQL Server 2014 Express	9/2/2016 11:06 AM	File folder	
Microsoft SQL Server Management Objects	9/2/2016 11:06 AM	File folder	
Microsoft Visual C++ 2013	9/2/2016 11:06 AM	File folder	
Microsoft Visual Studio 2010 Tools For Office Redist	9/2/2016 11:06 AM	File folder	
Open XML SDK 2.5 for Microsoft Office	9/2/2016 11:06 AM	File folder	
SharePoint Client Components	9/2/2016 11:06 AM	File folder	
Windows Indentity Foundation	9/2/2016 11:06 AM	File folder	

Role Tailored Client

This folder contains the configuration file for **Role Tailored Client** (**RTC**). It also contains all other essential component files that help RTC to connect to the middle tier. This folder is required in the later part of this chapter, in the ClickOnce installation in particular.

SQL Demo database

This is another very important folder, which contains the license file along with the precious SQL Demo database backup file. In most of the cases when we accidentally corrupt our demo database, we can easily restore this `.bak` file. This comes in very handy if we want to play with the database and objects.

Test toolkit

I personally believe this part to be the best part of Dynamics NAV 2016. It contains tools that can be used to test our customizations against regression issues. Most of us do not even know about this part, and I would like to go into detail over this in `Chapter 4`, *Testing and Debugging*. Some experts also call it the last missing piece to complete the big puzzle called *Road to Repeatability*.

Upgrade toolkit

This folder contains the tools that are key to the upgrade process. We will go into detail on the Upgrade toolkit in `Chapter 9`, *Upgrade and Migration*.

Windows PowerShell Scripts

This folder contains most of the PowerShell Scripts, which can be used for various PowerShell operations related to multi-tenancy, database, company data, Azure installation, and many others. In fact, most of the manual operations can be customized using PowerShell Scripts, which is available in this folder. Since this is an extremely useful topic, I have explained it in detail in the *Installation scenarios* section of this chapter.

Microsoft SQL Server requirements for Microsoft Dynamics NAV

The following are the Microsoft SQL Server requirements for Microsoft Dynamics NAV:

- Microsoft SQL Server 2014
    - Express, Standard, or Enterprise
- Microsoft SQL Server 2012 Service Pack 2
    - Express, Standard, or Enterprise (64 bit only)

- Azure SQL Database V12
  - Standard and Premium service tiers.

The components needed while installing SQL Server are as follows:

- Database Engineer Services
- Client Tools Connectivity
- Management Tools-complete

 This can be useful when we select every component while installing. It's always a good idea to know what are the requirements in particular to save time and memory. In this book, we will not cover basic installation of SQL Server assuming it to be the basic process that is similar to all the other older versions such as Microsoft Dynamics NAV 2013 and 2015.

Data encryption between MS SQL Server and Microsoft Dynamics NAV 2016

It is recommended to use **Internet Protocol security (IPsec)** for data encryption to maintain a secure channel between NAV and SQL System. IPSec uses cryptographic security services. For a better understanding of the concept, refer to the following diagram:

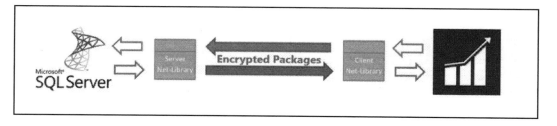

Using Azure SQL Database

In Microsoft Dynamics NAV, we can also use the Azure SQL database, which is a cloud service. It provides data storage, and the best part is that it is inbuilt in the Azure services platform.

We can directly connect the Microsoft Dynamics NAV Server instance to Azure VM.

 For better performance, VM and the SQL database must be in the same Azure region, and NAV Development Environment must be on the same VM in Azure as in the Microsoft Dynamics NAV Server.

Microsoft Dynamics NAV PowerShell

PowerShell is a very strong tool. It's useful in managing Microsoft dynamics NAV over Azure and Dynamics 365. It is also very useful for some out-of-the box installations such as Multitenant configuration. Moreover, it helps in carrying out major processes with just a few lines of code, and is often very fast. It fortifies our skills in administering Microsoft Dynamics NAV.

Dynamics NAV tools

The following are the tools that we use for development, administration, and object management purposes. As you can see, PowerShell can be used in all the areas, and so, this is the time when we should take PowerShell more seriously. Let's dive deep into PowerShell:

Development	Administration	Object Management/ Source control
C/Side	Administration Console (MMC)	Team Foundation Server (TFS)
Visual Studio Add Ins Extensibility Report Design	Role Tailored Client(RTC)	iFactor ReVision
Word Report Design		OMA
SQL Report Builder		Merge tool
PowerShell	PowerShell	PowerShell

Where in NAV are we with PowerShell?

With PowerShell, we are on the tooling side of NAV. For example, we have the report design (Visual Studio-SQL Report builder) tool and the MS Dynamics NAV Administrator tools.

Using PowerShell

Most of the Microsoft products are either already using or will be using PowerShell, and in the context of NAV, it is a growing trend to use PowerShell to make life easier for Administrators and Developers. In spite of that, we cannot do everything using a GUI, and so, Microsoft has provided backdoor processes using PowerShell command lines.

Getting started with PowerShell

The PowerShell works on objects so it is extremely useful. It can be useful while working with .NET Framework as well.

PowerShell **ISE (Integrated Scripting Environment)** can be taken as the development environment of PowerShell; it helps PowerShell look developer-friendly. It allows multiline editing, selective execution, context-sensitive help, debugging, command-exploration, snippets, and many more advanced functionalities, which makes it more than just a command shell.

Let's start with an example.

Let us assume that PowerShell is installed onto our system along with Microsoft Dynamics NAV.

There are three options [on right-click] to open it as one of the different authorities, as shown in the following screenshot:

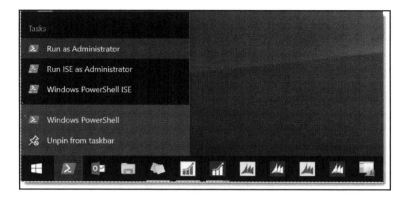

Generally, when we are coding, we might like to use the Windows PowerShell ISE option. This is because, if we create some file in the administrator mode, and if we want to edit the file later, we would have to open it with the administrator authority.

We will take an example of the Windows PowerShell ISE, which is the most common environment, just to make things simple:

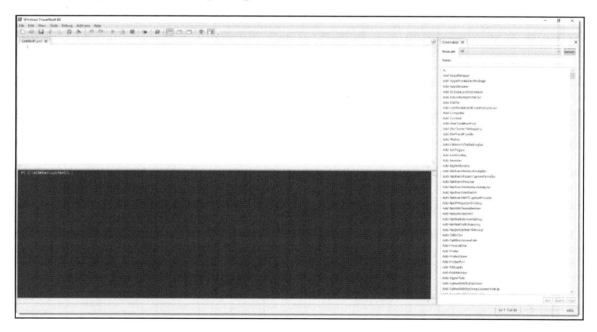

For administrative operations, we use the administrative mode. The following window does not have one:

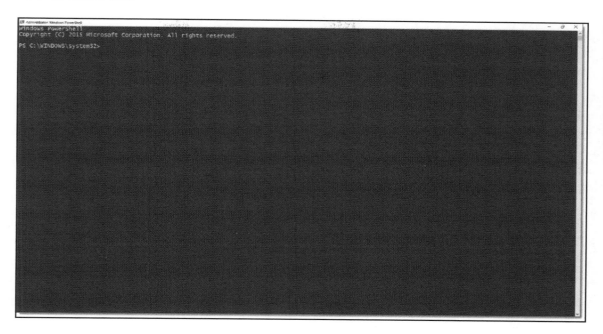

Dynamics NAV PowerShell has the following two modulus/snap-ins in particular:

- Microsoft.Dynamics.NAV.Management: import-module
  "${env:ProgramFiles}Microsoft Dynamics
  NAV90ServiceNAVAdminTool.ps1"

 This script is used to manage the service; it is a part of the Server management tool.

- Microsoft.Dynamics.NAV.Model.Tools: import-module
  "${env:ProgramFiles(x86)}Microsoft
  DynamicsNAV90RoleTailoredClientMicrosoft.Dynamics.NAV.Model.Too
  ls.psd1"

This tool can be used to work with the text object of NAV objects such as merging objects, comparing, creating Delta, creating objects, joining it, working with languages, and many more.

So, in general, we can take these snap-ins as the tools to hook NAV with PowerShell.

Patterns of scripting

It is essential for you to understand how different cmdlets function in order to harvest their full potential. Here in this section we are going to understand how cmdlets are written and we will also be examining some of the most useful cmdlets.

Understanding the PowerShell cmdlets

We can categorize the PowerShell commands into five major categories of use:

- Commands for server administrators
- Command for implementers for company management
- Commands for administrators for upgrades
- Commands for administrator for security
- Commands for developers

Commands for server administrators

The first category contains commands that can be used for administrative operations such as create, save, remove, get, import, export, set, and the so on as given in the following table:

Dismount-NAVTenant	New-NAVServerConfiguration
Export-NAVApplication	New-NAVServerInstance
Get-NAVApplication	New-NAVWebServerInstance
Get-NAVServerConfiguration	Remove-NAVApplication
Get-NAVServerInstance	Remove-NAVServerInstance
Get-NAVServerSession	Remove-NAVServerSession
Get-NAVTenant	Save-NAVTenantConfiguration

Get-NAVWebServerInstance	Set-NAVServerConfiguration
Export-NAVServerLicenseInformation	Set-NAVServerInstance
Import-NAVServerLicense	Set-NAVWebServerInstanceConfiguration
Mount-NAVApplication	Sync-NAVTenant
Mount-NAVTenant	

 We can set up web server instances, change configurations, and create a multitenant environment; we can only use PowerShell for a multitenant environment.

Commands for implementers for company management

The second category of commands can be used by implementers, in particular, for operations related to installation and configuration of the system. The following are a few examples of this category of commands:

Copy-NAVCompany
Get-NAVCompany
New-NAVCompany
Remove-NAVCompany
Rename-NAVCompany

Commands for administrators for upgrades

The third category is a special category for administrators, which is related to upgradation of operations.

Get-NAVDataUpgrade
Resume-NAVDataUpgrade
Start-NAVDataUpgrade
Stop-NAVDataUpgrade

The third category of commands can be useful along with the upgrade toolkit.

Commands for administrator for security

This is one of the most important categories, which is related to the backend of the system. The commands in this category grant the power of accessibility and permission to the administrators. I strongly recommend these make-life-easy commands if you are working on security operations. Commands in this category include the following:

Get-NAVServerUser	Remove-NAVServerPermission
Get-NAVServerUserPermissionSet	Remove-NAVServerPermissionSet
New-NAVServerPermission	Remove-NAVServerUser
New-NAVServerPermissionSet	Remove-NAVServerUserPermissionSet
New-NAVServerUser	Set-NAVServerPermission
New-NAVServerUserPermissionSet	Set-NAVServerPermissionSet
	Set-NAVServerUser

These commands can be used basically to add users, and for permission set.

Commands for developers

The last, but not the least, treasure of commands is dedicated to developers, and is one of my most-used commands. It covers a wide range of commands, and should be included in your daily work. This set of commands includes the following:

Get-NAVWebService	Join-NAVApplicationObjectFile
Invoke-NAVCodeunit	Join-NAVApplicationObjectLanguageFile
New-NAVWebService	Merge-NAVApplicationObject
Remove-NAVWebService	Remove-NAVApplicationObjectLanguage
Compare-NAVApplicationObject	Set-NAVApplicationObjectProperty
Export-NAVAppliactionObjectLanguage	Split-NAVApplicationApplicationObjectFile

Get-NAVApplicationObjectProperty	Split-NAVApplicationObjectLanguageFile
Import-NAVApplicationObjectLanguage	Test-NAVApplicationObjectLanguage
	Update-NAVApplicationObject

 This preceding category of commands can be used to manage web services, invoke codeunits, work with object files, and work with languages.

Practice with PowerShell

Here, in this section, I will break down the basic syntax of PowerShell Script, and explain how it functions:

```
Syntax: get-service -name "*net*"
```

The preceding syntax can be broken down into four essential parts. The first part, that is, GET, is a function, which is generally used as a verb that signifies the main action of the code. The second part is generally a noun, which defines the operation. Part one and part two combine to form a command, leaving part three and four to be the name and argument, which combine to form a parameter. This is better explained as follows:

Verb	Noun	Name	Argument
Get	Service	Name	Net
Command	Parameter		

I have drawn the following simple figure just to explain the process for a better understanding of the PowerShell Script. Every PowerShell Script can be understood by this method, and it's even easy to memorize and manipulate it if you can understand the structure of the scripts:

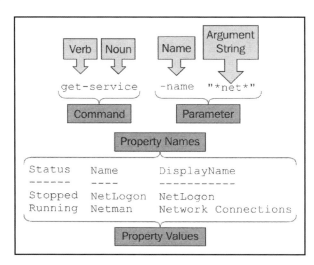

Installation scenarios

There are various ways of installing Microsoft Dynamics NAV 2016 on different platforms. We still use the conventional ways, which are optimized for a better experience. Installation of Microsoft Dynamics NAV 2016 On Premise is not in the scope of this book, as it is similar to the older version and the readers are supposed to have had that experience prior to starting this book. I have pointed out the most popular and most on-demand installation scenarios.

ClickOnce installation

ClickOnce is a component of the Microsoft .NET Framework. It helps to deploy a web application with just a link. The end user chooses a link to the Microsoft Dynamics NAV application installation. The link points to a shared file or a website. We can also deploy a mass installation if we want to carry out the process on multiple client systems.

Prerequisite list

The following is a list of prerequisites for this installation process:

- Microsoft .NET Framework
- Access to the Microsoft Dynamics NAV installation media (DVD)

High-level steps

The entire process can be understood in just a few steps, which are as follows:

1. Link to the application:
    - File Share
    - Website
2. Open the dialog box.
3. ClickOnce downloads all the installation files (implicit).
4. Run Windows client.
5. Install shortcut.
6. Check if a newer version is available.

Detailed steps

The steps mentioned in the preceding section can be understood in detail as follows:

1. Install all the prerequisites as mentioned in the preceding prerequisite list.
2. Install the ClickOnce Installer tools.
3. Run `setup.exe`, and install the ClickOnce Installer tools. The files will be installed in `C:Program Files (x86)Microsoft Dynamics NAV70ClickOnce Installer Tools`.

    Or find the folder in the NAV Installation DVD in `NAV.Installation.DVDClickOnceInstallerToolsProgram FilesMicrosoft Dynamics NAV90ClickOnce Installer ToolsTemplateFilesNAVClientInstallation.html`.

ClickOnce installation using File Share

You can also use File Share in order to install ClickOnce. You can follow the steps mentioned in the following section.

Prerequisite list

Following is the list of prerequisites for this installation process:

- Microsoft Windows SDK and .NET Framework
- Access to the Microsoft Dynamics NAV installation media (DVD)

High level steps

The entire process can be briefly understood in just a few steps, which are as follows:

1. Install the prerequisites Microsoft Windows SDK and .NET Framework.
2. Click on Installer Tools, as mentioned in the previous step:
   - `Setup.exe`
   - `C:Program Files (x86)Microsoft Dynamics NAV70ClickOnce Installer Tools. Or NAV.Installation.DVDClickOnceInstallerToolsProgram FilesMicrosoft Dynamics NAV90ClickOnce Installer Tools`
3. Update the settings in `ClientUserSetting.Config`.
4. Copy the template files.
5. Update the application, and deploy the manifest file:

   ```
   fileshareclickonceDeploymentMicrosoft.Dynamics.NAV.Client.ap
   plication
   ```

Detailed steps

The steps mentioned in the preceding section can be understood in detail as follows:

1. Copy the ClickOnce Toolkit from `C:Program Files (x86)Microsoft Dynamics NAV70ClickOnce Installer Tools` or from your installation DVD.

2. Create a folder called `Fileshare` in your system, preferably in the `C:/` drive.
3. Copy all the content from the `C:Program Files (x86)Microsoft Dynamics NAV90RoleTailored Client` folder and paste it into the `Fileshare` folder:

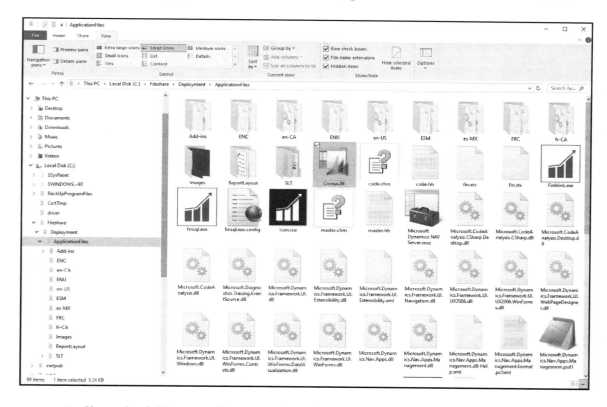

4. Share the folder over the network so that every user can access it and perform the installation process.

We can also use a website to host these files, for example, `http://Yourdomain/ClickOnceInstallFolder`.

Upgrading the Windows client using ClickOnce

The same process can be used to upgrade, using the setup file shared over the network of Windows machines:

1. Create a new folder, `ApplicationFiles`.
2. Update the application manifest.
3. Update the deployment manifest.
4. The deployment manifest's version is as shown in the following screenshot:

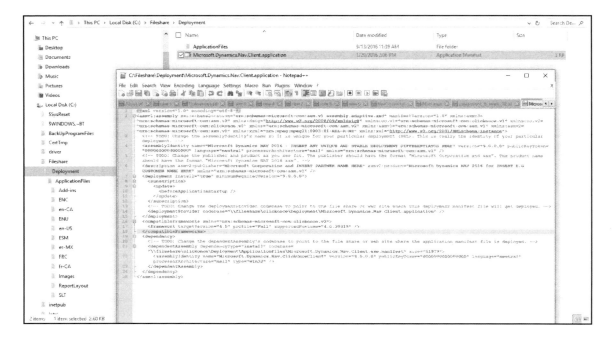

Manifest files are XML files, which are used to control all kinds of add-ins to work on all display targets.

Now the user can install the file at their end. Since the file is shared on the network, it's easy to follow the simple setup instructions, as shown in the following screenshot:

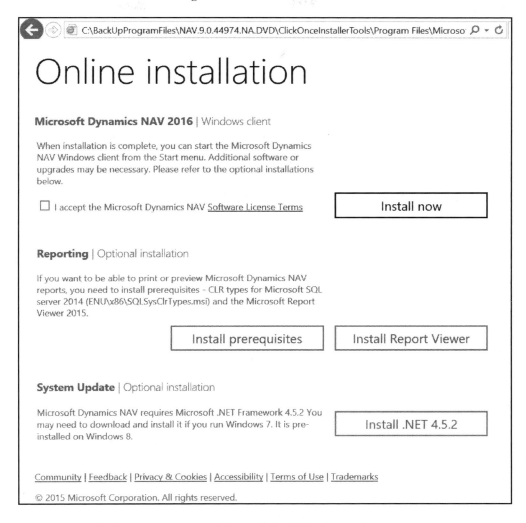

5. Accept the license terms, and install the Windows client.

And that's it! The installation process is simplified and distributed over the network. If the process implements an Internet protocol, then it's even easier to distribute the system.

Installing NAV on Azure VM using PowerShell

This is one of the most talked about topic in the Microsoft Dynamics Community. Most of the clients are looking forward to implement Azure machines as their System Server. We will try to explore how PowerShell can come in handy here.

Prerequisite list

Following is the list of prerequisites for this installation process:

- A Microsoft Azure subscription, and access to the Azure Management Portal
- Access to the Microsoft Dynamics NAV installation media (DVD)

High level steps

The entire process can be understood briefly in just few steps, which are as follows:

1. Prepare the Microsoft Azure subscription.
2. Prepare the provisioning computer:
   - Create a SQL database
   - Create a virtual machine

Detailed steps

The steps mentioned in the preceding section can be understood in detail with the following detailed steps. I have tried the Classic Portal. You can also try the new Portal; the steps will remain the same:

1. First get the Microsoft Azure subscription. We can easily subscribe for the free trial, and later upgrade to the full Azure subscription as per requirement. I will not go into details on how to subscribe for Azure, as this is not in the scope of this book. Subscription is the easiest process, where you just fill in the online form of subscription and log in. After logging in, you would be directed to a page, which is similar to the following screenshot:

2. Create a Microsoft Azure Storage account, which can be used for the later part of provisioning the computer.

3. Prepare the prerequisite for the provisioning as follows:

   Copy this folder from the Installation DVD into the cloud storage: NAV.9.0.Installation.DVDWindowsPowerShellScriptsCloud.

 These files contains all the PowerShell commands which can be used for the provisioning process.

4. Plan for NAV deployment.

5. The first model uses a single virtual machine to be created on Microsoft Azure, which hosts all the three servers. A firewall is configured for all the different client services for the clients using unique ports:

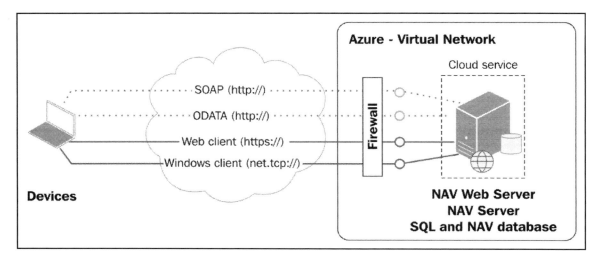

The second model uses two virtual machines, the NAV web server and service tier, and another VM for the NAV database. This is better for a system using huge databases:

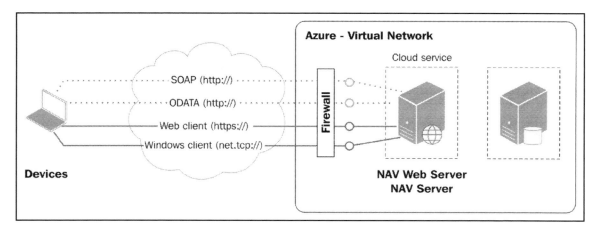

 From the client's perspective, both the models are same as they work in an exactly same manner on the client side.

Steps needed to prepare PowerShell commands

In these steps, I will explain how we can utilize the readymade command file, which is nothing but PowerShell Scripts prepared by Microsoft for administrative purposes:

1. Run PowerShell ISE as an administrator.
2. Change the `CloudHowTo` folder:
    - `Set-PartnerSetting.ps1`
3. Delete the #TODO (as explained in the following screenshot, highlighted in yellow):

 Update the values with the name of your subscription; here, replace `MyAzureSubription` with your Azure subscription.

Provide a value for the parameter as required, and save the file.

Now we can proceed with two types of deployment, deployment on single Azure VM and deployment on two Azure VMs. I will only elaborate on the first, since both deployments have similar steps.

4. Get ready for deployment (a single Azure VM):
   - Use `Example-1VM.ps1` using the PowerShell command present in `WindowsPowerShellScriptsCloudHowTo`
   - `Example-2VM.ps1` is used to deploy the system on two VMs, whereas `Example-1VM.ps1` is for a single VM

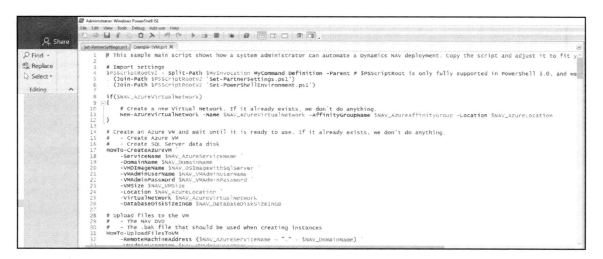

 Note that the cmdlets are to be run on a virtual machine, so copy the saved file onto your VM first.

The steps in this example file are explained as follows:

1. Create a new virtual network if it does not already exist.
2. Create a Azure VM, if it doesn't already exist, and wait until it is ready to use. Now create an **SQL Server data disk**.

3. Upload the following files to the VM:
   - The NAV DVD
   - The `.bak` file that should be used when creating instances
4. Install the SSL certificate that is used for HTTPS on the NAV Web Client as well as on the NAV server's OData and SOAP web services.
5. Install NAV on the VM.
6. Add a tenant (instance) on the VM.
7. Just select the code section, press *F8* or right-click on the code, and click on **Run Selection** under **Options**.

 Since all the cmdlets are already present in the file, CM on two machines also can be done similarly. The best part of the example file is that it is well documented and clear to read.

Deploying Microsoft Dynamics NAV 2016 database on Azure SQL database

Microsoft Dynamics NAV on Azure VM is more like an on-premise installation. Here we can create a SQL Server for hosting the NAV Database.

Prerequisite list

Following is a list of prerequisites for this deployment process:

- A Microsoft Azure subscription and access to the Azure Management Portal.
- Microsoft Dynamics NAV database is installed on an SQL Server Database Engine instance. SQL Server Manager is also installed on the same computer.
- Access to the Microsoft Dynamics NAV installation media (DVD).

To deploy a Microsoft Dynamics NAV database to an Azure SQL Database, the database must be exported as a data-tier application (DAC) file, which is known as a `.bacpac` file. This can be done using SQL Server Manager.

Creating a database in Azure

Creating a new database in the Microsoft Azure online portal includes some easy steps, which are explained as follows:

1. Click on the database link form on the left side of the page, fill in the information, and select an appropriate size of the SQL database:

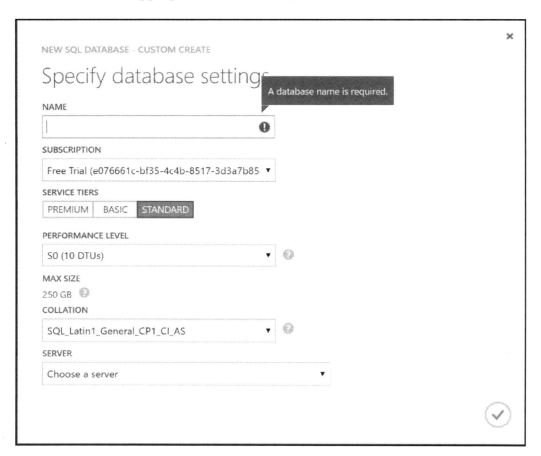

 We can manage Windows Azure at the following link:
https://manage.windowsazure.com/.

2. After you have entered the required values and created the database, you will be presented with a page displaying a list of SQL databases. In the following screenshot, you can see that both the databases are created under the same server:

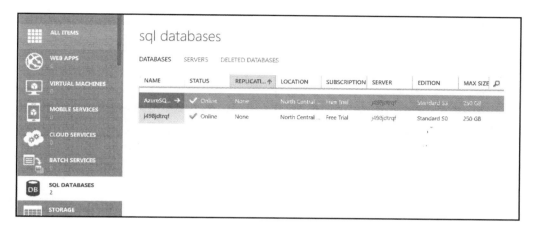

3. Click on the server, and then go to the **CONFIGURE** tab. Click on the **ADD TO THE ALLOWED IP ADDRESSES** arrow, and save the changes. Now only the IP is published on the Web, and we can access the database from any supporting management studio:

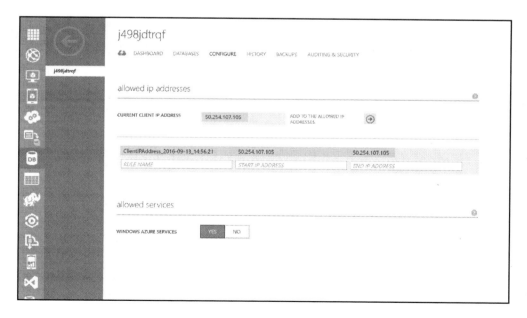

Let's test the connection from our local Microsoft SQL Management Studio. Before we start the connection, let's note down the information that will be needed for the connection. Go to the **DASHBOARD** tab of the server (similar to the **CONFIGURE** tab in the last step), and note down the administrator login information; this is the user name. From the dashboard of the database, note down the server name. In this case, the server name is **j498jdtrqf.database.windows.net**. Now let's use this information for the connection of the database engine. Use the password that we used while creating the database:

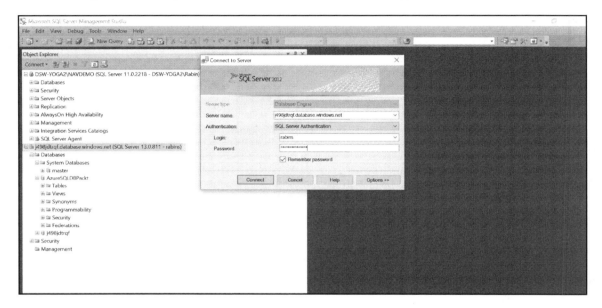

After successful connection, you can see the Azure SQL database on your SQL Management Studio Object Explorer. Now we can treat this database as any local database. But if we want to add any database to this server, then we will have to follow the steps which will satisfy certain criteria set by Azure Server.

Now, let's see how to replicate a database to the Azure SQL database:

1. Right-click on the database you want to replicate.
2. Select the **Tasks** option.

3. Now select **Deploy Database to SQL Azure…**:

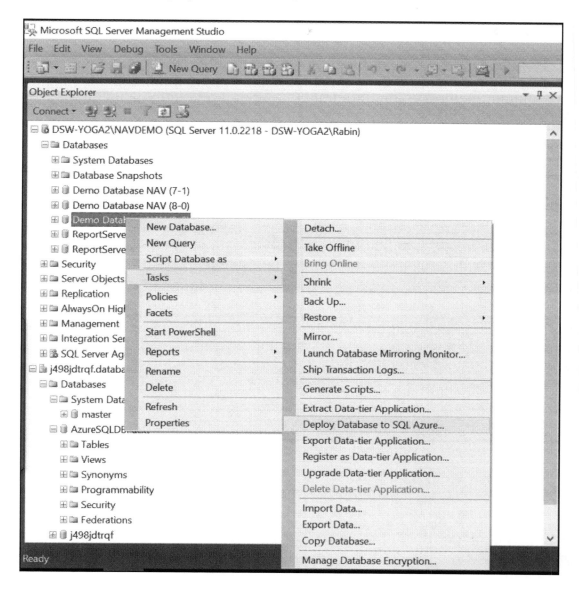

This will deploy a local database to SQL Azure and a connection is established between the local DB and the SQL Azure Database Server:

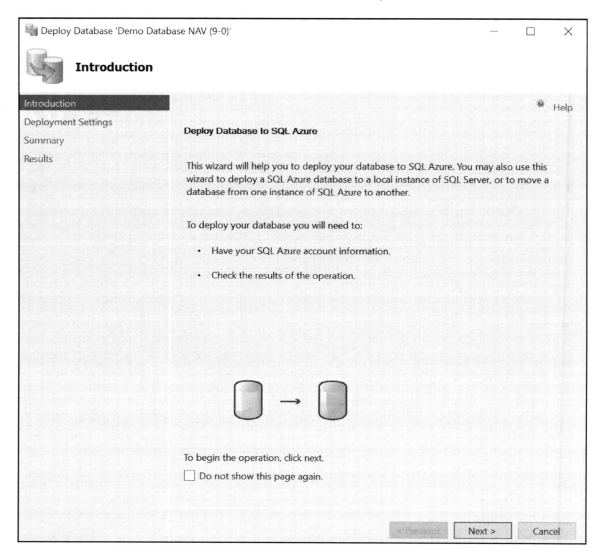

Now you just need to click the **Next** button, and you will be presented with the **Deployment Settings** page, which is an important one, because here you will have to connect to the Azure SQL database with your credentials, as shown in the following screenshot:

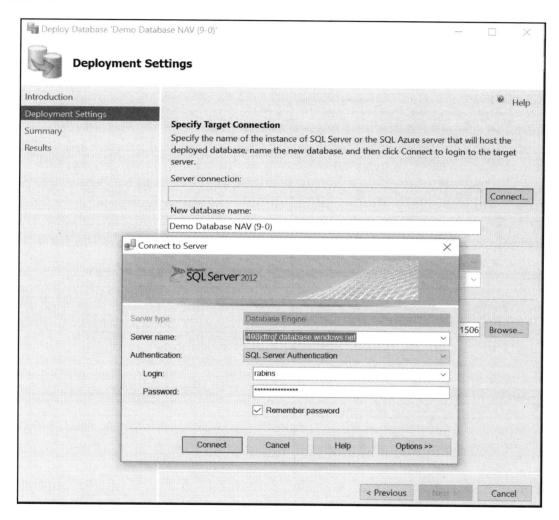

It takes a while depending on the size of the database.

After the process is sucessfully completed, we can see the same database in the SQL Azure database, as can be seen in the next screenshot:

Here, we have successfully connected an Azure SQL database using our SQL Server Management Studio, which is a local entity. You can see a database named **Demo Database NAV (9-0)** inside the database server, **j498jdtrqqf.database.windows.net(SQL Server 13.0.81 – rabins)**:

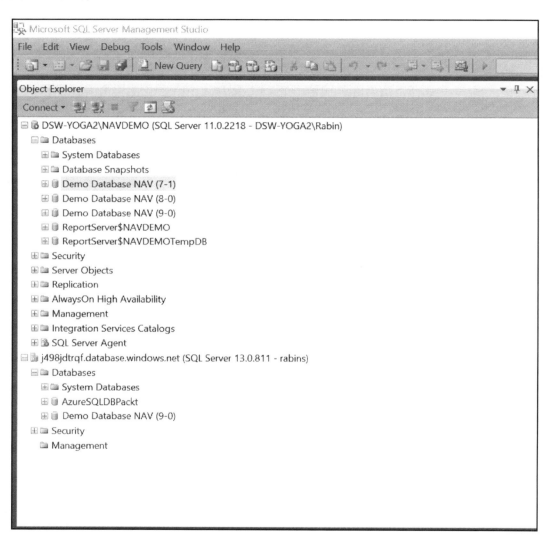

In case of an error, try to find the error, resolve it, and repeat the same process.

Creating a virtual machine

We will now create a virtual machine which will be used to host the Microsoft Dynamics NAV system. Follow the following steps:

1. From the **VIRTUAL MACHINE** icon, Create a new virtual machine from the **FROM GALLERY** option.
2. There are two options, **QUICK CREATE** and **FROM GALLERY**; use **FROM GALLERY** if you want to create a VM with the inbuilt Microsoft Dynamics NAV:

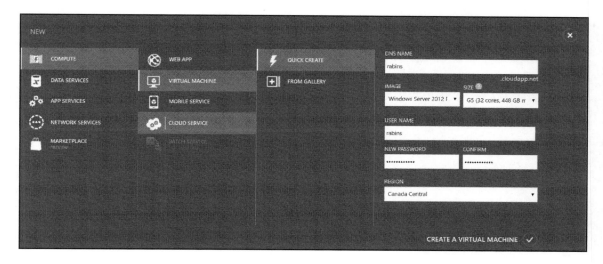

3. Select the appropriate Microsoft Dynamics NAV option from the list.

4. Select **Microsoft Dynamics NAV 2016** for this example, as shown in the next screenshot:

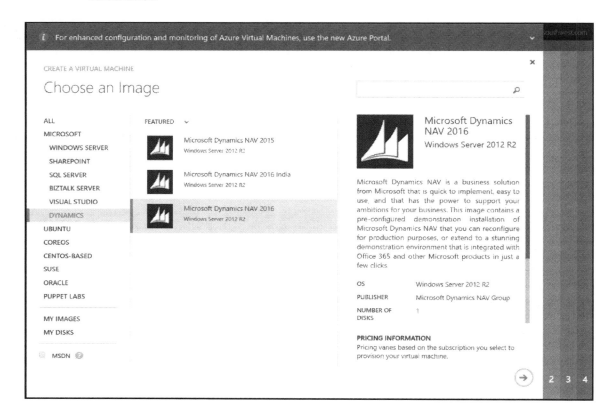

Generate the credentials for the login, and note down the password and user name, as this will be needed while connecting to this VM:

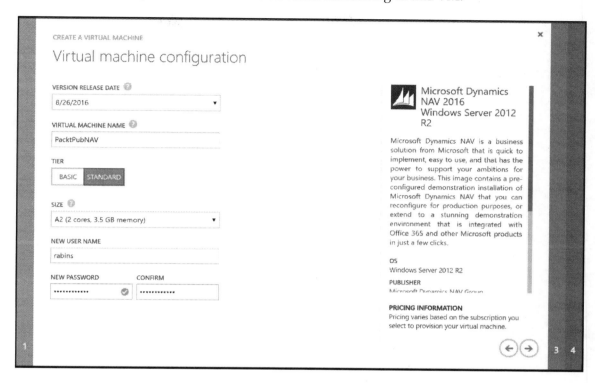

5. In the third step, we can change the port numbers if we want to. Also, we have to define the name of the Cloud Service DNS. Choose the best one that is available, as shown in the following screenshot:

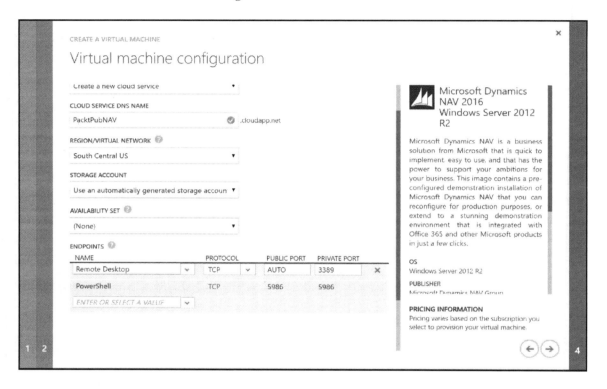

Just follow the steps and finish the process of creation of virtual machine with Microsoft Dynamics NAV installed in it.

6. In the following screenshot, I have created two virtual machines: one for testing purpose, which is just a plain VM without Microsoft Dynamics NAV, and one for using the gallery. We will be restricted as per the permission granted per subscription:

7. Now let the Azure System provision our virtual machine. These are straight-forward steps and should not be confusing.

8. After the virtual machine is running, click on the **Connect** option on the bottom tab, and it will get downloaded with an RDP, which can be used to log in to the virtual machine just like any remote server:

It is very fast and reliable.

9. Use the log-in credentials we used while creating the virtual machine:

And that's it. We have a brand new virtual machine up and running. Explore the properties and Firewall settings to ensure everything is perfect:

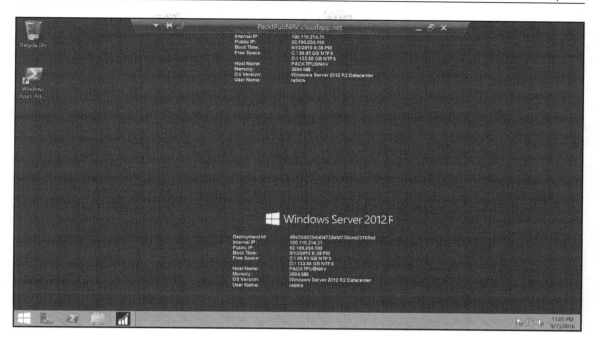

10. Go to the **Apps** section, and verify the presence of Microsoft Dynamics NAV, as shown in the following screenshot:

The NAV System should run its local database quite easily, since it is internally configured by the Azure Server while creating a virtual machine.

11. Let's connect the SQL Azure database which we created by replicating our local database, as explained in the following screenshot:

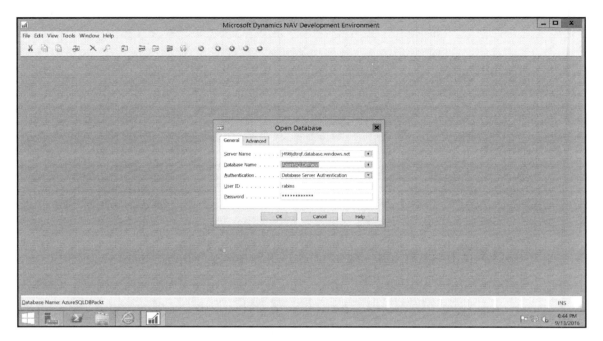

12. Use the credentials as shown earlier, and we should be good to go with the connection.

Now we can configure the instance setting in the Microsoft Dynamics NAV Administration tool, as shown in this screenshot:

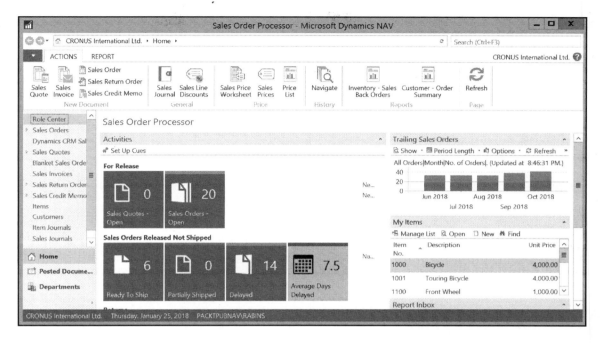

We can easily connect to the Role Tailored Client after the services are restarted.

Installing NAV on a multitenant environment

Here we will discuss the Installation process of Microsoft Dynamics NAV 2016 on a multitenant environment.

Prerequisite list

Following is the list of prerequisites for this installation process:

- The Microsoft Dynamics NAV database is installed on an SQL Server Database Engine instance. SQL Server Manager is also installed on the same computer.
- Access to the Microsoft Dynamics NAV installation media (DVD).

High-level steps

The entire process can be understood in just a few steps, which are as follows:

1. Prepare PowerShell for the operation.
2. Export the application database.
3. Remove the application database from the initial database.
4. Split the business data for each company.
5. Mount the application and business databases.

Detailed steps

We are first going to separate the application data from the business data.

The following are the steps for separating the application data:

1. Stop all Microsoft Dynamics NAV Server services.
2. Open the Microsoft Dynamics NAV Administration shell.
3. Then use the PowerShell cmdlets as follows:
   - `Export-NAVApplication`
   - `Remove-NAVApplication`

```
#cmdlet for removing Application
Remove-NAVApplication
    -DatabaseServer <Server name>
    -DatabaseInstance <Instance name>
    -DatabaseName <name of the original DATABASE>

#cmdlet for mounting Tenants
Mount-NAVTenant
    -DatabaseName <NAVDatabase>
    -Id <TenantID>
    -ServerInstance <NAVServerInstance>
    -OverwriteTenantIdInDatabase
----------
```

It is quite easy to get going with the PowerShell commands by just working around the codes.

For example, we can just write these commands and compile them as follows:

```
Set-ExecutionPolicy RemoteSigned -Force

Import-Module
'C:BackUpProgramFilesNAV.9.0.44974.NA.DVDWindowsPowerShellScriptsMultitenan
cyHowTo-MoveCompanyToTenant.ps1'
```

This will give you access to all the functions of the PowerShell file:

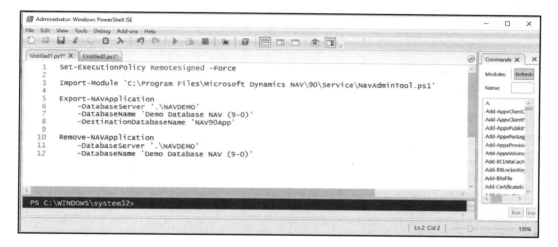

It is again the PowerShell cmdlet that makes like easier; just locate the folder
`WindowsPowerShellScripts/Multitenancy` in your installation DVD, and you are just
one step away from all the possible stuff you need in the multitenancy world.

Just import the file in Windows PowerShell ISE (run as administrator), and execute it to get
the result as follows:

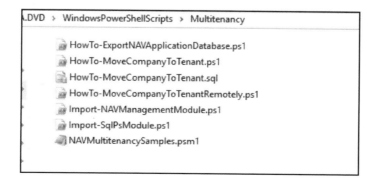

Some tips if you want to try your own customized code. Activate Intellisense, and import the PowerShell file you want to work with. Run the line, and you are good to go. You can now use all the functionalities of that file. It is the same like C# coding.

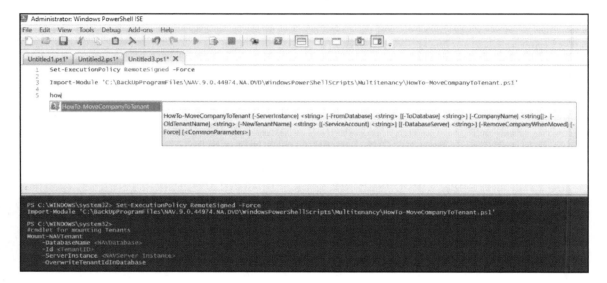

Post-installation operations

After the successful installation of Microsoft Dynamics NAV 2016, the administrator has access to the Microsoft dynamics NAV database. The database can be either on Cloud or On-premise. It can either be single tenant (traditional) or multitenant. The administrator can easily grant permission to other users using PowerShell commands, or he/she can manually grant the database owner role in the database in SQL Server Management Studio.

Summary

In this chapter, you learnt about the installation process of Microsoft Dynamics NAV 2016 in detail. We mostly covered the cloud platform. You also learnt ways to deploy the system on a multitenant environment. We explained how PowerShell can be better utilized to make life easier. Try to spend some time with PowerShell, and you will understand why Microsoft is trying to force most of the processes to be totally PowerShell-dependent.

In the next chapter, we will explore the latest features of Microsoft Dynamics NAV 2016 in detail, and the different design pattern that has been implemented into the Dynamics NAV system. The chapter will give you a better understanding of the business logic that has been implemented in NAV 2016.

2
Upgraded Features and Configuration in Dynamics NAV 2016

In the last chapter, we explained how Microsoft Dynamics NAV 2016 is well designed to suit different advanced technologies such as cloud technology, multitenancy, multi-environment installation, multi-client feature, and many more. We also discussed how we can use the PowerShell tool for different kinds of operations, and to increase the efficiency of Dynamics NAV Professionals. Here, in this chapter, you will learn about the latest features that have been added to Microsoft Dynamics NAV 2016 to make it more dependable and to reduce customization. We will also discuss their significance and effects on the overall system. We will discuss the workflow of these modifications, as well as try to understand the benefits of implementing these workflows.

The chapter requires some hands-on experience with the previous version, as I will be directly relating some of the features of its shortcomings. There will not be much explanation of things that are not modified to keep our focus on the scope of this chapter.

At the end of this chapter, we will understand the overall benefits of the new features and configurations, and find out the best possible way to harvest all these changes in the system. The main intention is to educate the reader about the reason and effects of implementing new features in the NAV system.

This chapter will cover the following points:

- Design Patterns of the system
- Technical details of the added features
- Comparison with older versions
- Different processes and workflows

Dynamics NAV 2016 Design Patterns

Design Patterns is the standard solution, which can be repeated to solve the most common problems. It is generally a part of the full system design. It can be taken as a proven concept in the application.

There are three different types of Design Patterns, which are clearly distinct in Microsoft Dynamics NAV 2016.

Architectural Design Pattern

Microsoft Dynamics NAV is highly based on Architectural Design Patterns, where highly reusable components are implemented so as to provide a dynamic structure to the system. It can be considered as a Software Design pattern.

Implementation Pattern

In Microsoft Dynamics NAV 2016, we use several Implementation Patterns, which are nothing but different development techniques. Most common Implementation Patterns are done for program organization and data structures.

Design Pattern

Design Patterns are reusable patterns that can be used to solve a specific problem. In Dynamics NAV, we use number series, blocked entity, and so on.

In most cases, a developer faces a problem where he/she needs to replicate the pre-existing functionality or some part of a module. It is essential that the developers understand about the design patterns implemented so as to get the best results and a clear understanding.

Implementing the Activity Log Pattern

The idea behind an activity log is that, whenever something happens, we can write down what happens and when it happens. We will follow the steps listed next for implementation of the Activity Log Pattern:

- Record the activity
- One centralized view
- Present to the user

The **Activity Log** feature records the activity, its outcomes, and success. We will assemble everything in one centralized view, and then present everything using filters.

We will start with the use of **Table 710 Activity Log**, as shown in the following screenshot:

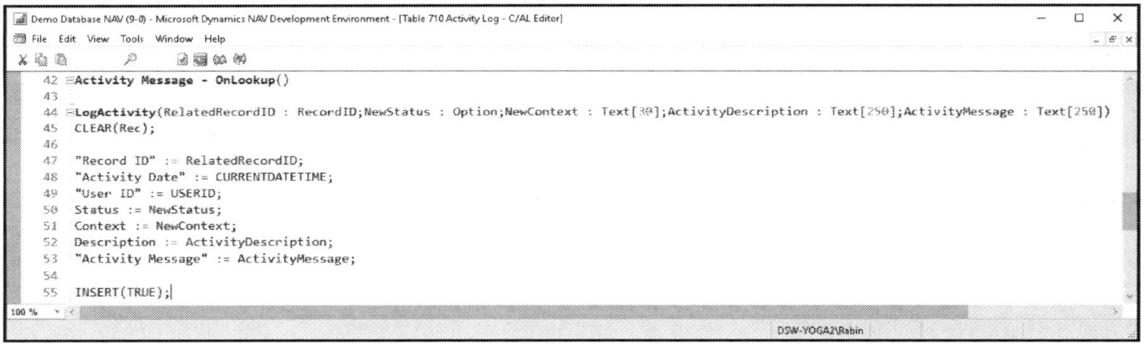

This is the part where the Activity Log Design Pattern captures the related detailed information on any kind of activity. The activity could be an error message, warning message, or just a confirmation message. There are three categories of log management:

- Log insertion
- Log modification
- Log deletion

The most common places where you can utilize these logs are Posted Sales Credit Memos and Posted Sales Invoices. You can click on the **Activity Log** button to view the activity in order to back trace what happened in the documents. The **Activity Log** feature always filters the view, which concludes our third step, Present to the user. This presents the proper message filter to the correct user. **Filter** also filters the **Activity Log** feature on the basis of date, and provides the exact log that the user is looking for:

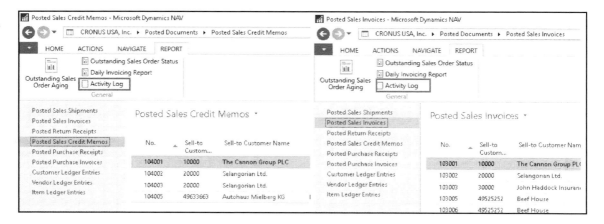

Now we will examine how this pattern outputs data, and presents it to the user.

We will take the example of a Posted Sales Invoice page, which has an action called **Activity Log**. It links the page with the logic that is connected to the **Activity Log** sub-system which implements the design pattern.

Let's examine the **Page** action of **Page 132: Posted Sales Invoice**. Here, you can find an action called **Activity Log**. We can find the code written on the **onAction()** trigger of this action by pressing *F9*, or by clicking the **C/AL Code** button in the header, as shown in this screenshot:

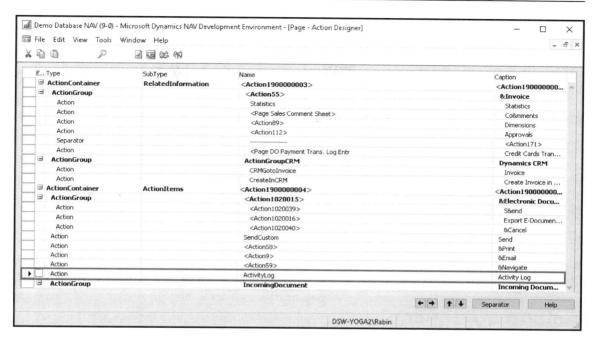

It has a function called **ShowActivityLog**. This function takes **RECORDID** as an argument, and passes it to the **ShowEntries** function of the **Activity Log** table:

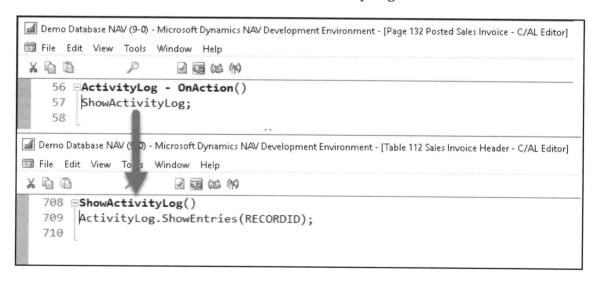

The function gets **RecordID** as an argument, filters the data as per the record and date, and presents the **Activity Log** to the user, as seen in this screenshot:

```
Demo Database NAV (9-0) - Microsoft Dynamics NAV Development Environment - [Table 710 Activity Log - C/AL Editor]

File   Edit   View   Tools   Window   Help

57  ShowEntries(RelatedRecID : RecordID)
58     SETRANGE("Record ID",RelatedRecID);
59     SETCURRENTKEY("Activity Date");
60     ASCENDING(FALSE);
61
62     COMMIT;
63     PAGE.RUNMODAL(PAGE::"Activity Log",Rec);
64
```

Setting up a change log

Open the Microsoft Dynamics NAV 2016 Role Tailored client, and perform the following steps:

1. Go to **Departments** | **Administration** | **IT Administration** | **General** | **Tasks** | **Change Log Setup**.
2. Click on the **Action** tab in **Change Log Setup**, and choose **Tables**.

   The **Change Log Setup (Table) List** window will open.

3. Select the table you want to include.
4. Select **Some Fields** or **All fields**.

   For the **Some fields** option, you need to define a list of fields that you want to select. Use the **Assist Edit** button to do so. Close the window.

5. Finally, in the **Change Log Setup** window, select the **Change Log Activated** field:

Your setup is complete.

Viewing the Change Logs Entries page

We can view all the changes logged in RTC in the Change Log Entries page. To view the logs, just go to the page with the help of the following path:

Departments | Administration | IT Administration | General | Change Log Entries

This will show you a list of all the change logs. This is crucial from the administrative point of view:

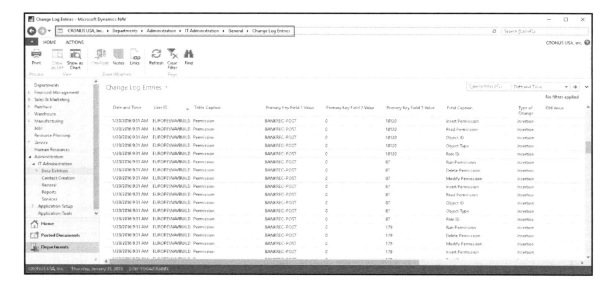

Redesigned C/AL Editor

The C/AL Editor has been redesigned to provide more coding capabilities. Coding in the new C/AL Editor is just as before except for some new features such as IntelliSense, name completion, change tracking, improved syntax highlighting, and colorization. The following sample code in the C/AL Editor clearly shows its capabilities:

```
 Demo Database NAV (9-0) - Microsoft Dynamics NAV Development Environment - [C/AL Editor]
 File   Edit   View   Tools   Window   Help
 X                     P           

 1  Documentation()
 2  //Different Colors
 3  Text := text
 4  Code:= 'CODE1234'
 5  Number := 12345
 6
 7
 8  OnRun()
 9  IF NOT CONFIRM('Constant' + COMPANYNAME + '___') THEN
10     EXIT;
11
12  ItemRec.no
13          No.
14          No. 2
15          No. of Substitutes
            No. Series
```

Event channels on Microsoft Dynamics NAV Server events

Monitoring is an essential part of software security and surveillance. You can monitor events on Microsoft Dynamics NAV Server to diagnose conditions, and troubleshoot problems that affect operation and performance. Microsoft Dynamics NAV 2016 introduces event channels on events that occur on Microsoft Dynamics NAV Server instances. Event channels provide a way to collect a view event data from a specific provider, which, in this case, is Microsoft Dynamics NAV Server, and for a specific type of event, such as Admin, operational, or debug. The implementation of event channels offers the following enhancements to event logging and viewing.

Microsoft Dynamics NAV uses **Event Tracing for Windows (ETW)**, which is a subsystem of the Windows operating systems. ETW provides a tracing mechanism for events that are raised by an application or service. ETW enables you to use industry-standard tools, such as Windows Performance Monitor, PerfView, Event Viewer, and Windows PowerShell, to dynamically collect data on trace events that occur on the Microsoft Dynamics NAV Server.

LOG	Admin	Operational	Debug
Description	Includes events that target end users and IT administrators. These events typically indicate a problem that requires action to resolve the problem.	Includes events that provide information about an operation that occurred on Microsoft Dynamics NAV Server instances.	Includes trace events that occur on Microsoft Dynamics NAV Server instances.
Example	An example of an admin event is a tenant database failing to mount on the Microsoft Dynamics NAV Server instance.	An example of an operational event is the shutting down of the Microsoft Dynamics NAV Server instance.	

Event Logs can be viewed using Windows Event Viewer.

To start Event Viewer, follow these steps:

1. Click on **Start**, and point at **Programs**.
2. Point at **Administrative Tools**, and then click on **Event Viewer**.

To collect and view trace events in Event Viewer, follow these steps:

1. In the console tree, choose **Applications and Services Logs**, **Microsoft**, **DynamicsNAV**, and then **Server**.
2. If the **Debug** log is not shown under **Server**, then in the **View** menu, select **Show Analytic and Debug Logs**.
3. Select the **Debug log** option, and then choose **Enable Log** in the **Actions** menu.

 Understanding how to read the event logs properly is vital if you have system-or application-level issues. We will discuss more about event logs in `Chapter 4`, *Testing and Debugging*.

Multiple namespaces on XMLports

In Microsoft Dynamics NAV 2016, you can define multiple namespaces on XMLports that import or export data as XML. This improves the ability to create XMLports that are compatible with XML schemas, which are used by the system that consume or provide the Microsoft Dynamics NAV data.

 For those who don't know what namespace is Namespaces are used to distinguish fields and provide uniqueness. The inclusion of namespaces enables parties to tag elements and resolve any ambiguity.

You can define a namespace in the new namespaces property of the XMLport object as shown in the next screenshot.

Each namespace is defined by a prefix and the namespace, which is typically a **URI** (**uniform resource identifier**).

You then apply the prefix to specific elements of the XMLport by setting the new `NamespacePrefix` property:

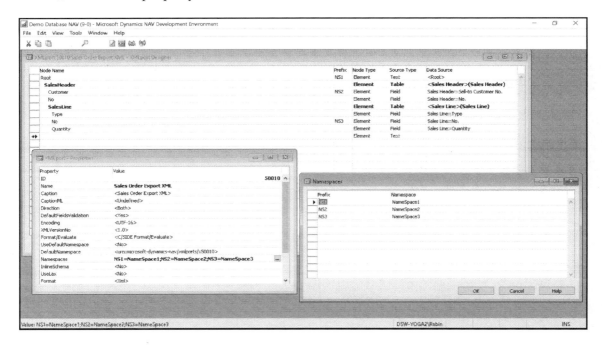

Select the **Export** option in the request page for the **Sales Order Export XML** report, and click on **OK**:

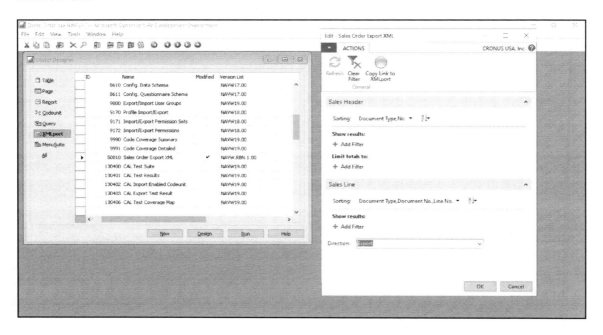

You will be prompted with a **Save/Open** dialog box, as seen in the following screenshot. Just select one option, and follow the steps:

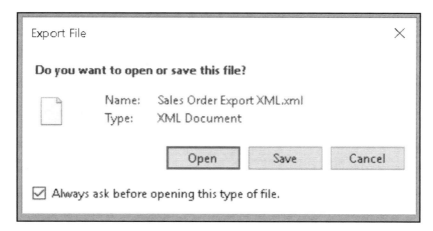

The XML file shown in the following screenshot clearly signifies that the different namespaces are assigned to the corresponding data, which can be utilized in the case of conflicts by differentiating elements or attributes within an XML document:

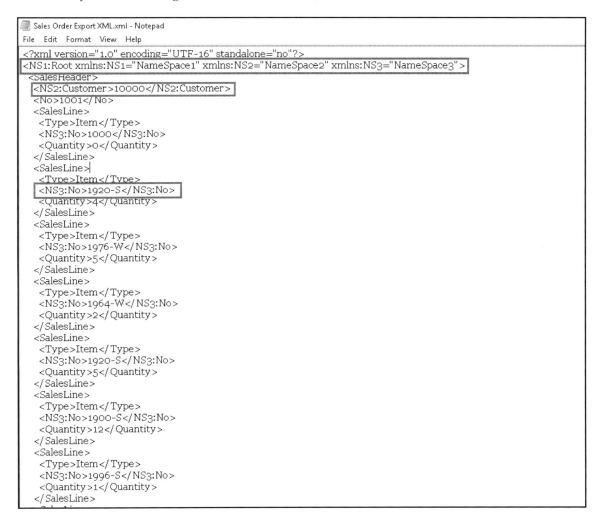

Updating custom report layouts using upgrade codeunits

In Microsoft Dynamics NAV 2016, a report has a built-in report layout by default; it can be a Word report layout, a Standard RDLC report layout, or both. You can update custom report layouts with the help of upgrade codeunits. It handles all the changes in the report datasets that affect the report layouts. Upgrade codeunits enable you to programmatically update multiple custom report layouts in the database to changes in report datasets, which cannot be resolved by users from the Microsoft Dynamics NAV client; however, there are certain changes to the dataset that the user is required to modify manually in the report layouts before they can be used. These types of change include, for example, deleted fields or field name conflicts as a result of renaming. Upgrade codeunits enable you to handle these breaking changes to report datasets and layouts without requiring end user interaction.

To design the report upgrade logic in an upgrade codeunit, you add the C/AL code that implements the report upgrade API (through .NET Framework interoperability) and a set of functions which are available in codeunit 9651: *Document Report Mgt.*. In the Microsoft Dynamics NAV application, codeunit 9651: *Document Report Mgt.* is the main component for running and maintaining customized report layouts.

We will talk more about this in Chapter 3, *The C/AL and VB Programming*.

 There are other C/AL upgrades such as the Try function, the FILTERPAGEBUILDER datatype, the HyperlinkHandler function type in test code, the Metadata Virtual table, the CLIENTTYPE option, and others, which are explained in Chapter 3, *The C/AL and VB Programming*, in detail.

Finance is an important business domain in Microsoft

The new and improved features in Dynamics NAV 2016 enhance the user experience for accountants and bookkeepers. The following are some of the main points I would like to emphasize in this section:

- Microsoft Dynamics NAV 2016 reporting enhancements
- Microsoft Dynamics NAV 2016 Preview Posting
- Microsoft Dynamics NAV 2016 Positive Pay
- Microsoft Dynamics NAV 2016 North America document totals

- Microsoft Dynamics NAV 2016 Deferrals
- Microsoft Dynamics NAV 2016 works natively with Azure SQL

I will try to explain these points with some basic examples.

Microsoft Dynamics NAV 2016 Reporting enhancements

In Microsoft Dynamics NAV 2016, we have several reporting enhancements. All these enhancements were included because of an increasing demand from Microsoft partners, and in order to reduce the implementation cost and time. Most of the reporting enhancements were initially separately developed on demand by Microsoft partners, but because of the increasing demand by the end users, these enhancements are included in this release.

In Microsoft Dynamics NAV 2016, a new feature called Report Enhancements updates the existing reports, and helps you create new reports.

 There are basically two releases which we will be taking into consideration here: NA Release (North American Release) and W1 (Worldwide Release).

The North American report updates include updating the paper size of all the reports to letter size when printing.

You can see wider reports in the W1 report since the updates include changing the 25 report to landscape orientation. This helps us to visualize the report better. Most of us have faced this issue where the user wants to see the landscape view of most of the journal reports.

Benefits for the users

We can now view more content displayed on the 25 report, which is now in landscape orientation. Hence, it is expected that most of the clients can directly start using these reports in North America in particular.

All reports in the North American installation default to letter-sized paper when printing. This has been done by keeping in mind the common working style of North American users. In my experience, almost all of my American Clients want the paper setup to be letter-sized.

The following screenshot displays the printer setup page where we can select the paper property and other options:

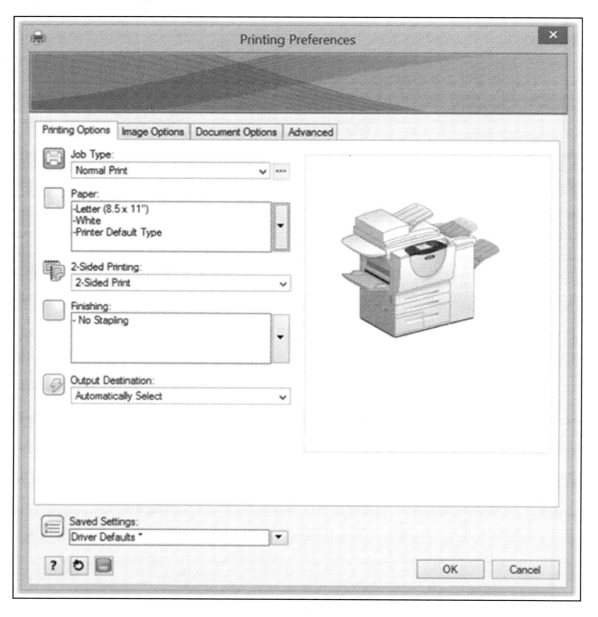

In addition, the new **Vendor Pre-Payment Journal** displaying invoices/credit memos per vendor is present in the system by default. The following is a screenshot of this report:

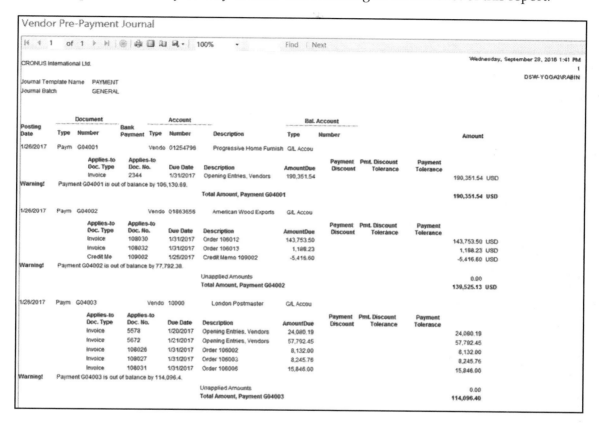

Here, in the **Account Schedule** report given in the next screenshot, you can see the contents are better visualized in the landscape view:

Account Schedule

CRONUS USA, Inc.
Period   01/01/15..09/28/16
Fiscal Start Date 01/01/16
Account Schedule   INCOME   Cash Flow Statement
Column Layout   ACT./BUD

All amounts are in USD.

Acc. Schedule Line: Date Filter: 01/01/15..09/28/16

9/28/2016
Page 1
DSW-YOGA2\RABIN

Description	FY17 Actual	FY17 Budget	Variance (Actual vs Budget)	Percent of Budget	FY16 Actual	YOY Change
Revenue	19,555,165.65	19,017,040.00	538,125.65	2.83	1,498,569.64	18,056,596.01
Cost of Goods Sold	13,282,752.84	10,676,550.00	2,606,202.84	24.41	899,732.08	12,383,020.76
Gross Profit	6,272,412.81	8,340,490.00	-2,068,077.19	-24.80	598,837.56	5,673,575.25
Operating Expense	7,354,283.67	7,032,540.00	321,743.67	4.58	520,819.49	6,833,464.18
Net Operating Income	-1,081,870.86	1,307,950.00	-2,389,820.86	-182.72	78,018.07	-1,159,888.93

These are simple, but wise, decisions made by Microsoft in order to make the new release more meaningful. These small modifications and features make a lot of difference, and reduce the number of modifications for any implementation.

Word forms and e-mail

In Microsoft Dynamics NAV 2016, you can create multiple custom report layouts using Microsoft Word. It also allows you to assign specific e-mail addresses to document types, enhancing the user experience. This is one of the most striking features, as most clients want reports to be more compatible with the e-mail features.

In Microsoft Dynamics NAV 2016, Microsoft Word forms for customer statements and for the North America vendor remittance reports enable you to easily create multiple custom report layouts.

You can simply use these layouts to be assigned to a particular customer by document type, a specific report, and an e-mail address for that document. For example, if a statement needs to be sent to the receivables department, but the invoice needs to go to Sales, you can have different e-mail message destinations. This feature is something you can use to impress clients during a sales demo:

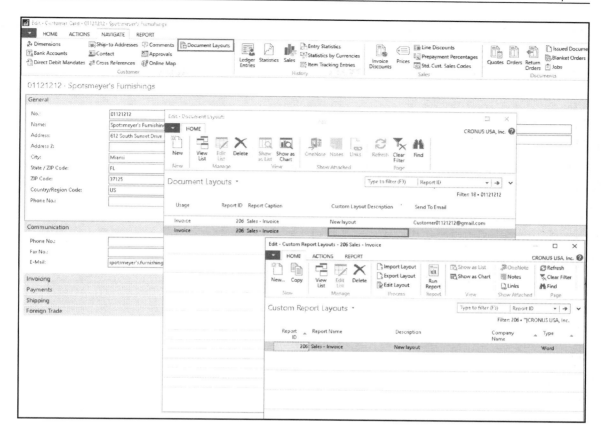

Microsoft Dynamics NAV 2016 Preview Posting

In Microsoft Dynamics NAV 2016, you can review the entries to be created before you post a document or journal.

This is made possible by the introduction of a new feature called Preview Posting, which enables you to preview the impact of a posting against each ledger associated with a document.

In every document and journal that can be posted, you can click on **Preview Posting** to review the different types of entry that will be created when you post the document or journal.

Benefits of Preview Posting

You can understand the system state prior to posting, which might affect the transaction and the related ledgers. It also reduces errors in posting, and the user can have confidence in the posting setup. In prior versions, we had test reports, which gave somewhat similar ideas, but this gives you the real perception before the posting process has been carried out. This can be a very useful tool while you are trying to test the posting setup in live companies.

To launch the preview, click on **Preview Posting** in the **Posting** group on the ribbon for the document:

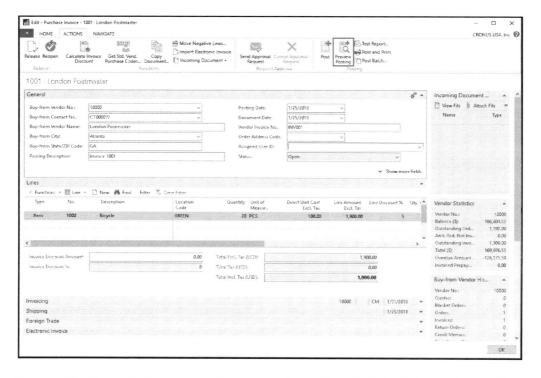

The **Preview Posting** window opens first, providing a list of all the ledgers that will be affected. From here, you can drill into the details for each ledger to see the impact against the ledger.

In the following screenshot, you can clearly see how the system actually posts the values temporarily so as to give you the real scenario without posting. These transactions are rolled back once the user exits the posting preview pages:

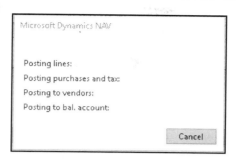

You can easily navigate through the ledgers, and see how it is going to impact the system and other data, as shown in the next screenshot:

You can click on the **All Ledger** entry on the number of entries link. It will navigate to the corresponding ledger entry view, as shown in the following screenshot:

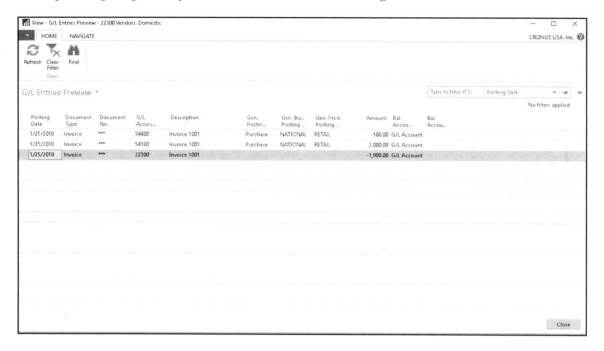

The Preview Posting functionality is available for the following sections of documents:

Journals	Receivables	Payables	Service
General Journals	Sales Invoice(s)	Purchase Invoice(s)	Service Credit Memo(s)
Recurring General Journal	Sales Credit Memo(s)	Purchase Credit Memo(s)	Service Invoice(s)
IC General Journal	Sales Order(s)	Purchase Order(s)	Service Order(s)
Job G/L Journal	Sales Return Order(s)	Purchase Return Order(s)	Service Lines
Cash Receipt Journal	Mini Sales Credit Memo(s)	Mini Purchase Credit Memo(s)	
Fixed Asset G/L Journal	Mini Sales Invoice(s)	Mini Purchase Invoice(s)	

Sales Journal	Apply Customer Entries	Payment Registration	
Payment Journal	Unapply Customer Entries	Apply Vendor Entries	
Purchase Journal		Unapply Vendor Entries	
Fixed Asset Journal			
Recurring Fixed Asset Journal			

Microsoft Dynamics NAV 2016 Positive Pay

Positive pay is one of the interesting features that have been implemented in Microsoft Dynamics NAV 2016. Bookkeepers can now use positive pay to ensure accuracy and reduce fraud. This is a totally new feature, which is called US positive pay. It basically enables users to send payment information to the bank to reduce fraud and minimize errors.

 Positive pay is a cash-management service used to prevent checks-related fraud. Generally, banks uses positive pay to match the checks that a company issues with those it presents for payment.

In Microsoft Dynamics NAV, you can create a file with vendor information and check number and payment amounts, which you can send directly to your bank using the Positive Pay feature. The bank then uses this file to verify any payments submitted against your account. If the payment isn't found, the payment isn't cleared.

Benefits of Positive Pay

With the use of the Positive Pay feature, you can create a Positive Pay file automatically from the system, for example, from the Payment Journal, and send it to the bank. The bank will not complete the payment if it is presented and doesn't match the positive pay information. There are many default formats which are available and can even be customized for your specific bank needs. Another advantage of Positive Pay is that it keeps a history, which includes detailed data. You can also use this history to recreate a positive pay file for your bank.

The following screenshot shows the screen where you can import and export the data for paycheck. Select the option **Positive PayExport** for exporting the data:

Microsoft Dynamics NAV 2016 North America document totals

The American release of Microsoft Dynamics NAV 2016 includes document total information, which is very crucial for American users.

Benefits

American users can display the total tax, total amount excluding tax, total amount including tax, discount amount, and discount percent for unposted documents. In addition, the total information can also be seen after they enter transactions in Sales and Purchase order processing.

Sales order processing

As you can see in the **Lines** section shown in the following screenshot, we have a special card type subpage, which somewhat serves like a fact box, and presents calculated values of the line entries. This also prevents the use of small-level reports, which are generated just to calculate totals:

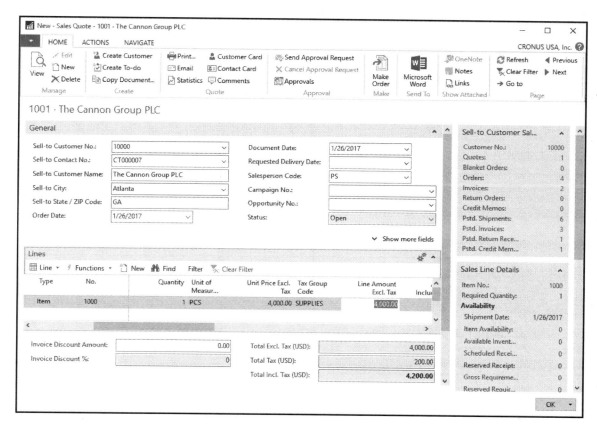

Similarly, you can see this in the **Sales Invoice** page. It is included in most of the similar documents in order to provide valuable information on the same page. This feature is highly appreciated by most of the clients:

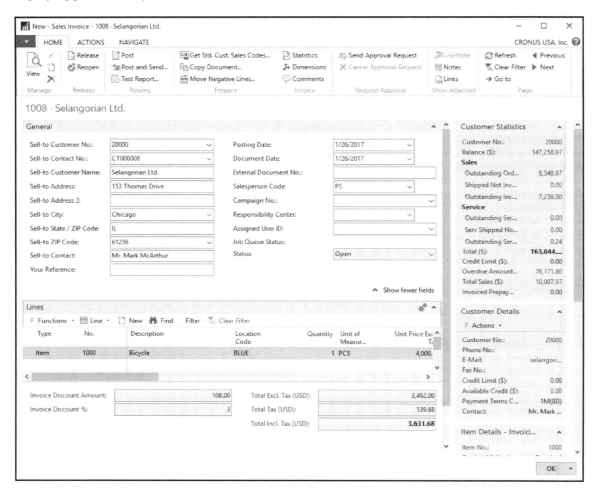

Microsoft Dynamics NAV 2016 Deferrals

Microsoft Dynamics NAV 2016 allows the process of deferring revenues and expenses to relevant accounting periods. This allows flexibility in the operation when you are not authorized to recognize any transaction directly at that current moment.

Deferrals means to defer or to delay recognizing certain revenues or expenses on the income statement until a later, more appropriate time. For example: annuities (`https://en.wikipedia.org/wiki/Annuity`), charges (`https://en.wikipedia.org/wiki/Fee`), taxes (`https://en.wikipedia.org/wiki/Tax`), income (`https://en.wikipedia.org/wiki/Income`), and so on.

Benefits

It enables additional financial functionality in Microsoft Dynamics NAV. This also reduces the time and effort required to defer revenues and expenses. It enables reporting on deferred amounts for customers, vendors, and account ledgers.

Set up deferral templates with the default settings used to build deferral schedules. The following screenshot shows how a deferral template can be created:

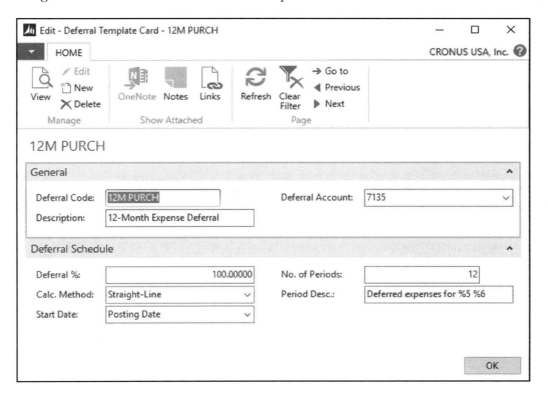

The next screenshot shows how the Item card can be set up for the deferral value. Define a default deferral template used for G/L accounts, items, and resources. Also, stockout warnings are generally turned off:

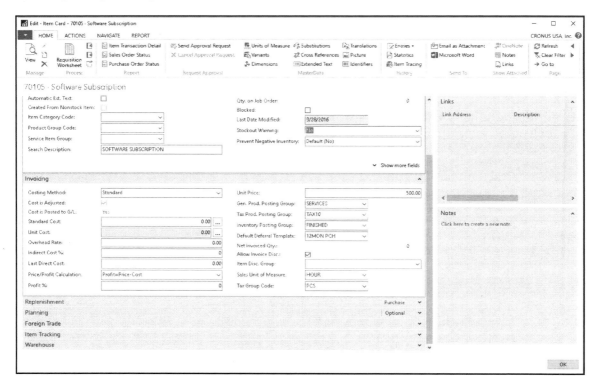

For each line item, you can view or modify the default deferral schedule, as shown in this screenshot:

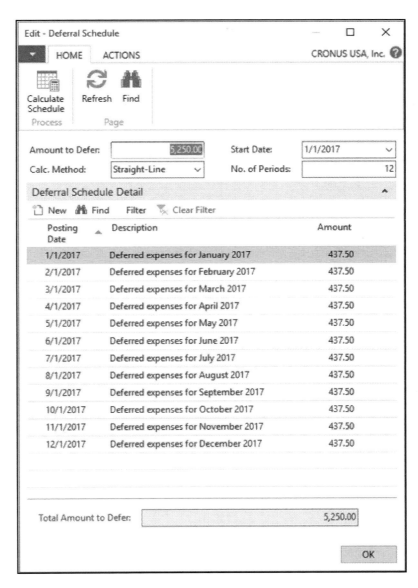

Now open the **Purchase Invoice** document, and complete the header section. Also select the item which is created with the assigned**Default Deferral Template** code, here, Item **70105: Software Subscription**:

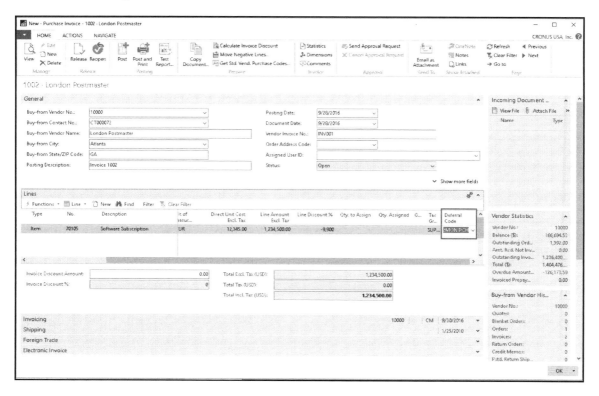

Select the deferral code, and click on **OK**. The next screenshot will show the posting accounts. We can check this preview using the feature called **Preview Posting,** and by selecting **G/L Entry** from the window.

The amount is posted to the deferral account, and recognized over the defined schedule:

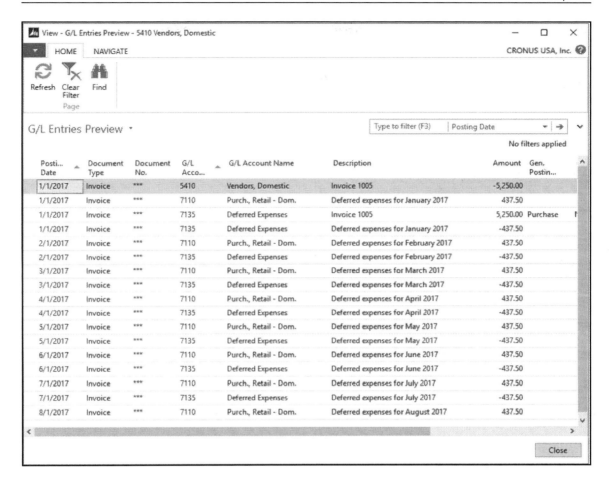

 View reports showing deferral balances by vendor, customer, and account.

There are three reports present in Microsoft Dynamics NAV 2016 for this purpose: **G/L** (General Ledger), **Sales**, and **Purchasing** summary:

	Type	ID	Name	Modified	Version List
	☐	1700	Deferral Summary - G/L		NAVW19.00.00.43402
	☐	1701	Deferral Summary - Sales		NAVW19.00.00.43402
▶	☐	1702	Deferral Summary - Purchasing		NAVW19.00.00.43402

A sample preview of the **Deferral Summary – Purchasing** report is shown in the following screenshot. Here we can easily see the landscape report containing the summary of all the deferral transactions carried out up to the date specified in the report filter:

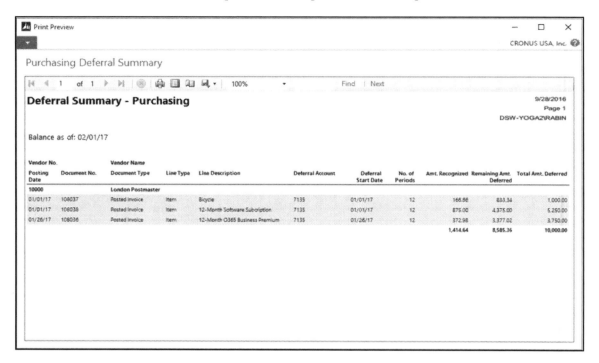

The deferrals feature is available on following documents:

Journals	Sales	Purchase
General Journals	Sales Invoices	Purchase Invoices
	Sales Credit Memos	Purchase Credit Memos
	Sales Orders	Purchase Orders
	Sales Return Orders	Purchase Return Orders

Microsoft Dynamics NAV 2016 works natively with Azure SQL

Microsoft Dynamics NAV 2016 can be configured to use Azure SQL as a relational database-as-a-service, eliminating maintenance and reducing costs.

In Microsoft Dynamics NAV 2016, you can configure your Microsoft Dynamics NAV Server instance to securely connect to a Microsoft Dynamics NAV database running within a managed relational SQL database-as-a-service or Azure SQL Database.

Azure SQL Database is a relational database service in the cloud, based on the Microsoft SQL Server engine, with built-in mission-critical capabilities.

Benefits for the user

There are several benefits of working with Azure SQL natively. I have tried to categorize them in the following section.

Cost

This is a very cost-effective plan, as you can now be billed hourly at a fixed rate instead of paying for an SQL license upfront. It eliminates hardware costs and results in near-zero administrative costs. And you can adjust the number of subscriptions as per your need, making it a more dynamic service.

Administration

There is built-in support service for high availability, automatic backups, data protection, and fault tolerance; the database software is automatically patched and upgraded by Microsoft Azure. This is crucial if your system is performing slowly; in that case, the system automatically reinstalls all your components on a new instance, providing you with the feel of a newly installed one.

Service -level agreement and compliance

Working with Azure provides a database-level availability SLA of 99.99%; Azure certifications include ISO, HIPAA BAA, and EU Model Clause.

Business continuity

There are multiple built-in business continuity features included along with features such as point-in-time restore, geo-restore, and geo-replication.

Benefits for partners

Working natively with Azure SQL is is beneficial for Microsoft Partners. I have tried to analyze this with the help of the following perspective.

Predictable performance and scalability

It automatically adjusts performance and scale without downtime, uses monitoring and troubleshooting features for index tuning, and queries optimization, hence making it an ideal service even for the organizations with a huge data flow.

Setup and admin

It focuses on rapid application development rather than managing the infrastructure; Microsoft Azure takes care of the physical resources of the underlying SQL Server instance.

Simple migration path

It is very simple to use as you can upload and manage your existing database using Azure Portal, SQL Server Management Studio, or an API which is connected securely from Microsoft Dynamics NAV 2016.

Familiar SQL Server tools and APIs

It can be accessed through REST API, PowerShell, Azure Portal, and SQL Server Management Studio. It is completely compatible with the SQL Server engine.

REST Stands for **Representational State Transfer**, which is nothing but a web service (`https://en.wikipedia.org/wiki/Web_service`), which provides one-way interoperability between computer systems on the Internet (`https://en.wikipedia.org/wiki/Internet`). Web service APIs (`https://en.wikipedia.org/wiki/Application_programming_interface`) that comply to the REST architectural constraints (`https://en.wikipedia.org/wiki/Representational_state_transfer#Architectural_constraints`) are called REST APIs.

Understanding Development Environment

We use Development Environment to develop Microsoft Dynamics NAV 2016 applications. The Development Environment has a similar look if we take Microsoft Dynamics NAV 2015 as a reference.

The basic object types are the same. We still have seven basic object types: Table, Page, Report, Codeunit, Query, XMLport, and MenuSuite.

 I assume the reader knows the basics of these seven objects, and have not included the descriptions in this section, saving space and your time.

Changing the database size

We can easily change the database size if we have sufficient space available by following these steps:

1. Go to **File** | **Database** | **Alter**, and then select the **Database Files** tab.

2. You will get a window similar to the following screenshot:

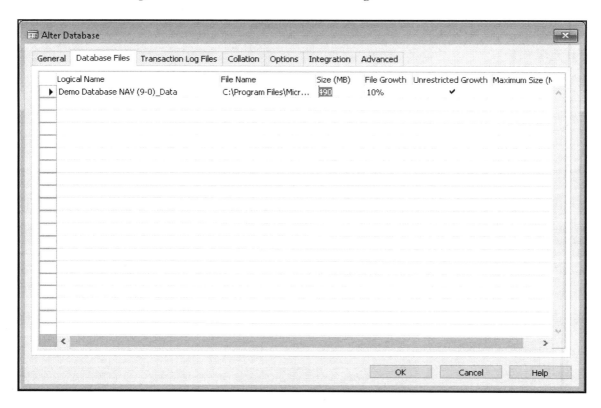

3. Increase the size in the **Size (MB)** column with a proper number. Then click on the **Transaction Log File** tab. You will get information related to the log file size of your database. Look at the following screenshot:

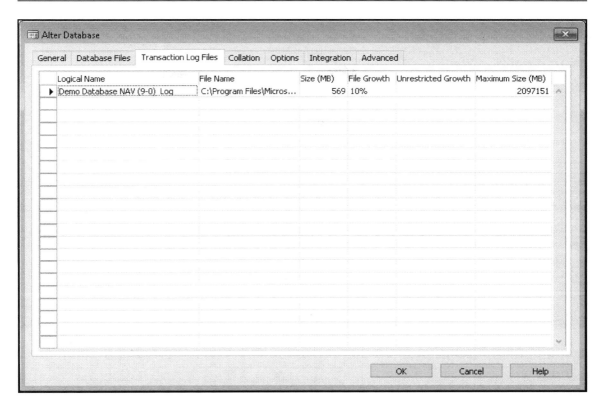

4. Change the value in the **Size (MB)** field, and click on **OK**.
5. Exit the Development Environment, and reopen.

Database schema synchronization

At certain times, **Microsoft Dynamics NAV object designer** might contain some modification of objects at the table level and they need to be synchronized to the **SQL Server** side, because the database is in the SQL Server itself. We have a **Schema synchronization** feature, which can take care of this synchronization operation as shown in the following screenshot:

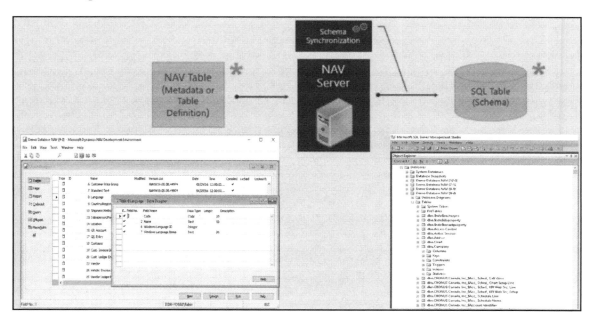

Whenever a modification is done in the table in Development Environment, it is stored as a metadata information. And at certain moments in time, you can synchronize the metadata of changes via the service tier towards SQL Server.

Whenever we work at the table level, for example, coding or making some modifications in the fields, while saving, the system automatically prompts the user to synchronize and compile. But there are times when you have done some drastic changes that might result in data loss. The system will not automatically synchronize the objects. Instead, it keeps it in the metadata, and then you can carry out the synchronization operation later. There are three options for synchronization.

To compile an object, you can either press the F11 button from your keyboard, or go to the Menu bar, and click on **Tool/Compile**. It will prompt you with the dialog box shown in the following screenshot:

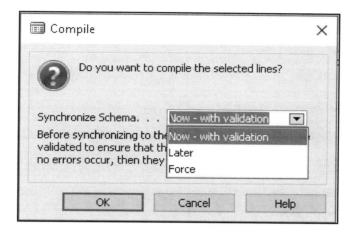

With the **Later** option, you can choose to synchronize later, and **Force** actually enforces the synchronization process; this might result in data loss. This is an interesting feature, and comes in very handy during the development phase. But these features should be handled with responsibility, since they might result in the loss of valuable data.

Workflows in Microsoft Dynamics NAV 2016

In this section, we will learn how to create and use Workflow in Microsoft Dynamics NAV 2016. This section will explain the new basic workflow functionality of Microsoft Dynamics NAV 2016, which is awesome.

We will cover the following steps to make you better understand the workflow functionality:

- Introduction to the workflow functionality
- Set up the prerequisites for a workflow
- Workflow demo

Introduction to workflow

Workflow enables you to understand modern life business processes along with the best practices or industry standard practice, for example, ensuring that a customer credit limit has been independently verified and the requirement of two approvers for a payment process has been met.

Workflow has these three main capabilities:

- Approvals
- Notifications
- Automation

Workflow basically has three components, that is, Event, Condition, and Response. **When Event** defines the name of any event in the system, whereas **On Condition** specifies the event, and **Then Response** is the action that needs to be taken on the basis of that condition. This is shown in the following screenshot:

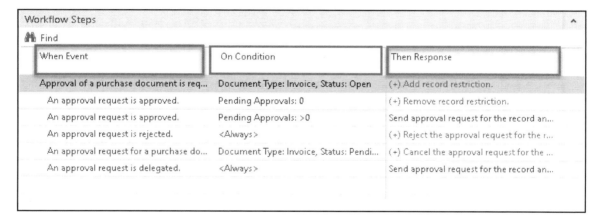

 We need to differentiate between a workflow, which is a collection of one or more **Event. Response** is designed and managed through a designer (as shown in the preceding screenshot) and **workflow Template**, which is a mechanism to deliver the workflow process to the NAV System.

Setup required before using workflow

The following setup is a prerequisite for the workflow functionality, which I will just discuss briefly:

- SMTP Mail setup
- Job queues
- Approval User setup
- Workflow User group
- Notification setup

SMTP Mail setup

For SMTP setup, go to the SMTP Mail Setup page from the RTC client, and fill in the **SMTP Server** name, **SMTP Server Port** number, and the **Authentications** option. You just need to make sure that your e-mail setup is working, as shown in this screenshot:

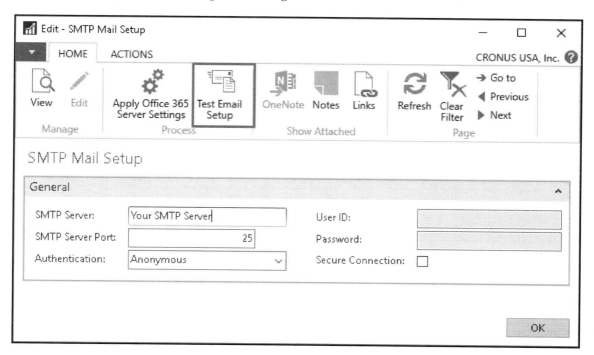

Job queues

We will use the default job queue just to make sure that the actions run in the background. Just click on **Start Job Queue**:

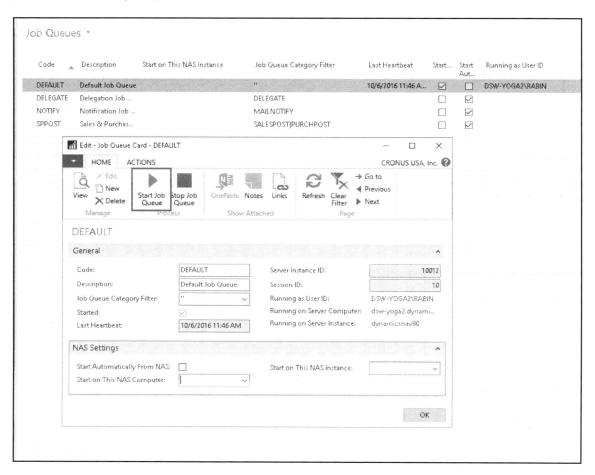

Approval User setup

Just make sure you have a well-defined Approver Setup. Microsoft Dynamics NAV 2016 has a very easy user setup process. You can take a look at the following screenshot to see how it can be done:

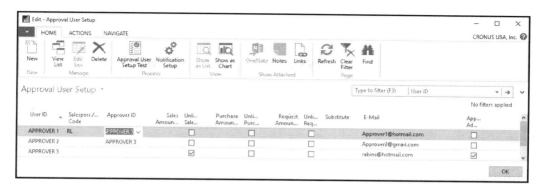

Workflow User Group

The **Workflow User Group** window is new in Dynamics NAV 2016. It introduces the possibility to create a user group for approvals. It includes a sequence number. As shown in the following screenshot, both users have the same sequence, which means that both users will get the notification at the same time. If it were different, then the notifications would be sent as per the sequence:

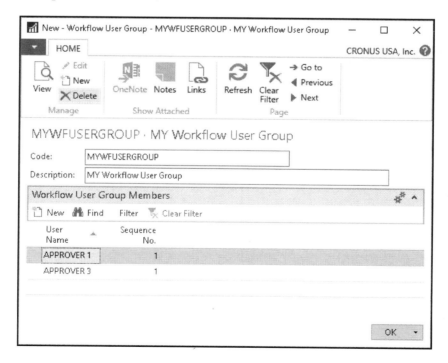

Notification Setup

In Microsoft Dynamics NAV 2016, we not only find different notification templates, but we can also create new ones. For example, by default, the standard notification for approvals is an e-mail. We can change the schedule as per our need. Open **Notification Setup**, and refer to the following screenshot to change the schedule:

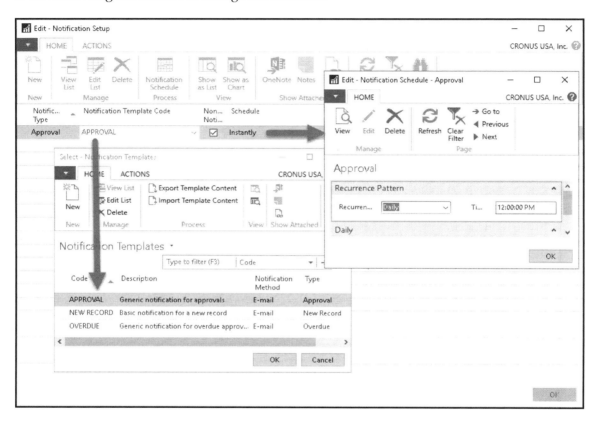

Workflow demo

We can use the workflow functionally for various operations. Let's take an example of the Customer Approval workflow. Here we will need to approve the customer if the credit limit is changed. We will set up our workflow accordingly to show a better picture of the process.

Setting up the conditions

Let's set up the scenario for testing the workflow functionality of Microsoft Dynamics NAV 2016.

Following are the steps to set up the conditions:

1. Follow this link for workflow in Role Tailored Client of Microsoft Dynamics NAV 2016:

   Departments | **Administration** | **Application Setup** | **Workflow** | **Workflows**

   Or you can directly type `workflow` in the **Search** pane.

2. Create a new workflow. Let's use **New Workflow from Template**. This will create a workflow with a template, which we can modify later. Refer to the following screenshot:

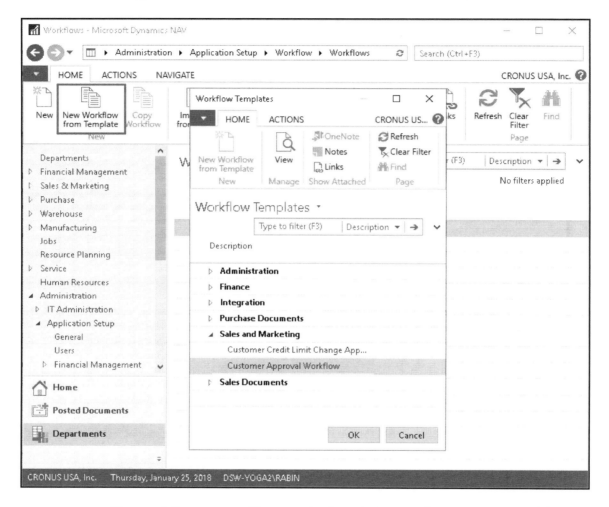

The workflow steps will appear in the window, and now we can modify as per our requirements.

3. To see how the workflow functionality works, let's take an example where a credit limit greater than 1,000 will trigger an event, which will generate some response.

> For this, click on the **AssisEdit** button in the **On Condition** column on the first line **Approval of a customer is Requested.**. Add the condition **Credit Limit(LCY) is > 1,000** in a new window:

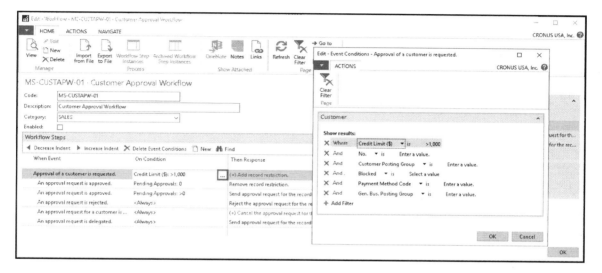

 We can add more responses just by clicking on the **AssistEdit** button of a record in the **Then Response** column. Then click on **Add More Responses**. You can also assign recipient information for that response.

4. Edit the reponses of the line. In the **Workflow Responses** window in **Approver Type,** select **Workflow User Group**, which we created for this demo. Now select the **MYWFUSERGROUP** code in the **Workflow User Group Code** field:

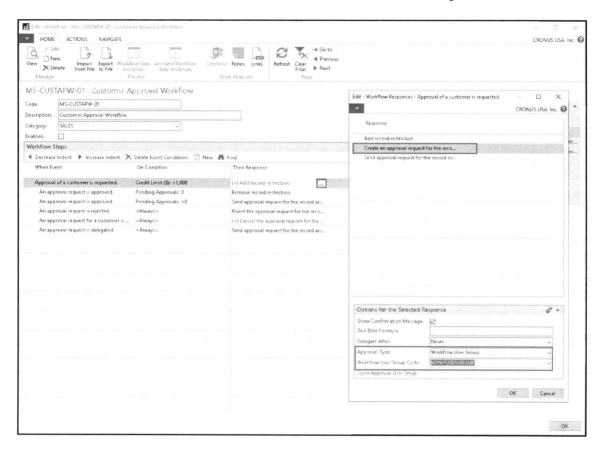

5. Click on the **Enable Boolean** button, and then you are done with configuring the workflow setup:

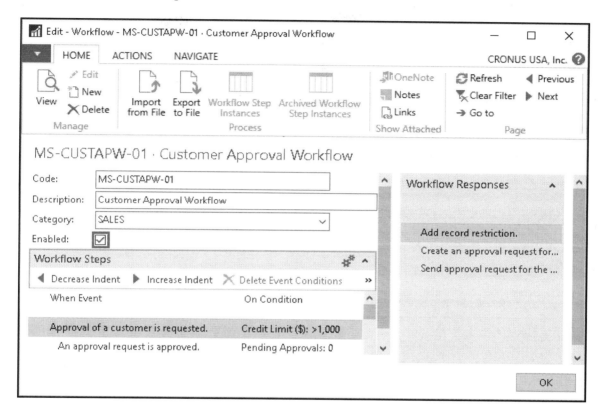

Testing the workflow

Now we will run the system to test the workflow functionality and get impressed.

Following are the steps to test the workflow:

1. Go to a customer card-for example, customer number 2000, and change the credit limit to a value greater than 1,000(here, **1,200.00**):

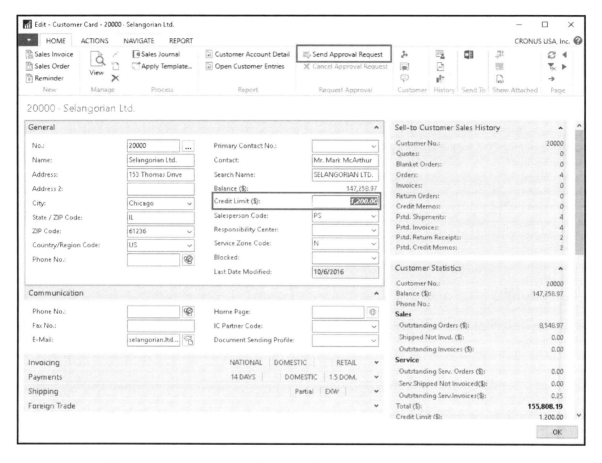

Here we set **1,200.00** as the credit limit value, and click on the **Send Approval Request** button on the ribbon bar.

Now we will see how the whole logic works in the system.

 Here the customer will be restricted, since it violates the workflow rules. Just make sure your workflow is set to active, or else no response will be observed.

2. Now we will create a **Sales Invoice** page with **Sell-to Customer**, the customer whose credit limit we just changed, that is, customer number 2000, and **Post** the **Sales Invoice** page:

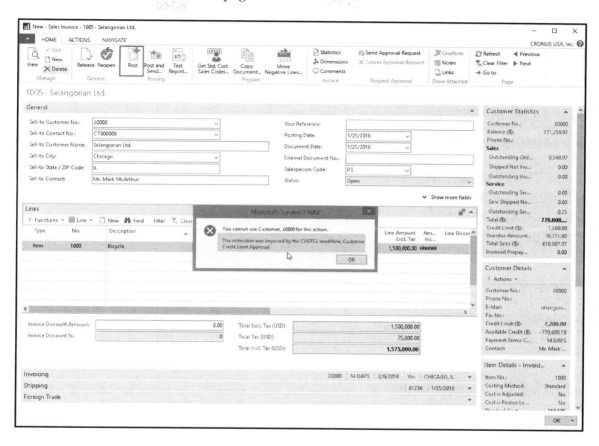

Output of the workflow

The steps that we performed in the previous section will create lines in the **Approval Request Entries** page, one for **Approver 1** and one for **Approver 3,** with the same sequence number as to which our setting was defined.

This will also create notifications for both users, which can be seen in the **Notification Entries** page.

Once the approver approves the customer, the process can move further, but until then, the customer will be blocked for any kind of similar transactions.

Hopefully, you must've understood how the workflow feature can be utilized to make our process flow more precisely, and to restrict any unauthorized activity.

Latest features in Microsoft Dynamics NAV 2016

There are various interesting features that have been integrated to make Microsoft Dynamics NAV 2016 even better to use and present to the customer. Some of the features explained here might be useful for the developer, while some are highly preferred by the end users.

Test automation suites

We can easily automate regression tests of your application code using the Test Runner code unit. Test runner code units enable the execution of test code units without a user interface and without the integration of Test management and reporting frameworks. You can review the test output in your mailbox after the test finishes. The details about testing are explained in `Chapter 4`, *Testing and Debugging*.

Universal App on all devices

The best thing about Universal App is that it allows accessibility of the same system on different kinds of gadgets, from big-screen laptops and desktops to small-screen tablets and phones. It helps in discrimination of brands, as now you can access NAV on Apple and Android phones, tablets, and phablets. It also provides similar kind of interface, so the user can easily resume their work when they want to switch between different gadgets as per their convenience.

The following image clearly explains the range of accessibility of Universal App. Except on laptops and desktops, which require Windows OS, Universal App can be literally installed on every kind of operating system:

You can easily find Universal App by typing Dynamics NAV in the Windows store for desktops and laptops:

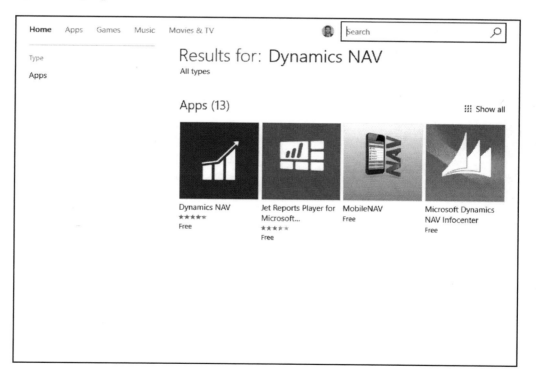

It is easy to find and install Universal App on Windows, Apple, and Android phones. Just find Dynamics NAV Universal App on the online phone store. Then install and provide the connection string, which is constant throughout the range of devices. You also need to provide the credentials before you enter into the system just for security purpose, which is obvious:

 It is easy to install and use Universal App in a mobile environment. In most cases, mobile clients are used by users when they are away from their desks, for instance when they are driving or have just left work. It increases the productivity of the user by responding to the process on-the-go.

The Web Client enhancements

Web Client is something that needs your attention. Microsoft has spent a tremendous amount of effort for enhancing the web experience of users. It is much cleaner. The startup time when launching app is significantly faster. The navigation time is extremely fine-tuned. Nice animation and smoother transition between different animation events is another great feature. The **Activity** button is more descriptive. There is an exciting horizontal scroll feature, and fast tabs are more interactive.

There are over 60 enhancements to the web client targeting simplicity, productivity, and performance.

In the following screenshot you can see the web client interface, which at first glance might look similar to the previous release but, internally there are tons of prominent changes, improving the user experience with the system:

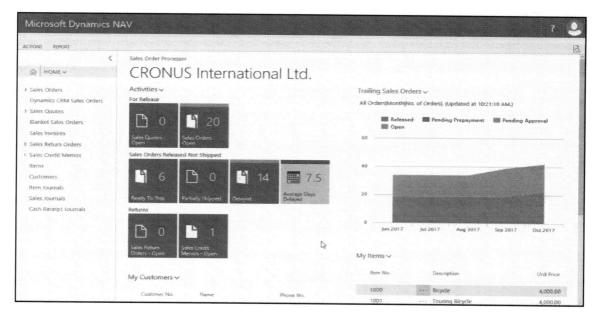

In Microsoft Dynamics NAV 2016, you can have a first-class desktop experience. It is designed for fast and fluid mouse and keyboard interaction. The best aspect of using web client is that you can use it on the go, from anywhere. The dynamics flow of role center for different browser sizes and to support high-resolution screen has also been increased.

It has also improved performance while fetching data over the Internet. In the case of list page, web client does not fetch all the list values at once, but rather fetches data on the go, as the user scrolls down the page. It significantly increases the performance of the system on the Web.

Working with Microsoft Dynamics CRM

With Dynamics NAV 2016, Microsoft has enabled the tight integration between two solutions to allow for caching the processes more efficiently. It also enables the user of the two solutions to make a more informed decision without switching products. In case they need to switch, tight integration enables this informal bit generic navigation action. Integration is enabled with a default definition from within Microsoft Dynamics NAV, which is simple to set up and use.

We just need to go to **Microsoft Dynamics CRM Connection Setup**, and enter the details in **Dynamics CRM URL: User Name** and **Password**, and then enable the settings by checking the **Enabled** check box, as shown in the following screenshot:

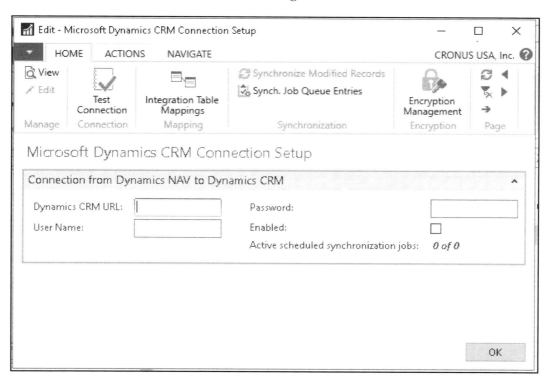

The benefits are of integration are as follows:

- Shared information
- Efficient order processing
- Easy integration

Now with the integration, we can make better real-time decisions allowing growth of our business and generating better results.

Working natively with Azure SQL

If you missed Chapter 1, *Microsoft Dynamics NAV Installation*, of this book, then I would like to request you to read that first to understand how we can work natively with Azure SQL. We can connect to Azure SQL using our local SQL Server Management Studio and work natively. We just need the connection credentials, which are the username, password, and the link to the server.

Extensions

It is one of the biggest changes in the product. This is a new development capability in Microsoft Dynamics NAV 2016. It enables you to modify Microsoft Dynamics NAV without directly changing source recourses. Because of this feature of extensions, Microsoft Dynamics NAV is now highly scalable and easy to deploy, manage, and upgrade.

We will cover extensions in detail in Chapter 11, *Extending Dynamics NAV 2016*.

Document management

Microsoft Dynamics NAV 2016 has implemented document management and Optical Character Recognition capabilities. **Optical Character Recognition (OCR)** capability means the identification of printed characters using photoelectric devices and utility computer software.

The main intention behind this modification was to reduce the paper-based process, and to optimize the environment for smooth operation. This also helps improve the speed and accuracy of the operation, and is actually more economical for small- and medium-sized businesses.

It is now easy to implement the service provided by the OCR service providers.

Workflows

Microsoft Dynamics NAV has enhanced the following workflow capabilities:

- It is essential in the current business environment to focus more on visualization, notifications, and similar visual enhancements. Microsoft Dynamics NAV 2016 addresses most of these with its enhanced workflow capabilities.
- It also enables the end users to configure relevant workflows with no need to pay a billable for a technical resource for the modification.

E – Everything

Microsoft Dynamics NAV 2016 has a high level of E-Services integration. Most of the reports now can be directly sent over the Internet, and can also be configured for direct delivery without user intervention. This change has made the system more acceptable for the high tech environment. It is extremely compatible with different e-commerce software. Data can be directly sent to a website using inbuilt web services, which just need a simple configuration.

Microsoft Dynamics NAV 2016 heavily supports the E – Everything concept. It has the ability to enable smooth integration with other cloud-based products and services. Even the connectivity steps are well documented and organized to reduce the time you spend on doing so.

Power BI

You can easily understand the pattern of data in Microsoft Dynamics NAV 2016 using intelligent tools like Power BI. It helps us analyze data and get meaning out of it for different purposes such as decision making, resuming purchase and sales process, carrying out a manufacturing process, and so on. Power BI retrieves your data, both sales and financial data, and then builds an out-of-the-box dashboard and reports based on that data. The dashboards are very user-friendly, and easy to change as per your choice. Since this is a very useful tool and highly recommended, we will discuss more about Power BI in `Chapter 11`, *Extending Dynamics NAV 2016*.

Office 365 integration

Microsoft Dynamics NAV supports federated user authentication with Microsoft Azure Active Directory. Microsoft Office 365 uses the same Identity provider service, and thus, NAV System can be easily integrated with the Office 365 platform service. A Single Sign-On (SSO) user experience can be implemented for both Microsoft Dynamics NAV 2016 and Office 365, where a single sign on works on both the applications. If you use web client, then you do not need to sign in to another application if you have already signed in to one; this makes everything run smoothly.

The following screenshot will show you a common interface where all of the applications can be accessed from a single login:

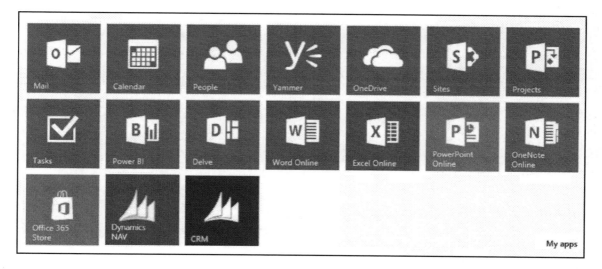

Microsoft Dynamics NAV 2016 can be configured to use Azure SQL as a relational database-as-a-service, eliminating maintenance and reducing costs.

We need these cloud services in order to do the following:

- **Eliminating maintenance**: Reduces pressure on the internal IT teams
- **Reducing costs**: Upfront investment is significantly reduced, as monthly payments for SQL services are possible

Strategy and roadmap

If you remember, Microsoft Dynamics NAV 2016 was released as the code name **CORFU**. The strategy of the system has changed drastically, and Microsoft is still planning to alter the roadmap so as to best address the needs and demands of the current user.

Microsoft Dynamics NAV 2016 has been meticulously designed, with the focus being on modern technological aspects and integration guidelines such as Cloud technology integration with Microsoft Azure, smoother workflow, better data security, integrated multi-client environment, and much more.

It is highly customizable, but with many added features, Microsoft has made sure the system can be more flexible, reducing the need of more customization. Microsoft Dynamics CRM and Office 365 can be directly linked to it and can be accessed with common user credentials, which is great from the user's point of view. We are soon expecting the 2017 release, which will probably have some more powerful tools intractability and is expected to provide more freedom to the developers and programmers. At the time of this content writing, the Demo version of Dynamics NAV 2017 is already released:

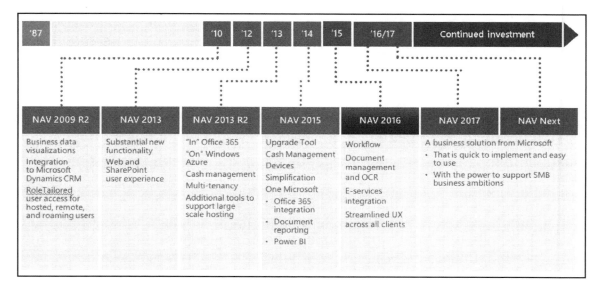

Summary

In this chapter, you learnt about the different components that take part in configuration processes. We also covered most of the latest features and its implications in Microsoft Dynamics NAV 2016. We briefly discussed design pattern and its significance on the system. In order to understand these new features properly, it is recommended that one should practice the steps mentioned in the chapter, and try to implement real-life data to observe the behavior of the system.

In the next chapter, we will go into details on the security aspect of Microsoft Dynamics NAV 2016, which is one of the least discussed topics in this field. We will try to understand the implications of poor security measures, and how it affects the system components and data. We will discuss the preventive and curative aspects as well.

3

The C/AL and VB Programming

In the last chapter, you learned about the latest features that have been added into Microsoft Dynamics NAV 2016. It gave you an idea about what you can now expect from the system, and it also gives you space to predict future changes in the system. We also discussed the significance and effects of these features on the overall system.

Here, in this chapter, we are going to deliberate on the core programming aspect and related topics in Microsoft Dynamics NAV 2016. The main focus will be on the backend of the code, providing the reader with a glimpse of how the code interacts with the system.

The chapter requires some hands-on experience with C/AL Programming, and unlike other materials online, the chapter will not go into a list of functions and their syntax in any depth; instead, we will learn the most general aspects of C/AL. Compilation details and hierarchy of code will be presented in the chapter just to give the reader a broad angle about the system they are using. The chapter will also include a part on Visual Basic programming, where we will understand the core aspects of the programming language used for Dynamics NAV report design, which is one of the least-talked-about topics.

At the end of this chapter, you will understand how the C/AL code is actually written and compiled. You will also understand how the software interacts with the hardware, and commands it to perform the task it is instructed to perform by the code. This is very essential for all programmers to understand before they actually start coding.

This chapter will cover the following points:

- C/AL code core
- C/SIDE compiler design
- Different aspects of good programming practice in C/AL
- VB programming basics

Coding with C/AL

The C/AL programming language in Microsoft Dynamics NAV 2016 is similar to the older version of NAV. Coding with C/AL has always been easy because of one extra layer of preprocessing before all of its code is literally converted into C# code; it then follows the same compilation process as any other .NET program. A mediocre programmer can easily understand the previous code and make some changes in it. This is one of the reasons for the popularity of Microsoft Dynamics NAV among developers and consultants.

Connectivity of NAV with SQL is governed by the .NET standards. Especially, the interoperability with other third-party programs outside C/AL is directly controlled by the .NET architecture. This is also one of the reasons we need to install the .NET prerequisites into our system before installing Microsoft Dynamics NAC.

Later in this chapter, we will discuss how the codes are preprocessed into C# code, which all NAV developers need to understand.

Reusing code

One of the main intentions behind this chapter is to provide the reader with some guidance towards **Good Programming Practice (GPP)**, and one of the best ways to follow the guidelines of GPP is to reuse the code. Reusing code makes developing applications faster and easier. In addition, it also saves memory space when the code is passed to the compiler for compilation by reducing the amount of code needed to be processed by the compiler system. If you organize your C/AL code as suggested by NAV standards, then your applications will be less prone to errors. By centralizing the code, you will not unintentionally create inconsistencies by performing the same calculations in many places, for example, in several triggers that have the same table field as their source expression. If you have to change the code, you could either forget about some of these triggers, or make a mistake when you modify one of them.

 Code reuse has been practiced from the earliest days of computer programming. Programmers have always reused sections of code, templates, functions, and procedures. This significantly helps if you are customizing code.

Best programming practice for C/AL code

There are many standards available in different fields of computer science when it comes to coding in a system. All standards feature the core objectives while dealing with the code part. Here are a couple of the main points that I would like to put forward:

- Always prefer using the codeunit to write code instead of on the object (page/table/report) on which it operates. This promotes a clean design, and provides the ability to reuse code. It also helps enforce security and also boosts the speed of code during code compilation.
- In case you need to put some lines of code on an object instead of in a codeunit, then put the code as close as possible to the object on which it operates. For example, put code that modifies records in the triggers of the table fields.

Multi-language functionality

Microsoft Dynamics NAV 2016 has a multi-language feature. This was one of the most discussed topics among Microsoft Professionals and clients, which is smartly presented in this release. The main idea behind the multi-language feature is to make translation easier between different languages, and allow it to switch between different languages at the level of the user interface.

All C/AL code should be entered as English (United States). The main benefit of using the same language for code is to provide a smooth maintenance process. It also helps to keep different add-ons as the base for translation.

Activating objects

One of the most general errors that you get is a less informative error message in case of null values. It is important that we use relevant patterns of programming in computer science. In computer science, we are supposed to activate and test the variable before using it. It is the same in C/AL programming as well. Here we use the TESTFIELD function to actually test the value of the variable we are going to use. The system can provide better informative error messages, and hence prevent extra error handling. It also allows a simple level of exception handling if the value is null or blank. This is depicted in the following code:

```
GLEntry.TESTFIELD("Department Code");
Dept.GET(GLEntry."Department Code");
```

```
GenJnlTemplate.TESTFIELD("Report ID");
REPORT.RUN(GenJnlTemplate."Report ID")
```

The Dialog.OPEN function

You should use the `Dialog.OPEN` function only to indicate that the system is doing something, such as a process in progress:

```
Syntax: Dialog.OPEN(String [, Variable1],...)
```

If possible, use a progress indicator.

Example of a progress indicator

The following example explains how progress indicators can be implemented into your solution. It is always recommended when you are dealing with slow reports or processes which cannot run in the background:

```
MyNext := 0;
MyDialog.OPEN(Text000,MyNext);
REPEAT
  // Do some processing.

  MyNext := MyNext + 1;
  MyDialog.UPDATE();    // Update the field in the dialog.
UNTIL MyNext = 9999;
SLEEP(1000);
MyDialog.CLOSE()
```

The following are the variables and constants used in the preceding code:

- `Text000` is a text constant, which progresses from 0 to 9999@1@@@@@
- `MyDialog` is a value of the `Dialog` type
- `MyNext` is an integer variable

The following screenshot shows the output:

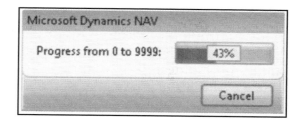

In Microsoft Dynamics NAV, the following are the recommended guidelines:

- Enter messages as text constants.
- Write messages using the active voice. For example, write `Processing items` instead of writing `Items are being processed`.
- Align the # and @ fields to the left with at least one space character between the text and the variable.

> If you use the @ character instead of the # character, then the variable value is used as a percentage, and both the percentage and a progress indicator are displayed. The percentage value that is displayed is the percentage of the variable value from 0 to 9999.

Some basic rules

Following are the most important rules you can use to achieve greater interactive messages for the end users. These not only provide information, but also establish the relationship between the user with the system:

- Always use active voice for messages. For example, `Processing items`.
- Use `Text Constants` for messages. For example, `Text001="This is a Message"`, and use `Text001` in the code instead of typing the message in the code.
- End a message statement with an ellipsis for the running process. For example, `. . . .`

- In order to insert some extra space, you can use two backslashes at the end of a line with the message. For example, :
  - Text002=Batch Name 123456Checking lines #2######
  - Always align an extra white space to the left of the field containing hash (#) and the longest text. Also put a whitespace between # and @. For example, refer to the example shown in the next section, *Variables and constants*.
  - The minimum length of the text field before # and @ must be 16, which includes the whitespace, which is always the final character before any of these symbols start, as explained in the previous point.

Variables and constants

The following example will explain all the rules in the preceding section. Here we can see how text constants can be used to make the code more efficient and clean. Also, the use of #, @, and are explained in the following example:

```
Window.OPEN(Text0001);

//ConstValue = Processing items...
Window.OPEN(Text0002)
ConstValue=Batch Name 123456Checking lines #2######
@5@@@@@@@@@@@@Checking balance #3######
@5@@@@@@@@@@@@Posting lines #4###### @5@@@@@@@@@@@@
```

 Dialog windows that are opened by an object are closed when the object terminates. Dialog windows are automatically sized to hold the longest line of text and the total number of lines.

Avoiding deadlock

Certain rules must be observed to avoid deadlock and maintain consistency in the database. The Microsoft Dynamics NAV database has a deadlock protection, which prevents the entire system from locking up, as shown in the following diagram:

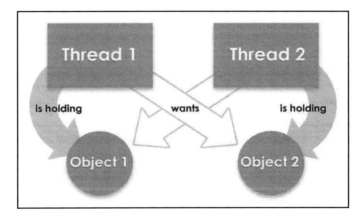

 In a computer program, deadlock is, effectively, a situation in which two computer processes or threads sharing the same resource/object prevent each other from accessing the resource, resulting in both the programs ceasing to function, and thus none being able to accomplish their task.

In day-to-day life, multiple users might try to access the same table (generally for posting purposes). There might be an issue because of this action at the system level, creating the problem of deadlock in the system. The following hierarchy must be followed in order to respect the locking pattern of the tables. Here I have made four categories into which the tables can be divided in order to prevent the system from getting into the state of deadlock. I highly recommend all coders to keep this in mind while dealing with table-level coding:

- Journals
- Non-posted lines and headers
- Posted lines and headers
- Ledger entries and registers

Locking orders

The following table explains the order in which the respective tables should be locked. Most programmers do not care about table locking, resulting in a bad experience for the end users in a multiuser environment:

Order	Journals	Non Posted Lines and Headers	Posted Lines and Headers	Ledger Entries and Registers
1	Journal Line	Purchase Line	Purch. Rcpt. Header	G/L Entry
		Sales Line		
2	Batch Name	Purchase Header	Purch. Rcpt. Line	G/L Register
		Sales Header		
3	Journal Template		Sales Shipment Header	
4			Sales Shipment Line	
5			Purch. Inv. Header	
			Purch. Cr. Memo Hdr.	
			Sales Invoice Header	
			Sales Cr. Memo Header	
6			Purch. Inv. Line	
			Purch. Cr. Memo Line	
			Sales Invoice Line	
			Sales Cr. Memo Line	
7			Purchase Line	
8			Purchase Header	
9			Sales Line	
10			Sales Header	

The core of all these rules is to always lock tables at the lowest level first. If you can determine the lowest level, then you can easily understand this pattern.

Journals

In general, a journal has three levels: templates, batches, and lines. Templates are at the highest level, batches are at the middle level, and lines are presented at the lowest level, close to the user. In every process, journal records follow the locking pattern, where template, batch, and line act as the keys which can be used to better lock the record. During the deletion process of a journal, the Dynamics NAV system first deletes the journal lines, and then automatically locks them. It then repeats the process with the batch names, and finally, the template can be deleted. The pattern is the same for all journals, and if you customize some code, then you must pay close attention to this order.

Non-posted lines and headers

In the previous version of NAV, the database was different from the current version. We now have the standard MS SQL database, and now database consistency in the application is very important. In order to keep the records of the table consistent, you should always lock the sales line before locking the corresponding sales header table. This is crucial because of the structure of these tables and the manner in which they are linked with each other. When a user tries to push a record into a new sales line, the `Sales Line` table is automatically locked. Since the tables are locked at this instance, none of the users can carry out delete operations on the sales header at that particular time. This is because the sales lines have to be deleted before a sales header can be deleted, which is again because of the structure in which the tables are linked. This is the core concept in all the Header line combination documents in NAV. Because of this, there will never be a sales/Purchase line without a corresponding sales/purchase header. This is the case for all other header-line document systems in NAV.

Posted lines and headers

Similar locking patterns are also found in posted tables, but there are some conceptual differences in the case of posted tables. In case of posted tables, the posted headers are locked before posted lines, and purchase tables are locked before sales tables. This is the critical point: sales tables have a lower locking privilege in comparison to purchase tables. Also, posted tables are locked before non-posted tables. In most cases, we can deal with posted sales and purchase tables separately, but when we need to use them by the same logic, then we must make sure all these locking patterns are followed.

Ledger entries and registers

In Dynamics NAV, it is important that a ledger entry table is always locked before its analogous register table. This is true for all the ledgers and its corresponding registers.

Most of the programmers make the mistake when they lock the table before carrying any activity which touches the locking pattern, that deal with the database activities.

Naming conventions in C/AL

A naming convention is nothing but a set of rules for adopting the character sequence to be used as an identifier, which includes variables, types, functions, and so on. These are a precise and consistent phrasing, which help the programmer better regulate the programs so that they can be properly understood by broader professionals. These abbreviating objects also help developers to understand the Cronus system internally before he or she can start customizing or applying some changes for the fulfillment of a requirement. This also helps in developing the features faster. The main difference it makes is when we need to review or make some changes to our code after some years-if we maintained some convention, then it would be easy to understand, whereas the lack of any pattern of a naming convention would make the whole process a cumbersome task.

 The compiler does not give a warning when using a local variable with the same name as the global variable. The system will always use the local variable first.

In Microsoft Dynamics NAV, we have been recommended several guidelines for naming objects, captions, local and global variables, functions, constants, and so on. I believe the developer can use any naming convention he or she likes. I do not want to point out the rules that one must follow, and at the end of the day, nobody really cares about the rules if the code works properly. The main concern should be defining descriptive names of the objects and variables. In some of the worst cases, I have seen crap like SL3 for Sales Line; this is not a standard by any means. In Microsoft Dynamics NAV 2016, the system generates the record type variable name automatically when you enter the name or number of the object in the variable page. It can be taken as the reference point, and you can see how the variables should be defined with simple descriptive names such as SalesLine for Sales line record. You can still append prefixes such as lSalesline for the local variable of sales line and gSalesLine for the global one. It all depends on what makes your program better and easier to understand so that the next time you or your teammates see your code, you are able to understand it easily.

 I highly recommend using suffixes such as temp for record variables of temporary tables. This really makes sense when you are deleting the record from the temporary variable.

Compiler design

In this section, you will understand the concept of a compiler in brief. It is recommended that everyone who codes in Dynamics NAV should understand the basics of compiler design.

The main aim of a compiler is to convert a high-level language such as C# and JAVA to a low-level language like machine-level language. The question is, Why do you need to do that? The reason is that we are not comfortable writing a problem in 0's and 1's, which is the form in which a computer system understands the commands. The figure shown in the *Assembler* section explains how the whole compilation process can be sliced into different entities, which handle different operations, leading to the transformation of a high-level language into machine-level bits. The first layer in most of the high-level development environments is the preprocessors.

Preprocessor

A preprocessor is nothing but a language-specific program, which processes the input high-level code into the output code that can be passed on to the compiler. It basically breaks down the complex chunk of code for the convenience of the compiler. Here, in the C/SIDE development environment, you can take the preprocessor as the code that converts C/AL code, and converts it into a C sharp equivalent code. Actually, this is not real compilation. It is just changing the form of the code. The output of the preprocessor is transferred to the compiler.

Compiler

A compiler is also a computer program or programs, which work together to transform the output source code of a preprocessor into another form, usually into another computer language. Here I am taking the preprocessor as the first layer, but in many cases, the source code is directly passed on to the compiler. In most cases, the output of the compiler is assembly code, and the code is passed on to another layer called the assembler.

Assembler

An assembler is the entity which translates assembly-level language into object files or machine code bits. The basic functions used in assembly language are basic arithmetic operations, because a computer just knows how to compute. The operations are add, subtract, move, compare, shift, and so on. This is the last layer where there is some user-readable form of code. The output of the assembler is the bit of 0's and 1's, which is binary programming language, also called machine-level language.

A computer only understands binary language, because it can be then transformed into the electrical form, 1 for electrical potential and 0 for no electrical potential, and then the processor can carry out operations at the hardware level. Hence, whatever be the output of the operations, it is again converted back into a user-readable format, and the user is able to see the result.

The main intention behind explaining these core terminologies is to give the reader a very brief knowledge about code transformations thus providing knowledge about the system and the implications of very complex code, which can make system response time slower.

The next diagram explains how high level languages are broken down into chunks of bits when it passes through different processing units such as the preprocessor, compiler, and assemblers. Some of them have their own **context free grammars** (**CFG**) which they use as the tool while breaking the code that is meaningful to the humans into relevant machine level codes and vice versa:

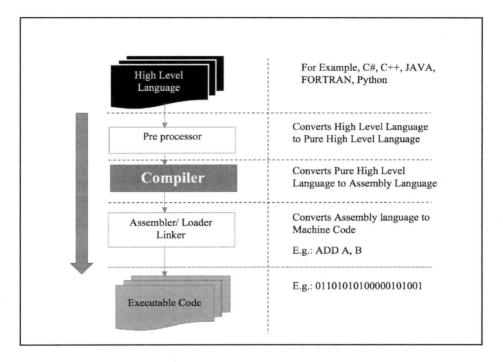

Now let us examine the internal structure of a compiler, since all of the major operations such as lexical analysis, syntax analysis, and semantic analysis are carried out by different programs which are a part of the main compiler program set.

Whenever any code is passed on to the compiler, it is converted into tokens or a stream of tokens. Tokens are nothing but strings with an identified meaning. Every compiler has a set of strings in its dictionary. In the next layer, these tokens are matched with the strings in the predefined dictionary. But in this layer, the code is just converted into small chunks of tokens, and passed on to the syntax analyzer.

A syntax analyzer is also called a parser. The compiler contains the rules and grammar. It arranges the tokens into a parse tree so that in the later part it can be checked for its correct grammar and rules. The parse tree is then passed on to the semantic analysis process.

Semantic analysis is the process of relating the parse tree with the phrases where the compiler understands the meaning of the code. It also verifies for correct grammar and correct semantics of the code (parse tree). This then passes through other layers where the code gets reduced in size, and where the comment section is truncated from the actual code, making the code ready to be converted into assembly-level code. Finally, the assembly-level code is generated.

This preceding process is the same such as when you translate a non-English language into English: you first break down the words, and then arrange the words as per the meaning and its semantics, and finally, understand the meaning of those arrangements.

The following figure explains the internal structure of different layers that we examined in the previous section. Here we can see how difference processes are carried out inside the compiler to break the high-level code into assembly level code:

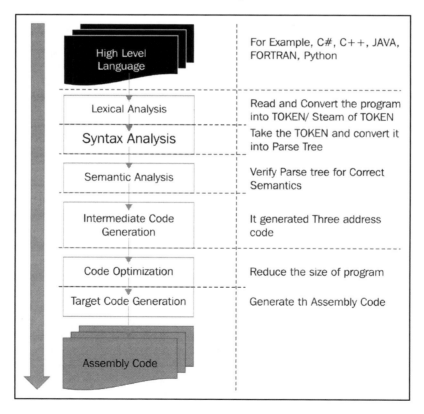

Hence, the code is processed and checked. There are many layers which perform different tasks. It is important to understand how the C/SIDE development environment does all this for a programmer.

Preprocessing into C# code

Whenever you write C/AL code in Dynamics NAV, you must understand that the ultimate goal is to provide the command to the computer to perform operations like add, subtract, move, and many such basic operations. C/Side just provides an additional layer of simplicity over C# code compilation. We all must understand that all C/AL codes are ultimately converted into C# codes, and then processed accordingly. We will now examine how we can see the C# code for the corresponding C/AL code. For this, we need to make some changes to our configuration file so that the system can generate a C# code, which is nothing but the counterpart of the C/AL code.

Perform the following steps to get the corresponding C sharp code:

1. Go to the following address in the system where Dynamics NAV is installed:

   `C:Program FilesMicrosoft Dynamics NAV90Service` and find the file named `CustomSettings.config`.

2. Open the file, and search for the `EnableDebugging` key.

3. Change the value of `Key` to `True`:

```
CustomSettings.config  ×
    <!--
        With the EnableDebugging flag set to true the Microsoft Dynamics NAV Server
        will start with debugging mode enabled.  This mode has three main functions:
        1)  Upon first connection by a RoleTailored Client all C# for that application
            will be generated.
        2)  C# files will be persisted between server restarts.
        3)  Application Objects will be compiled with debug information.
    -->
    <add key="EnableDebugging" value="True" />
    <!--
        Specifies whether C/AL debugging is allowed for this Microsoft Dynamics NAV Server instance.
    -->
    <add key="DebuggingAllowed" value="true" />
    <!--
        Sets the maximum number of items to serialize or deserialize.
    -->
    <add key="ClientServicesMaxItemsInObjectGraph" value="512" />
    <!--
```

4. Save the file.

5. Restart the service from **Services.Msc**.

   For this, open the Run command (*Ctrl + R*), and type `services.msc`. Locate the Microsoft Dynamics NAV 2016 Service, and restart it as shown in the following screenshot:

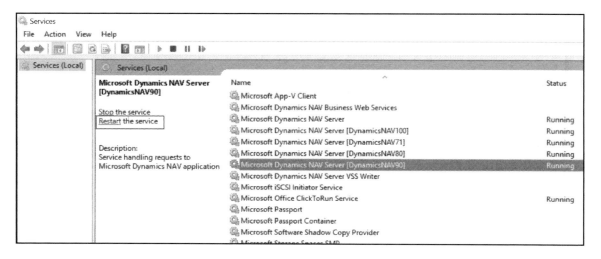

6. Now run the Role Tailored client of Microsoft Dynamics NAV 2016.

Locate the folder C:ProgramDataMicrosoftMicrosoft Dynamics NAV90ServerMicrosoftDynamicsNavServer$DynamicsNAV90source:

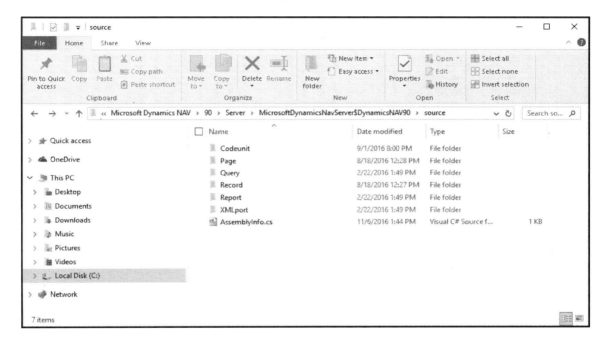

The folders seen in the preceding screenshot are those which contain the CS file, which contain the corresponding C# code. Microsoft Dynamics NAV 2016 has come a long way since the code started preprocessing into C#, which was first introduced in version 2009. The following screenshot is the C# equivalent code for Page 48: Sales Orders, which is not that easy to understand. But if you take a look at the earliest version of C# code of the same page, then it will be easy to understand for the sake of this discussion. So, I will try to explain this concept with the help of a C# code of Microsoft Dynamics NAV 2009 (RTC):

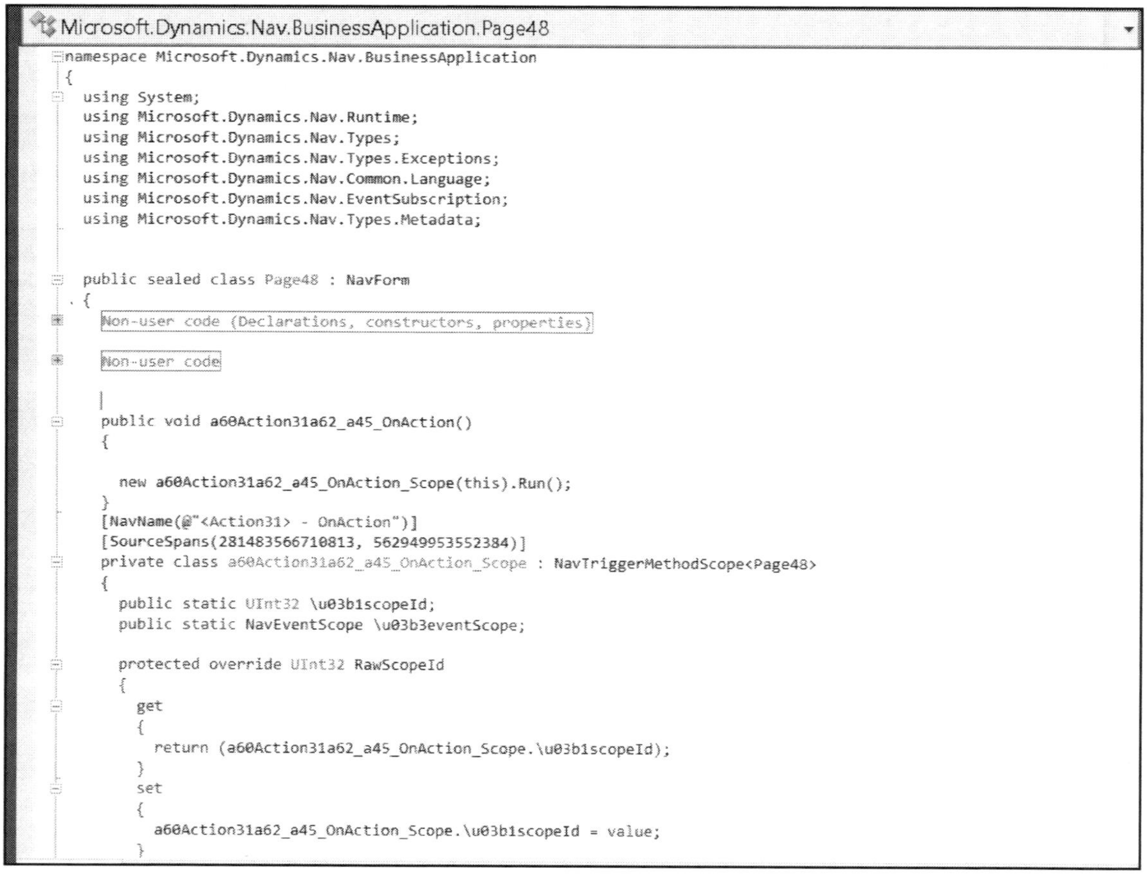

```
Microsoft.Dynamics.Nav.BusinessApplication.Page48                                    ▾

namespace Microsoft.Dynamics.Nav.BusinessApplication
{
  using System;
  using Microsoft.Dynamics.Nav.Runtime;
  using Microsoft.Dynamics.Nav.Types;
  using Microsoft.Dynamics.Nav.Types.Exceptions;
  using Microsoft.Dynamics.Nav.Common.Language;
  using Microsoft.Dynamics.Nav.EventSubscription;
  using Microsoft.Dynamics.Nav.Types.Metadata;


  public sealed class Page48 : NavForm
  {
    Non-user code (Declarations, constructors, properties)

    Non-user code


    public void a60Action31a62_a45_OnAction()
    {

      new a60Action31a62_a45_OnAction_Scope(this).Run();
    }
    [NavName(@"<Action31> - OnAction")]
    [SourceSpans(281483566710813, 562949953552384)]
    private class a60Action31a62_a45_OnAction_Scope : NavTriggerMethodScope<Page48>
    {
      public static UInt32 \u03b1scopeId;
      public static NavEventScope \u03b3eventScope;

      protected override UInt32 RawScopeId
      {
        get
        {
          return (a60Action31a62_a45_OnAction_Scope.\u03b1scopeId);
        }
        set
        {
          a60Action31a62_a45_OnAction_Scope.\u03b1scopeId = value;
        }
```

Let us examine the C sharp code for the release function, which is present in **Page 9305 Sales Order List**:

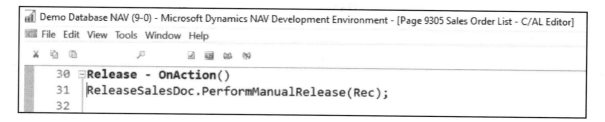

In the last screenshot, we can easily see that a function `performManualRelease` is being called by passing Record as the parameter. Now we will examine the C# code for the same page in Dynamics NAV 2009 to make things clearer. Even in version 2009, the process of generating C sharp code and the location is similar to what is shown in the following screenshot:

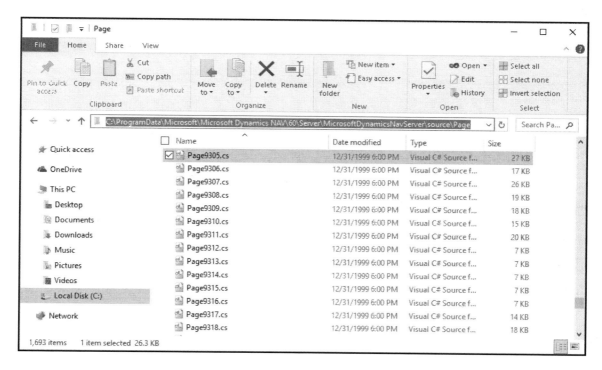

Now let's open the code, search for the `PerformManualRelease` function, and examine the code:

```
Page9305.cs - Microsoft Visual Studio

File   Edit   View   Project   Debug   Tools   Window   Help

                                                          performmanualre

Page9305.cs X   Page48.cs      Page48.cs      CustomSettings.config

Microsoft.Dynamics.Nav.BusinessApplication.Page9305

        }

        public void Control1102601049_OnAction()
        {
          using (NavMethodScope __local = new NavTriggerMethodScope(this, @"Cont
          {
            NavCodeunitHandle releaseSalesDoc = new NavCodeunitHandle(__local, 4

            // ReleaseSalesDoc.PerformManualRelease(Rec);
            releaseSalesDoc.Target.Invoke(2, new Object[]{Rec});
          }

        }

        public void Control1102601050_OnAction()
        {
          using (NavMethodScope __local = new NavTriggerMethodScope(this, @"Cont
          {
            NavCodeunitHandle releaseSalesDoc = new NavCodeunitHandle(__local, 4

            // ReleaseSalesDoc.PerformManualReopen(Rec);
            releaseSalesDoc.Target.Invoke(3, new Object[]{Rec});
          }
```

It is clear that the C/AL code has been commented out, and the corresponding C Sharp code is generated. Now it is clear how the complexity of different concepts has been simplified into a single line of C/AL code, which is another reason for the success of Microsoft Dynamics NAV. Since the year 2009, Microsoft has been working to optimize the code and make it more secure. Thus, the present version of the code, which is more robust and efficient, has evolved. If you want to know more, then try this with version 2009 and then relate it to Version 2016.

Triggers

In Computer Science, a trigger is a method that commences an action when an event which is related to it occurs. In general, the events resemble key-press events, mouse events, and automatic events from a timer. But here, we are dealing with events that are directly or indirectly relevant to the database fetch or push operations like insert, delete, modify, and so on. There are the following three kinds of triggers in Microsoft Dynamics NAV:

- Documentation triggers
- Event triggers
- Function triggers

Documentation triggers

These are actually not triggers; these are used to write documentation for a particular object. Many developers use this space to document their modifications to standard objects. Every object has a documentation trigger. The code written in this trigger is eliminated in the section of code optimization of the compiler, and no code written in this section actually runs:

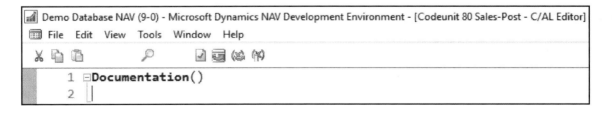

Event triggers

Event triggers are the most commonly used triggers. These triggers take action when any events are set. They always start with the word `On`, such as `OnRUN`, `OnInsert`, `OnDelete`, and the like. We can write code in all of the triggers. For event triggers, the code runs when the event related to it occurs. For example, the code in the `OnRun` event trigger is executed when a codeunit that contains the trigger is run. Other examples are shown in the following screenshot:

Function triggers

Function triggers are the triggers which are created automatically when the function is defined in the **C/AL Global** window. The C/AL code can be written in the `Trigger` section, and is executed when the function is called.

The following triggers are available for different objects in Microsoft Dynamics NAV 2016:

- Report and data item triggers
- Table and field triggers

- XMLport triggers
- Page and action triggers
- Codeunit triggers
- Query triggers

Exception handling

Exception handling is a new concept in Microsoft Dynamics NAV. It was imported from .NET, and is now gaining popularity among the C/AL programmers because of its effective usage.

Like C#, for exception handling, we use the Try function. The Try functions are the new additions to the function library, which enable you to handle errors that occur in the application during runtime. Here we are not dealing with compile time issues. For example, the message `Error Returned: Divisible by Zero Error.` is always a critical error, and should be handled in order to be avoided. This also stops the system from entering into the unsafe state. Like C sharp and other rich programming languages, the Try functions in C/AL provide easy-to-understand error messages, which can also be dynamic and directly generated by the system. This feature helps us preplan those errors and present better descriptive errors to the users.

You can use the Try functions to catch errors/exceptions that are thrown by Microsoft Dynamics NAV or exceptions that are thrown during the .NET Framework interoperability operations.

The Try function is in many ways similar to the conditional `Codeunit.Run` function except for the following points:

- The database records that are changed because of the Try function cannot be rolled back
- The Try function calls do not need to be committed to the database

Creating a Try function

Let's see how the Try function can be created in C/AL. For the sake of example, let's create a codeunit: `50001 - Exception Handle`.

Phase 1

1. Create a global function called `Try`.

2. Define two parameters for the `Try` function:

   ```
   ItemCode of Type code and Length 20
   ItemDescription of Type Text and Length 50
   ```

3. In the property section of the `Try` function, change the value of the `TryFunction` property to `YES`. This will help this function to be identified as the Exception handler in the system, which can be called from another codeunits:

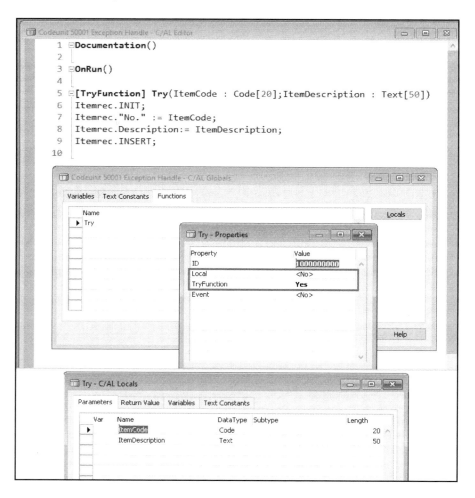

4. Let us write code to push a new item record into the item table. So, create a new record type variable called `Itemrec`.

5. Write the following simple code to push a value into the item record:

```
[TryFunction] Try(ItemCode : Code[20];ItemDescription :
  Text[50])

Itemrec.INIT;
Itemrec."No." := ItemCode;
Itemrec.Description:= ItemDescription;
Itemrec.INSERT;
```

6. Save the codeunit, and follow phase 2.

Phase 2

In phase 2, we will create a new codeunit, `50002 - Application`, which will show how the codeunit created in phase 1 can be utilized. Actually, we will call the function through this application codeunit where the exception will he handled:

1. Create a function called `AddItem` with no parameter.

2. Create a variable of codeunit **50001- Exception Handle** as `ExceptionHandle`:

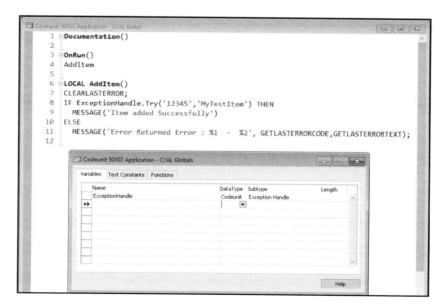

3. Write the code to provide the exception message if the process meets any exception. If the item is already there in the current case, then print the error message with the description presented by the inbuilt functions called GETLASTERRORCODE and GETLASTERRORTEXT. And in case of success, present a success message:

```
LOCAL AddItem()

CLEARLASTERROR;
IF ExceptionHandle.Try('12345','MyTestItem') THEN
  MESSAGE('Item added Successfully')
ELSE
  MESSAGE('Error Returned Error : %1  -  %2',
    GETLASTERRORCODE,GETLASTERRORTEXT);
```

4. Also call this local function, AddItem, into the OnRun trigger as follows:

```
OnRun()
  AddItem
```

5. Finally, run the Codeunit **50002- Application**.

The first time you run it, a new item with item number 12345 will be created:

6. Run the codeunit once again; since the item is already present, it will generate an error message as seen in the following screenshot:

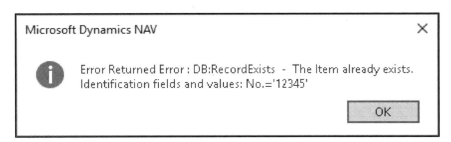

Hence, we achieved the exception handling functionality in Microsoft Dynamics NAV, which is very exciting to implement and use.

Microsoft Dynamics NAV Reports

There are many ways to understand the purpose of reports in Microsoft Dynamics NAV. Reports can have different purposes, but the main purpose is to visualize the data/information from the database repository in a structured way. The best example of a report is a list of customers, vendors, or items. It can even be a list of the top 10 customers, or statistical reports for goods sold.

In addition to statistical reports, which provide information about different resources, there is another category of reports called document reports. Document reports are used to communicate with third parties like sales invoices, credit memos, sales quote, and so on.

Reports can also be used in the system for processing purposes or batch events. These reports do not have a particular layout, or might have some level of layout for interaction purpose. These reports are very important for processing purposes, since they help complete the pending process or calculation process, which is crucial for the data that we process. Here, in this section of the chapter, we will focus mainly on the technical aspect of report design.

Report design

In Microsoft Dynamics NAV 2016, the look and feel of reports have been kept the same as in the previous releases, just keeping in mind the comfort level of users. Creating a report in NAV involves two basic steps: first you have to design the data model/ dataset, and the dataset determines the data that is extracted or calculated from the Microsoft Dynamics NAV database tables, which can be used in a report. After the dataset has been designed, you design the visual layout of the report. There are two tools that you can use for the latter process: Visual Studio Report Designer or SQL Server Report Builder. After you design a report, you can make it available to applications that are running on the Microsoft Dynamics NAV Windows client.

The request page

Most of the reports contain a request page. It is the first thing you see when you run a report. Let's take an overview of the request page:

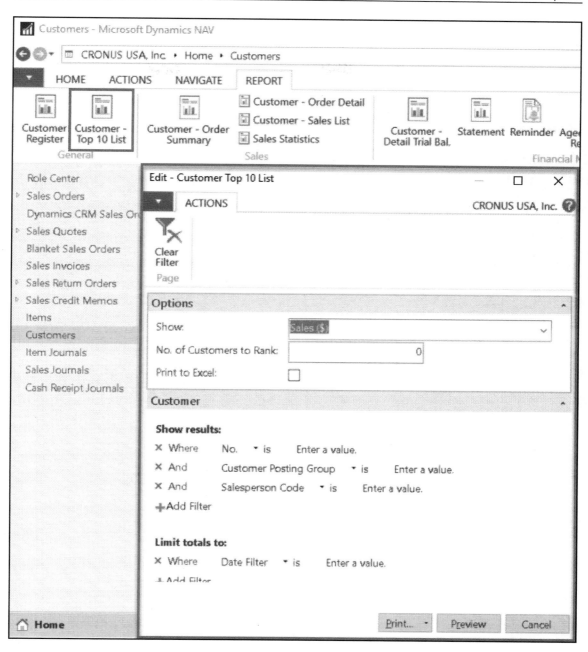

In the preceding screenshot, we can see a request page of the **Customer Top 10 List** report. It is the place where you can determine how to view the report. You can provide all the options that a user needs to filter out the data for the reports and a default option to make it more user-friendly.

The report viewer

The report viewer is now more interactive and expressive. As you can see in the next screenshot, the inbuilt graph expresses the data more clearly. Like the previous versions, we can make the report interactive, where the user can click and interact with the data. This feature gives the Microsoft Dynamics NAV report a huge boost:

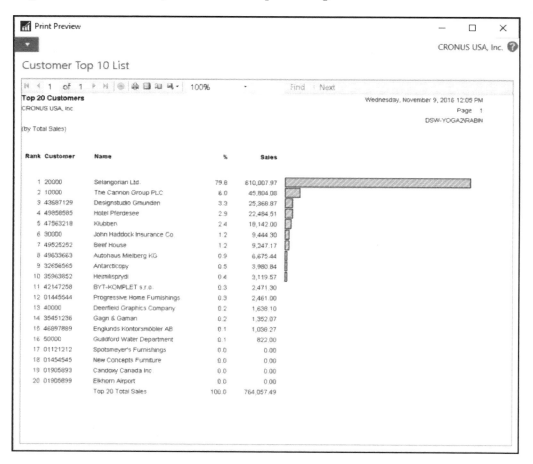

We will learn how to make the report interactive in the following section.

Interactive sorting and visibility toggle

Similar to the previous version of Microsoft Dynamics NAV, we can make the report interactive, and toggle around with the data. Let's create a new report called `itemReport`, and use this report for all the interactive features that we are going to discuss. After you create a simple item-table-based report, perform the following steps:

1. Open Object Designer, and select the `ItemReport` report. Then choose **Design** to open it in Report Dataset Designer, as shown in the following screenshot:

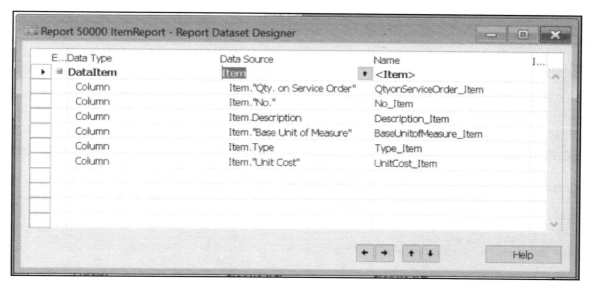

2. In the **View** menu, choose **Layout**. The report opens in Visual Studio.
3. Select the **No Item** text box in the first row, first column. Open the shortcut menu, and then choose **Text Box Properties**.
4. In the **Text Box Properties** window, choose the **Interactive Sorting** tab.
5. Select the **Enable interactive sort action for this text box** checkbox.

6. In the **Sort by** drop-down list box, select **[No_Item]** from the list, choose **fx** to open the expression window, and then verify that the **Set expression for: SortExpression** textbox contains the value =Fields!No.Item.Value. Click on the **OK** button:

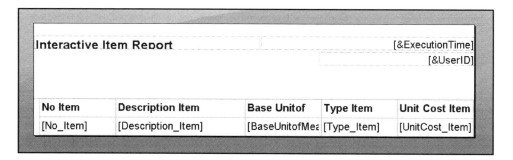

7. Click on **OK** to close the **Change interactive sort options for this text box** window as seen in this screenshot:

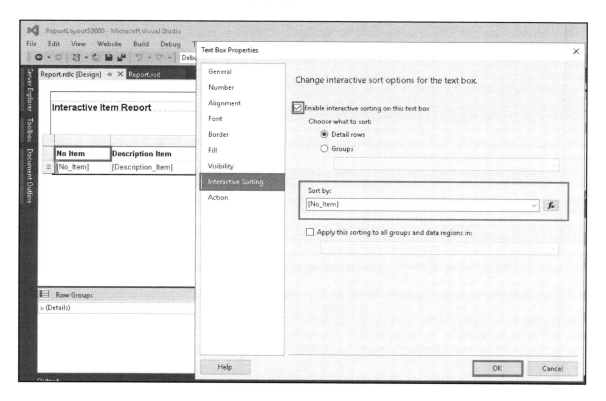

8. Repeat the same process for the **Description** field.

   Select the **Respective** option.

9. In the **File** menu, choose **Save Report.rdlc**, and close Visual Studio.
10. **Run** the report.

11. As you can see in the preceding screenshot, the report is now interactive. When you click on the item caption, there is a small icon to shuffle the sort in ascending or descending order. The following screenshot shows the sorted results:

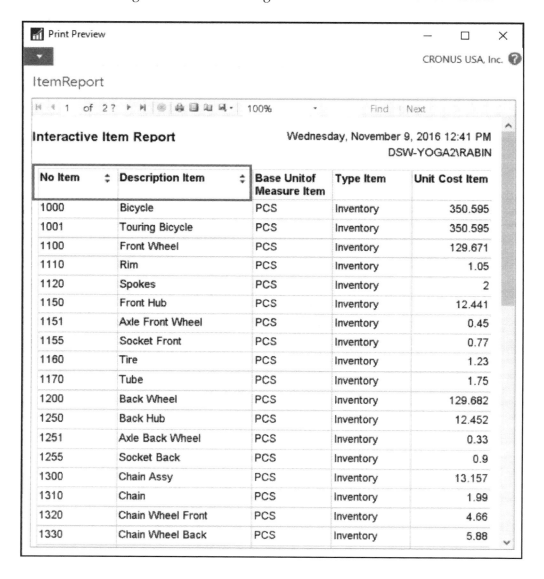

Visual Basic programming

Visual Basic (VB) is an event-driven programming language. It is also an **Integrated development environment** (IDE). If you are familiar with the BASIC programming language, then it will be easy to understand Visual Basic, since it is derived from BASIC. I will try to provide the basics about this language here, since it is the least discussed topic in the NAV community, but very essential to be understood by all report designers and developers.

Here we do not need to understand each and every detail of the VB programming language, but understanding the syntax and structure will help us understand the code that we are going to use in the RDLC report.

An example code of VB can be written as follows:

```
Public Function BlankZero(ByVal Value As Decimal)
   if Value = 0 then
     Return ""
   End if
     Return Value
End Function End Sub
```

This preceding function, `BlankZero`, basically just returns the value of the parameter. This is the simplest function which can be found in the code section of the RDLC report. Unlike C/AL, we do not need to end the code line with a semi-colon (;):

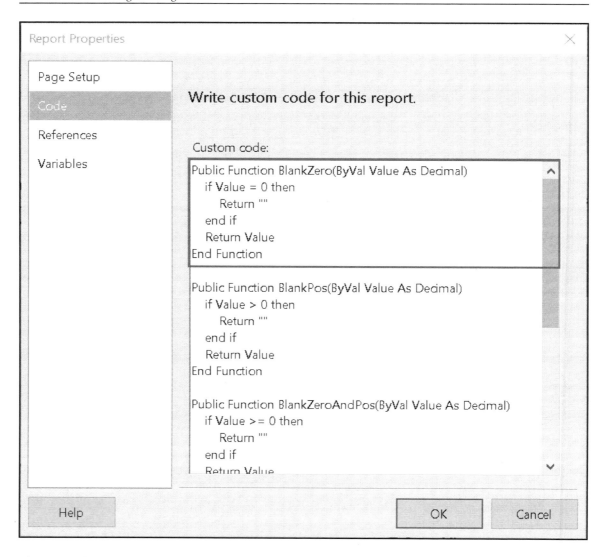

The preceding screenshot, taken from the code section of the report, can be seen when you right-click on the blank section of the report, and click on **Report Properties**. Then, in the **Report Properties** window, click on the code option in the left pane. This is basically the section where the basic functions are defined, which serves as the main function for the operation of report data.

Business logic should not be written in a report layout. Most functions you create and use in a report layout are formatting and conditional formatting functions only. Try to keep all business logic on the NAV side.

The following functions can be seen in this report:

- BlankZero
- BlankPos
- BlankZeroAndPos
- BlankNeg
- BlankNegAndZero

To call a custom function from within an expression, you need to use this syntax:

```
=Code.NameOfFunction(Parameters,...)
```

These functions are used for some basic functions such as to format numbers. For example, if the quantity for an item is zero, you can show an empty value instead of a zero via the following expression:

```
=Code.BlankZero(Fields!Quantity_ItemLedgerEntry.Value)
```

You can write functions in this way, which basically serve for the whole report in this section. You can also do formatting like colors for the quantity which is above a certain value, or underline the decimal or integer values depending on your requirements.

Creating variables

You can define variables in the same area where you code the function. An example of variables can be written as follows:

- Shared Data1 as object
- Shared Data2 as object
- Shared NoOfCopies as integer

These variables, Data1, Data1, and NoOfCopies, can be used in functions as in any other programming language. In document reports, shared variables are used to store information that needs to be available on all pages of a report, in the page header or footer. Since you cannot use data regions in a report header or footer, you add the fields from the dataset on to the body of the report, usually in a list container, and then you store the values in the shared variables using Set and Get functions.

Set and Get functions

Set and Get are the most common functions used in VB to set some values to a variable, and then retrieve that value from the same variable when needed. It's like assigning a temporary variable to hold some information.

For example:

```
Public Function SetNoOfCopies(Value as integer)
NoOfCopies = Value
End Function
Public Function GetNoOfCopies() As integer
Return NoOfCopies
End Function
```

Since we have already defined the Set and Get function, we can now call the function and carry out the set-get operation on the variable. When you type =Code.SetNoOfCopies(5) in an expression, the value 5 is stored in the shared variable NoOfCopies, and when you type =Code.GetNoOfCopies(), the expression returns the value 3, stored in the shared variable NoOfCopies. This might look a little different, but with just some practice you can easily understand these syntaxes.

Decision functions

Decision functions are conditional functions, which help give a dynamic look to the report. You can use the following functions to carry out the operation:

```
Iif() function
```

```
Switch() function
```

The IIf() function

This is a way to write a case expression in VB. It basically evaluates the Boolean expression passed as the first argument. It is equivalent to the conditional operator which works on certain conditions:

```
=IIf(Len(Fields!FieldName.Value) <= 30, "9pt", "6pt")
```

Here in the following screenshot you can see where you can write the IIF statement code. You can find this in the **Property** section under the **Font** category:

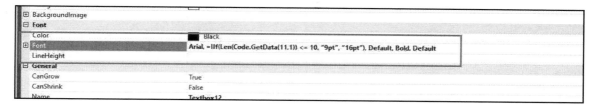

The preceding code detects the length of the fieldname, and if the length of the fieldname variable is less than or equal to 30, then the size of the value to be displayed is adjusted to 9pt, or else to 6pt. Hence, we can do other tricks like coloring different values depending on their value or length. This function comes in very handy while formatting RDLC reports. You can place this code anywhere-in the property section or in the **Expression** section, depending on the requirement and convenience.

The Switch() function

Instead of using it for two cases, we can use this in more complex cases with the help of the switch case:

```
//Using Switch Case for Color

=Switch(Len(Code.GetData(11,1) <= 5, "Green",
Code.GetData(11,1) >=10 AND Code.GetData(11,1)<=15 , "Amber",
Code.GetData(11,1) >15 , "Red")
```

The following screenshot shows where you can use the preceding code to adjust the color of the text:

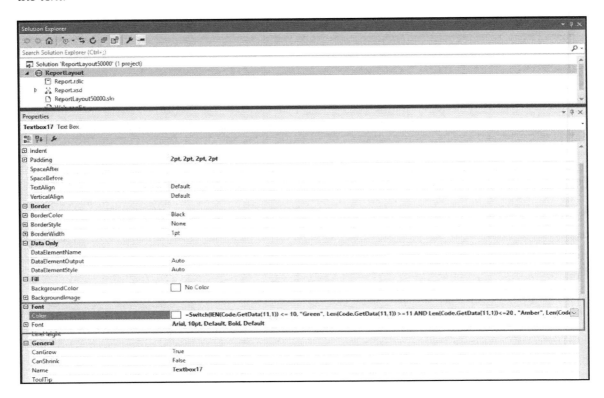

The preceding code basically categorizes the values in three different ranges: the first being less than or equal to 5, the second category being greater than and equal to 10 and less than or equal to 15, and the third category being greater than 15. So the data whose length is smaller and equal to 5 will get displayed in the green color. The data with size greater than 5 and smaller than 10 will be displayed in the default color, the value in the second category will get Amber color, and the last category (length greater than 15), will be printed in red.

Summary

In this chapter, we discussed the core concept of coding with the C/AL programming language and compilation details. You also had some hands-on practice with VB programming. The main intention of this chapter is not to provide details about the functions and features, but the chapter is designed to provide the core concepts in order to boost the concept of computer programming with respect to the C/Side Development Environment. This chapter is highly recommended to not only technical professionals, but also for a non-technical reader.

In the next chapter, we will go into customization, development, and implementation considerations of Microsoft Dynamics NAV 2016 in depth. The next chapter intends to provide an eagle-eye perspective towards the system, and will help in getting prepared before an NAV professional actually starts any customization and development activity. It will also highlight the implications of any changes, and provides suggestions on how to avoid those implications before time. The chapter is intended for developers, consultants, and implementers.

4
Testing and Debugging

In the last chapter, we discussed the core **programming** concepts and related topics of Microsoft Dynamics NAV. We discussed how codes in Dynamics NAV get compiled into other code forms, and how we can sneak through the back door to understand the complex logic behind the simple look and form of the C/AL code. We also saw how VB programming has been integrated into the Dynamics NAV family to overcome the complexity of reporting.

In this chapter, we will focus solely on the testing part of C/AL codes. We will discuss the testing pattern implemented by Microsoft in its release of the 2016 NAV version. We will explain, in detail, how to write your own Test codeunits, and how to utilize automated testing, which is life-changing for consultants and developers. We will also see how the Visual Studio debugging technique can be utilized to debug the C/AL code, providing programmers of other programming languages with something familiar and a rich technique.

At the end of this chapter, we will cover the testing techniques that have been implemented in Microsoft Dynamics NAV 2016. We will see the idea behind the inclusion of a test tool kit in this release. You will also learn to develop your own test case and test code to test the C/AL code.

This chapter will cover the following points:

- The concept of testing and generating a test case
- Test tool kit
- Unit testing
- Automated testing
- Visual Studio debugging technique

Software testing lifecycle

Before you release any software, you must go through the software testing process. For the Microsoft Dynamics NAV world, this might not be the case since a majority of consultants do not follow the software testing standards, and in the remaining cases, it has been observed that each professional follows his or her own standards. Microsoft Dynamics NAV has been trying to include the testing standard or tool into the system so that the developer can easily test the code. Finally, with the Microsoft Dynamics NAV 2016 release, Microsoft has included the Test tool kit in the package, which looks very robust.

Microsoft is trying to implement the C sharp standard of functions and exception handling techniques to make C/SIDE more flexible for code development. You might know these ideas already, but let us approach this new concept in a pattern so that you get a clearer understanding of the concept.

The following diagram shows the steps that make up a software testing lifecycle. You may or may not follow all of the steps, but the pattern must be followed:

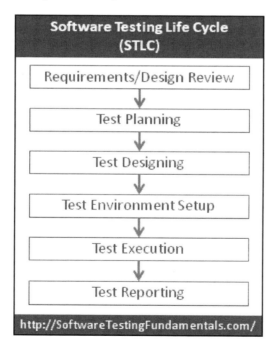

Testing in Microsoft Dynamics NAV 2016

We, as C/AL programmers, should accept the fact that we have had a very poor culture of testing our code. Microsoft has been trying to get the best possible solution that can replace this culture, and bring in a culture where we will optimize our coding skills:

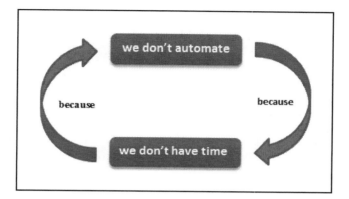

Coding is not always about a successful code; it also is about whether the code generates the result in an optimal time and without affecting other people's work. Microsoft Dynamics NAV 2016 came up with a modified and concrete solution in the form of automated testing, which is customizable, and allows us to test the system without really putting on an effort. Microsoft has presented this version in a ready-to-implement package of codeunits, which can be run to check if the different processes involved in different transactions are successful or not, thus enabling the personnel to quickly identify the root cause of the problem.

Automated testing

Automated testing is one of the best features of Microsoft Dynamics NAV 2016. It simplifies the testing process, and allows less experienced consultants and programmers to test the most complex process of the NAV system. In the past, testing used to be done manually, and it needed experience to test the process with different variances, and to test if the whole process is correct. All that is history now. Now you can use the automated testing mechanism to test the state and process of the system. It also helps programmers quickly understand how their code affects the overall system, and thus act quickly on any kind of bugs. Let us delve into the world of automated testing in Microsoft Dynamics NAV.

Previously, some of the smart coders used to write a codeunit that deletes the value after the process so that they could continue the test. Now you do not need to bother about that as well. You do not need to test manually unless you have to present the system with the value, and show the results with the report output.

The following diagram shows how automated testing might look a lot of work at the beginning, since you are creating extra codes to test the development you have done. But in the long run the manual process of testing consumes most of the project time when done repeatedly:

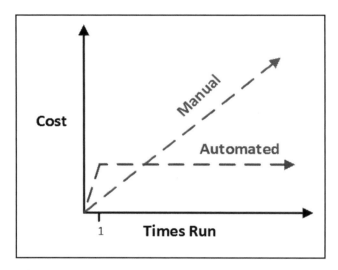

The following are some of the main points that we will achieve with automation testing:

- To allow rerun of test collateral frequency
- To show that the existing functionality is still working as it should
- To estimate that the test covers all known scenarios
- To explain that the code is efficient enough to be accepted
- To demonstrate a technical documentation along with UAT
- To reduce the risk of system failure

Lack of automation makes testing expensive and tedious. It also consumes a lot of time just to confirm if the customized code is correct or not, or whether it affects another part of not. It also helps follow the pattern of Microsoft releases, where Microsoft releases a number of versions and hotfixes frequently. In order to keep our system in a consistent state, we must keep all our test cases running every time we import any object from the latest hotfixes or release.

The good news for all developers and consultants is that Microsoft has promised that the Test tool kit will be a part of the product in future as well, and they are going to upgrade the test codeunits in order to optimize the time consumption of automated testing.

Testability framework build in NAV

If you have worked with C# code, then this part will be easy to relate to. All the functions have a prefix that defines the characteristic of the function. This is new in Microsoft Dynamics NAV, and personally, I think it is cool to have this in C/AL. The following screenshot shows a few examples of functions with prefixes:

In the essential part of the testability framework, we have the following four main parts:

- Test codeunits
- ASSERTERROR
- UI handlers
- Test runner/test isolation

The codeunits have a subtype. The subtype has a number of options such as **Normal**, **Test**, **TestRunner**, and **Upgrade**. If we select Test as a subtype of our codeunit, this means that we are able to create code here as a test code:

 The code which inserts a value inside a table written in the Test codeunit does not actually enter the value into the table. The process is confined to only testing purposes. It virtually pushes the data and tests the success or failure condition.

When you create a function inside the test codeunit, then the [Test] tag is assigned to the function as a prefix.

Now let's see how we can import the Test codeunits from the Installation DVD folder into our Dynamics NAV system:

1. As shown in in the following screenshot, locate the **TestToolKit** folder in your installation DVD folder. Choose the file appropriate to your Dynamics NAV system:

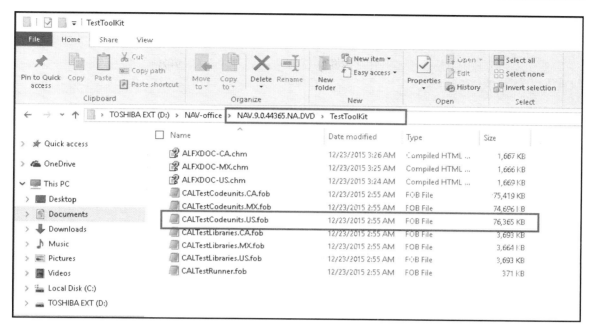

2. Now let's use the **Import** object functionality from the development environment of Dynamics NAV system and import the object pointed in Step 1. The following screenshot shows how the import operation will create new objects:

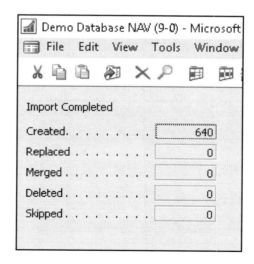

3. Confirm the newly created objects from the development environment as shown in in the following screenshot:

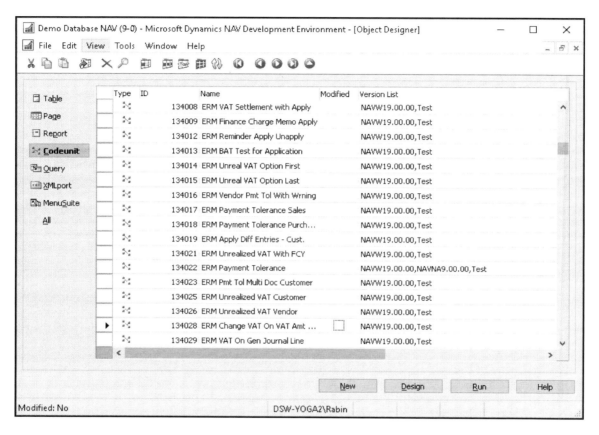

These codeunits can be used to test different testing operations and are redesigned in Microsoft Dynamics NAV 2016.

Now let's understand the basics of Test codeunits. A Test codeunit is very similar to any other codeunit except that its subtype property is defined as Test, which allows the system to recognize it as a Test codeunit. The first thing you should do when creating a codeunit is to go to the property and change the subtype of the codeunit to Test as shown in the following screenshot:

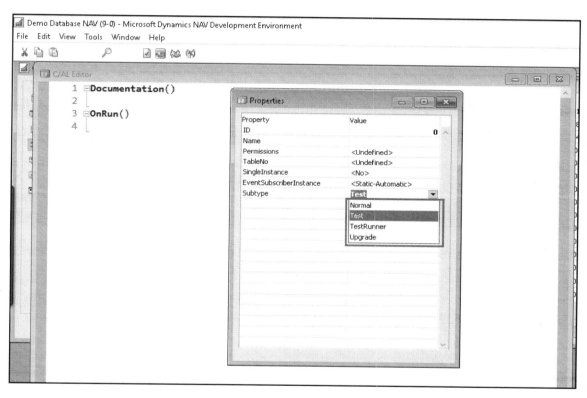

The job of these functions is used to return a success or failure value. So, whatever function is mentioned in the codeunit will either return success or failure as a return value:

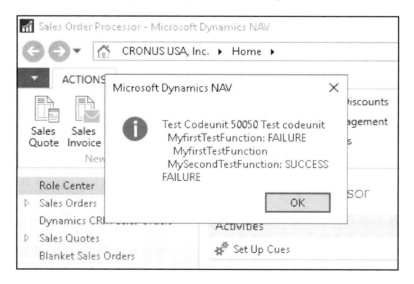

The output of the function in the preceding screenshot is presented like this:

The ASSERTERROR statement is used in test functions to test the behavior of the function at the time of failing conditions.

The ASSERTERROR statement guarantees smooth execution of the code when expected errors occur in the statement of the test function. You can always get the error text of the statement by using the GETLASTERRORTEXT function.

But in case the code that is followed by the ASSERTERROR keyword does not get an error, then the ASSERTERROR statement generates the error as follows:

```
TestAsserterrorFail: FAILURE
An error was expected inside an ASSERTERROR statement.
```

This returns the Failure result. So this is a very important system statement, which can be used to test the failure states while allowing the code to proceed:

Handler function

We should not put messages in the test code, since it takes some time to handle the error message. So we use error handlers, which will help us test the codes that contain different options such as yes or no for different operations. For example, if there is a confirmation dialog box that should only proceed with the post operation on option Yes, it can be tested using the handler function. This function is basically used to catch the message and proceed with the test process.

There are various types of handler functions such as the following:

- MessageHandler
- ConfirmHandler
- StrMenuHandler
- PageHandler
- ModalPageHandler
- ReportHandler
- ReportHandler
- RequestPageHandler
- FilterPageHandler
- HyperlinkHandler

Do not ever put the message or confirmation messages in the Test code with other test statements. Always try to keep these test cases in message. You can take this as good programming practice.

The following screenshot shows a list of handler functions that you can implement:

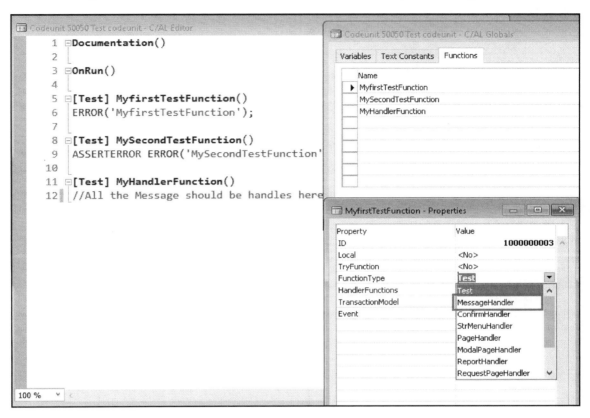

These handler functions are directly derived from C#, and like C# they have the same functions.

You need to link your handler function to the test function so that whenever a certain event associated to the test process occurs, it is then handled by the handler function, making the code efficient.

In the last chapter, you studied how exception handling is done in C/AL. You can relate this handling event to exception handling. Actually, both processes have a similar pattern.

We can link the function to the handler function by assigning the handler function name in the `HandlerFunctions` property of the test function, as shown in the following screenshot:

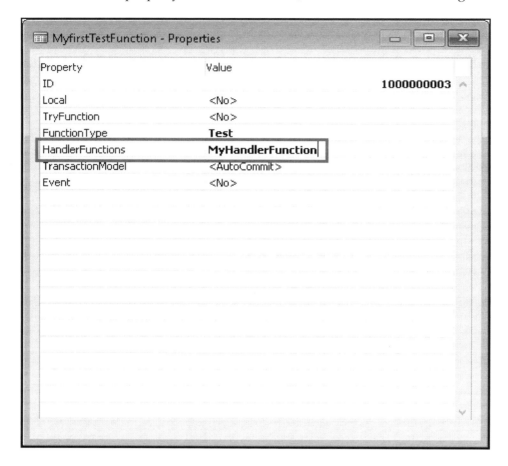

 Note that you have to manually type the name of the handler function. Make sure the name of the function you type is correct.

Now since we have already seen how the Test codeunit really works from outside, let's first understand how multiple Test codeunits can be run from a single point to achieve better handling of the codeunit. After that, we will discuss how to write a simple codeunit to test a test case.

The TestRunner codeunit

There is a codeunit that handles the run operations of all other test codeunits. The ID of the Test Runner codeunit is **130400**. This codeunit allows you to run all the Test codeunits, catch the result, and present it in a single-page view. This makes life easier for the test engineers to understand how his or her code works along with other pre-existing codes.

 Always make sure you build your own test codeunit and, once your codeunit passes the test, run all the codeunits to see if your code has affected other existing processes. I highly recommend doing so at least once before you deliver your modification codes or objects.

Test Runner codeunits run in isolation, and roll back all the changes to the database to maintain the consistent state of the system. This is also important if you are doing iterative testing. You can see how the Test Runner codeunit works in the following screenshot:

```
OnRun(VAR Rec : Record "CAL Test Line")
  IF GLOBALLANGUAGE <> 1033 THEN
    ERROR(LanguageErr);

  CALTestSuite.GET("Test Suite");
  CALTestLine.COPY(Rec);
  CALTestLine.SETRANGE("Test Suite","Test Suite");
  RunTests;

LOCAL RunTests()
  WITH CALTestLine DO BEGIN
    OpenWindow;
    MODIFYALL(Result,Result::" ");
    MODIFYALL("First Error",'');
    COMMIT;
    TestRunNo := CALTestResult.LastTestRunNo + 1;
    CompanyWorkDate := WORKDATE;
    Filter := GETVIEW;
    WindowNoOfTestCodeunitTotal := CountTestCodeunitsToRun(CALTestLine);
    SETRANGE("Line Type","Line Type"::Codeunit);
    IF FIND('-') THEN
      REPEAT
        IF UpdateTCM THEN
          CodeCoverageMgt.Start(TRUE);
```

In the preceding code, the records are copied from CALTestLine, which is a record type of the CAL Test Line table. Actually, the records contained in this table are Test codeunits. Whenever we select a codeunit, which is Test-by-property from the Role Tailored Client side, this codeunit basically scans all the codeunits and runs to generate the result. The following screenshot shows how to carry out run operations from the RTC side:

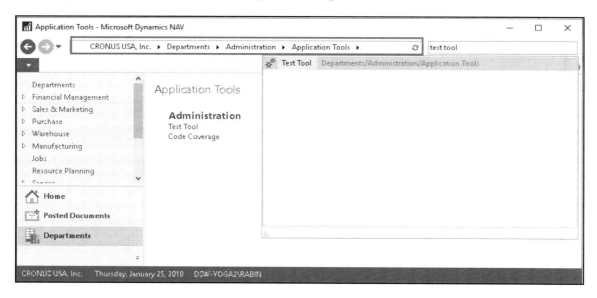

You can either search for test tool from the search bar, or go to the following link:

Departments | Administration | Application Tools

Then open the **Test Tool** page, and click on **Get Test Codeunits**:

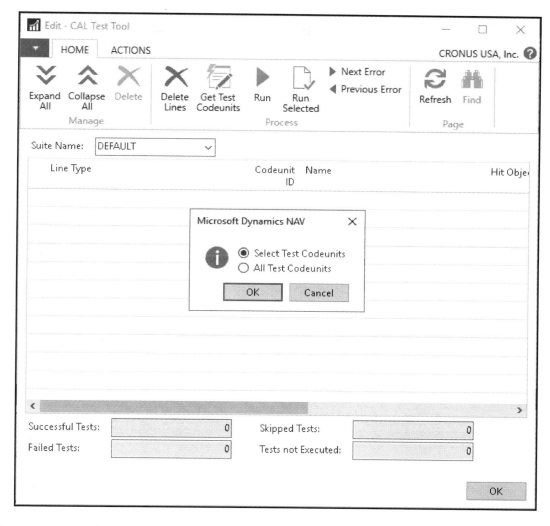

Here, you can either select **Select Test Codeunits** or **All Test Codeunits**. If you select **All Test Codeunits,** then it will scan all codeunits in the system (Development Environment) whose property is **Test**. But if you want to select a specific one, then select the first option as shown in the preceding screenshot. It basically scans the system, and adds all the Test codeunits:

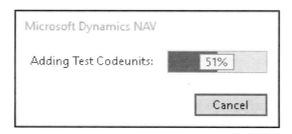

Then the page is presented with a list of Test codeunits:

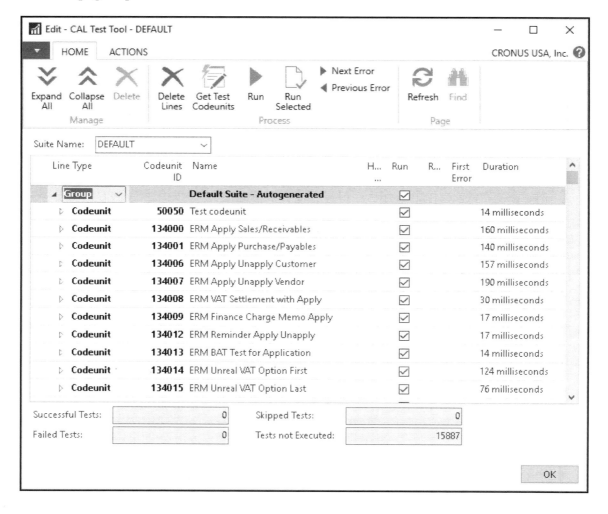

Now you can select a specific codeunit and run it, or select all the codeunits and run them. Whenever you will run a codeunit, you will be presented with two options. After you run the codeunit it will present you with a success or failure result. It will also give you some kind of reason for the failure case.

Writing your own Test unit

Writing your own Test unit is very important, not just to test your code but also to give you an eagle's-eye view on how your code is actually interacting with the system. It gives your coding a meaning, and allows others to understand and relate to your development. Writing a unit test involves basically four steps as shown in the following diagram:

We first set up our data, or create the records that we will be testing later, using some statements. A statement might be an error message, value checking, confirmation, and others. After we get the statement in exercise, we verify our result with the result that is intended from our code that is being tested. If the verification is complete, then we tear down the setup data, and present the success and failure result so as to document the test.

For the sake of writing a simple unit test, let us take an example of a simple error message. While creating a new item, if you choose the item tracking code whose **SNSpecific Tracking** is false, then while changing the costing method to **Specific**, the system will generate an error **Text018: SN Specific Tracking** must be **Yes** in item tracking code %4 when costing method is **Specific**. This is clearly explained by the code in the following screenshot:

```
Demo Database NAV (9-0) - Microsoft Dynamics NAV Development Environment - [Table 27 Item - C/AL Editor]
File  Edit  View  Tools  Window  Help

299
300  Costing Method - OnValidate()
301  IF "Costing Method" = xRec."Costing Method" THEN
302    EXIT;
303
304  IF "Costing Method" <> "Costing Method"::FIFO THEN
305    TESTFIELD(Type,Type::Inventory);
306
307  IF "Costing Method" = "Costing Method"::Specific THEN BEGIN
308    TESTFIELD("Item Tracking Code");
309
310    ItemTrackingCode.GET("Item Tracking Code");
311    IF NOT ItemTrackingCode."SN Specific Tracking" THEN
312      ERROR(
313        Text018,
314        ItemTrackingCode.FIELDCAPTION("SN Specific Tracking"),
315        FORMAT(TRUE),ItemTrackingCode.TABLECAPTION,ItemTrackingCode.Code,
316        FIELDCAPTION("Costing Method"),"Costing Method");
317  END;
318
319  TestNoEntriesExist(FIELDCAPTION("Costing Method"));
320
321  ItemCostMgt.UpdateUnitCost(Rec,'','',0,0,FALSE,FALSE,TRUE,FIELDNO("Costing Method"));
322
```

Now I will try to show a two-level, yet one of the simplest, unit test that you can write for your code or for testing the existing code if it is not present in the test code collection provided by Microsoft:

1. Create a new Test codeunit:
    *   Test codeunit is a codeunit with the **subtype** property **Test**
    *   Test codeunit can have multiple Test functions, as we discussed in the last section
    *   Instead of just running the OnRun trigger, a Test codeunit runs all of its test functions one after another, and the final success message means that all the Test functions inside the Test codeunit are successful

2. Create a Test function called `DemoUnitTest`.

3. Write a `SETUP` section to create `Item Tracking Code` as follows:

```
ItemTrackingCode.INIT;
ItemTrackingCode.Code := 'NewITCode';
ItemTrackingCode."SN SPECIFIC TRACKING" := FALSE;
ItemTrackingCode.INSERT;
```

In case of failure, always use the debugger. Using debugger will allow you to point out the missing statement, since there might be some of the required fields that need to be entered for the success state.

4. Write a `SETUP` section for `Item` creation:

```
Item.INIT;
Item."No." := 'Test Item';
Item."Item Tracking Code" := ItemTrackingCode.Code;
```

5. Write an `EXERCISE` section, where we will `Call Validate` trigger on the `Costing Method` item:

```
ASSERTERROR Item.Validate("Costing Method", Item."Costing
  Method"::Specific);
```

6. Write the `VERIFY` section, where the code will verify that the error message is correct:

```
IF STRPOS(GETLASTERRORTEXT, 'SN Specific Tracking Must be
  Yes') <= 0 THEN
    ERROR('Wrong error message');
```

7. Run the Test codeunit.

If you have managed to write the code correctly, you should be able to see the success message in the **Role Tailored Client** dialog box.

In the preceding steps, we followed the exact pattern of creating a new item with a new item tracking code. The overall steps might look confusing, but the core is to simulate the steps similar to the steps carried out in RTC environment. The values sent are not important, but should match the datatype of the field. The following screenshot shows the code that we have mentioned so far:

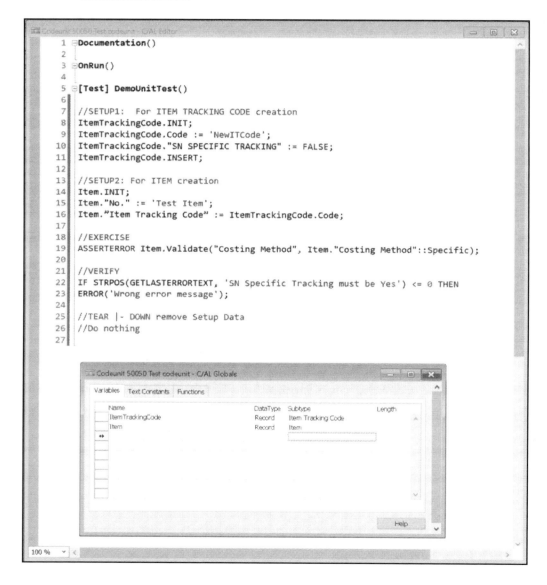

8. The last step that should be added to the function is TEAR DOWN.

   In TEAR DOWN step, we do nothing, since here the success state is an error message of the OnValidate trigger of Costing Method, and the failure state is the error message of Step 7. But in the other Test unit, you might have to roll back all the data to maintain the same steps:

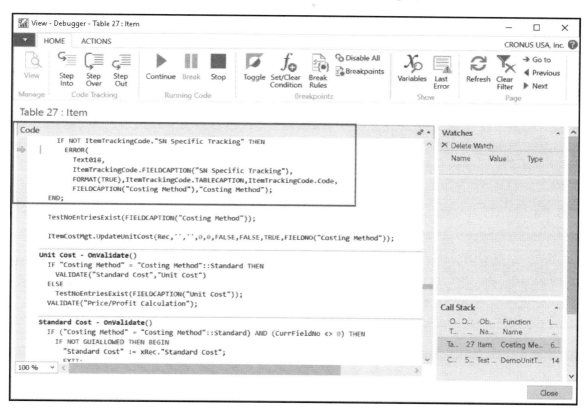

After you run the Test codeunit using the debugger mode, you can easily see how the ERROR function is being hit. When you continue with the debugger mode, you will be presented with a success message as shown in the following screenshot:

Debugging using Visual Studio Debugger

In the last chapter, you saw how we can find the corresponding CS code of a C/AL code. Now we will move a step forward, and see how we can use Visual Studio Debugger to debug the C/AL code.

Let us see the steps that you need to follow in order to start debugging using Visual Studio Debugger.

Here I assume you have changed the settings mentioned in Chapter 3, *The C/AL and VB Programming*, and followed the steps under the *Preprocessing into C# code* section. Just make sure that the value of **Enable Debugging** is set to **True**.

1. Open Visual Studio as an administrator.
2. Make sure the service Microsoft.Dynamics.NAV.Server.exe is running.
3. Now open the **C Sharp (CS)** file in visual studio, which is present at C:ProgramDataMicrosoftMicrosoft Dynamics NAV90ServerMicrosoftDynamicsNavServer$DynamicsNAV90sourcePage.

Since we are not following the conventional method to debug, we might use the CS file of the older version, Microsoft Dynamics NAV 2009, similar to the *Preprocessing into C#* section in Chapter 3, *The C/AL and VB Programming*. We are doing this to make it easy to relate the function to its base.

To explain the concept better, let us take **Page: 9305 | Sale Order List** as an example.

4. Let us try to check the release operation and debug it. So, copy the function `PerformManualRelease`, which is the function being called inside the `OnAction` trigger of the `Release` action, and find the function inside the CS file of NAV 2009. We will use the older version as a bridge between NAV and the modern version's CS file.

5. As I mentioned in the last chapter, NAV is continuously making the code efficient and secure. This is the reason most of the CS functions have also been changed.

6. Copy the C/AL function name, `releasesalesDoc`, from the NAV trigger function, and find the function in the CS file of Microsoft Dynamics NAV 2009. Now copy the respective CS function, which is `releaseSalesDoc.Targe.Invoke`, and find it in the CS file of Microsoft Dynamics NAV 2016, as shown in the following screenshot:

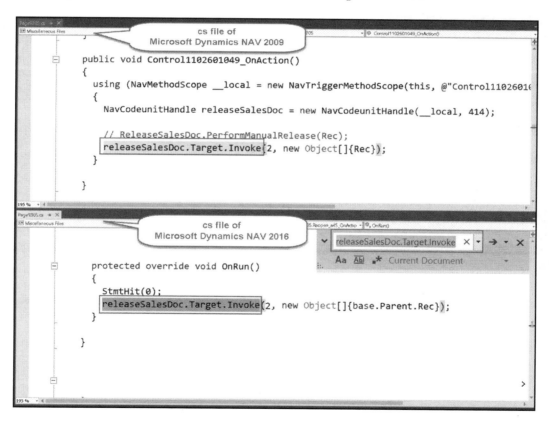

7. Set the break point on the `releaseSalesDoc` function.

You can set the breakpoint by just clicking on the left gray area. Or right-click on the line, and select the **Insert Breakpoint** option from the **Breakpoint** option:

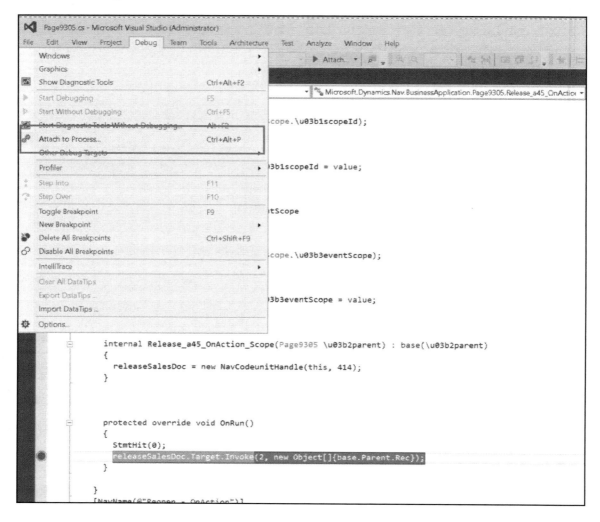

A new window will open where you have to attach a process to this debugging session.

8. Click on **Show Processes from all users**, select the
   `Microsoft.Dynamics.NAV.Server.exe` process, and click on **Attach**:

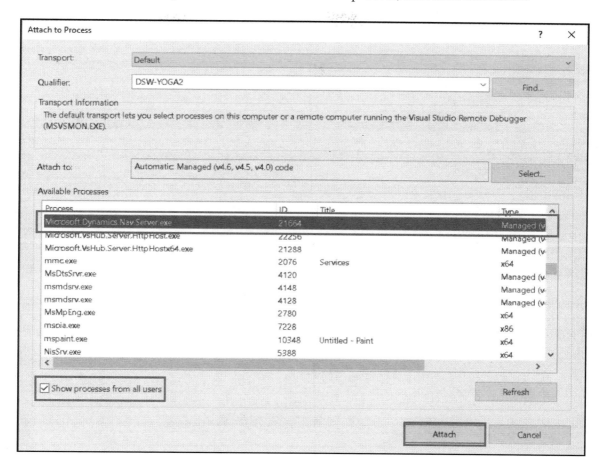

Here, in the following screenshot, you can see how the Visual Studio Debugger is very much dynamic, because it is C sharp in nature. It allows you to run through the values of the record. If you have a core programming background, then you will definitely love this concept:

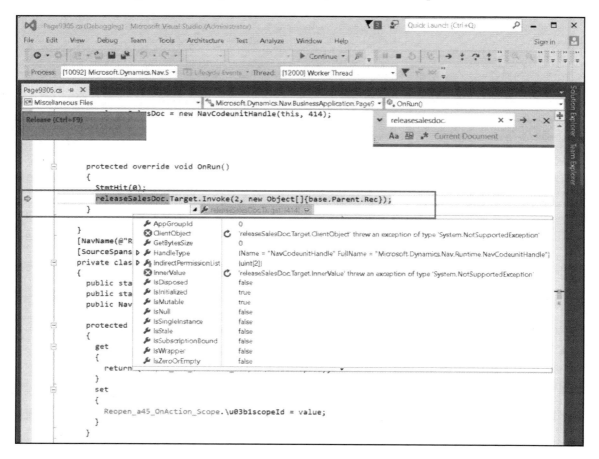

Now you are all set to debug the NAV system using Visual Studio Debugger. This is how we attach the Debugger to a process that is running on the NAV server.

9. Run the process using the Microsoft Dynamics NAV Client application.

Use the `Release` process from `Sales Order List`.

By using the debugger, you could basically run through the code. It is very similar to NAV Debugger, it has step into and step over, which can be of great importance while walking through the codes. Visual Studio Debugger is more robust, and gives broader debugging features.

If you debug the RTC, then you have to run the entire RTC. It is not user-wise debugging, so make sure other users are not using the system. Make sure you do not run it on a live system. This is highly recommended for informative purpose, and it helps solve some of the complex problems with ease. And I am sure the ones with a C# background will love this.

By just setting the breakpoint to any place, and attaching the process to the NAV Server, the debugger automatically catches the errors when you run an NAV process with an error. This is shown in the following screenshot:

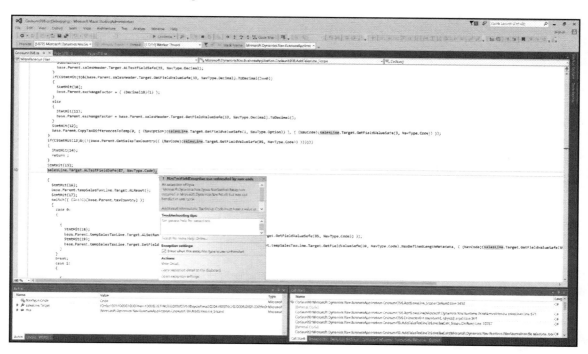

This is just a matter of confidence and being comfortable with these tools. I would recommend you to try these tools, and see how it suits you.

Summary

In this chapter, we explored the testing technique in Microsoft Dynamics NAV 2016. I personally believe that every consultant and developer should master this concept, since C/AL code is approaching C sharp by many means. Hence, in this chapter, we tried to present the views from the core programming angle. You learnt how to write your own test code and test the applications by yourselves. In addition to the self-generated unit test, we examined the Test codeunits provided by Microsoft, which are more than 600 in count. You learned how they can be used to test the standard process; this was the core of the chapter. We also reviewed the core concept of testing and its principles, which should be implemented for a better coding experience.

In the next chapter, we will discuss the application design and workflow of Microsoft Dynamics NAV. That chapter, being more functional, will be of greater interest for consultants and techno-functional consultants. Programmers can also get a better understanding on how the process actually works. This will give consultants a bigger picture of the Dynamics NAV system. The main intention of the chapter will be to include the latest designs and workflows that have been integrated and implemented in the NAV 2016 release.

5
Design and Development Considerations

The previous chapter focused on the testing and debugging of Dynamics NAV. The chapter tried to present the views from a core programming angle, and you learned how to write test code and test the system developed. We examined the test code unit provided by Microsoft, which is more than 600 in count. We also discussed how Microsoft Dynamics NAV 2016 is enriched with the advanced features that boost the testing experience.

In this chapter, we will understand how the designing process works in Microsoft Dynamics NAV. We will understand the design, customization, and development considerations. We will also discuss the difference between customization and development and how to decide what is best for the given condition. There are many standard good design practices and good programming practices in the software world; we will try to relate these practices with the practices of Dynamics NAV. We will look at how data flows into the system and how the posting process works. This is one of the core concepts that we are going to understand in this chapter.

At the end of this chapter, we will understand the different considerations that we need to follow while designing, developing, and customizing the Dynamics NAV subsystem. We will also understand the process we should adapt while working on the development activity.

This chapter will cover the following points:

- System design
- Customization and development
- Out-of-the box setup and system flow
- Test posting
- Design and development considerations

Starting the customization process

In Microsoft Dynamics NAV, we need to be very careful about when to start a development process and change the business logic. Generally experienced consultants can come up with very minimal customization and development and yet fulfill the customer requirement. In this chapter, the focus will be on how to better understand the system and fit the gaps with the out-of-the-box technique used by skillful consultants. There is a lot more functionality out-of-the-box than the basic order processing and accounting functions. The key to unlocking the full potential of Dynamics NAV is to get a basic understanding of the functions and what they're capable of.

The consistency in the look and feel of Dynamics has proven to be one of the key features behind the success of the product. The interface you design or modify should be consistent with the existing interfaces. This is to make it easier for the existing user to easily adapt to the added portion of the solution. It also helps train the new user when all the sections of the solution have the same interface flow.

 To understand more about user acceptance guidelines, you can visit `https://msdn.microsoft.com/en-us/library/jj128065(v=nav.80).aspx`. Version 2015 can be taken as a reference for 2016 as well.

In addition to these, you should always be aware of the consequences your modification can bring to the entire system. I consider these to be sins of Dynamics NAV development. It is always good to provide the user with new features and tweaks to the existing features, but you should make sure your part does not disturb the flow and logic of the existing system.

Dynamics NAV setup and customization

Dynamics NAV is a dynamics system that can be set up differently to fit different ranges of environment, and this is the reason why every consultant should have a strong hold over its setup before diving into customization. One must be very clear about the requirement and should be convinced that the existing setup meets the criteria to fulfill the requirements provided by the customer. Customization should be chosen only if the existing functionality and setup do not solve the problem.

When you set up a new company in Dynamics NAV, you will have to consider many setup tables, roughly 200. In addition to setup tables, there are setups related to journals and its subsections in different modules. Payment terms and the dimensions are another aspect of Dynamics NAV setup. It is highly recommended that you make a checklist of all the setup tables that are related to the module you are planning to implement and that are properly set up. There are certain variations in the setup table that significantly alter the nature of the system, so you must be very clear on what the requirement of the user is and what the possible feature variations provided by the Dynamics NAV setup tables are.

Secondly, you should be very much open to the design pattern of the Dynamics NAV, which suggests that if you are customizing the existing subsystem, then you should follow the norms of the pattern; for example, if you are inserting any field that is general to the setup, then you should inset the field in the respective setup table so that end user does not need to learn how to set up the subfunctionality developed by you. It might sound simple and unnecessary, but it really makes a difference between a proper customization and a haphazard one.

Let's discuss this with the help of a flow diagram:

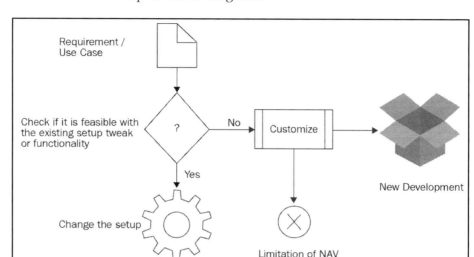

In this figure, we can see how we should approach any use case, if presented. We must be 100% sure that the solution is present inside the system. This will not only save our effort for the development, but also save our time and the efficiency of the system.

It is normal that the consultant or the developer does not know about the existence of all those small features found all over the application. But doing research and discovering these features every time we face a new situation is a great way to expand our knowledge in Dynamics NAV and provide more value to our work.

Convincing the customer

Customers are the ones who pay for what we design and develop for them. Many consultants take this as a source of income and the chance to show that they can design whatever the client has asked for. This is one of the worse practices. We must be able to convince the customer that the change required is a huge one in order to achieve a very minimal difference in the user experience. At the end of the day, this will reflect the amount of paycheck the client needs to release. I have also seen cases where many consultants are always ready to make changes to the system as per the requirement change without considering its consequence, which can affect the whole project and delay the implementation. It also increases the cost of maintenance after the project is implemented and the overall performance of the solution might get affected as well.

The following are the benefits of a successful convincing process:

- Reducing the load on the developer
- Reducing the cost of customization
- Less customization means a fast user experience
- Less bugs and low maintenance cost
- Timely project completion
- Satisfied customers

Most of the new consultants believe that convincing is equivalent to bargaining, but it is nothing more than blind belief. If your concept is clear about your solution and if you have properly studied the use case, then your solution would be highly appreciable. There might be certain group of clients that are hard to convince, but we are taking the most general case here.

But before you approach the client with a possible out-of-the-box solution, you must be sure about the solution and the use case, or else you might make a fool of yourself. Let's look at the steps you should follow before approaching the client with a solution:

- **Partner source**: Microsoft Dynamics NAV has a great Partner Source Archive, which includes both video and text formats of documentations and a stepwise walkthrough of most of the process flows. Reading and understanding these manuals helps you understand the process better and thus it will help you to take a better decision.

 People think that expert consultants do not need to keep reviewing these materials. However, they read and go through these manuals when they are first released and they keep reviewing them when they face any confusion. So always prefer these sources as the primary source if you have any confusion.

In addition to these manuals, you can find other books related to the specific topic in our online library at https://www.packtpub.com/.

- **Online source**: You should be always active on online communities if you are looking to solve problems that are not conventional. Online communities for Microsoft are very active, and you can find Dynamics NAV experts posting for the solutions of a variety of problems posted by different developers and consultants there. Some of the examples of online communities that I recommend are https://community.dynamics.com/nav/, http://mibuso.com/, and https://dynamicsuser.net/nav/. You can always post your problems in these communities.

In addition to these, you can find also multiple blogs written by experts in the field. They will provide you with their view toward the process and their techniques. It is not certain that you can find the exact solution on the go, but if you search with the right keywords and spend some time on Google, in most of the cases, you can find the related hints for the solution.

- **Expert advice**: Taking expert advice can save you and your company time and money. We all face problems, and in such cases, you must talk to the teammates and seniors in your team. I have seen that in most of the cases, posting your question online gets you some kind of help about the solution, but if you do not get anything from online sources and Microsoft partner resources, then you must try to organize a meeting inside your team and ask for suggestions and alternative approaches. Sometimes, the errors can be fixed by writing to Microsoft about the bugs, but before that, you must have done sufficient research.

  In a worse-case scenario, you might have to contact professional, paid consultants. Even in that case, you must be totally prepared so that you can understand this solution quickly and thus save money and time in understanding their solution.

Always make it a habit to save your solution somewhere. Many people write their blogs when they face problems and find the solution, which is unique or different. Or, you can always keep it personal so that the next time you or your team members face the same problem, you can easily refer them to the solution you get.

Customization and development

Once you have finished all the steps mentioned in the previous section to identify and resolve the problems using the default ways, you finally reach to a conclusion to develop your own customization to the system. This is a very critical part since this will involve precise designing, interconnectivity, testing, and a specific maintenance task to follow. Here, I will try to explain the broader part of the development picture. Let's discuss the life cycle of any customization and development activity in Microsoft Dynamics NAV.

Customization and development might seem confusing, but you must be very careful while presenting this to the customer as it affects many sections of the project, including the finance and due date. Customization is the process where you tweak the system to achieve the requirement. Some consultants also call it an out-of-the-box feature.

Development, on the other hand, needs a separate designing, code writing, integrating, testing, implementing, training, and maintenance subprocess. In almost all projects, development process increases the duration of the project and also increases the risks of the high maintenance cost after the implementation:

The preceding figure explain how customization and development can be understood. In a customization process, we usually deal with the system and subsystems within the Dynamics NAV product and the team members can accomplish the customization process as the project moves forward. It takes comparatively lesser time.

Let's talk about an exception example. In my experience, one of our clients wanted to change the outlook of each page by altering the name of almost all the pages and in many cases also wanted to change the datatype of the fields. In addition, they also wanted to change all the NAV reports to their standard report. They did not order any development work but wanted to customize the entire product. It took almost 4-5 months for two technical consultants just to achieve these customizations. Since they were willing to pay, we did not mind working for it. But this example shows how clients can come up with different requirements for customizations.

Application lifecycle

The application lifecycle is composed of six main steps, that is, design, development implementation, production, tuneup, and fit/gap, as shown in the following figure. This is a recursive process since the requirement is directly proportional to the life of any software. If any new requirement comes, then you can analyze the gap and find whether the problem can be resolved using the default setting, and if it needs additional development, you can go for it:

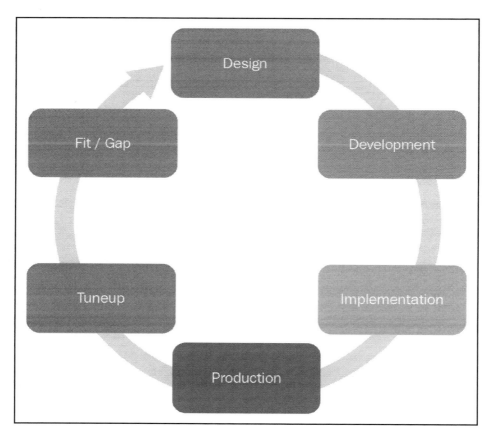

In this chapter, we will focus only on design and development considerations. The implementation and tuneup processes are covered in the upcoming chapters.

Design

Software design should be treated as any other engineering design and should be as simple and as compatible as possible. You should be able to design the system so that the end user who is going to use your system along with the standard system must not get confused with your development, and it should also not be alien in look and feel to the standard parts of the system. It is essential to use the same design principles and structure everywhere in your development. This is very essential because you as a developer do not want to make your development harder to implement and maintain. This also reduces the cost of training.

It is essential that the design you are going to create be totally in sync with the requirement of the customer. And another point you always need to keep in mind is that, if two different designer team are working on the common solution, then the level of complexity standard of both the section should be similar. It not only gives the user a smooth interface but also boosts the natural flow while using the system.

It is not always possible to design the best solution, but we should always keep the basic fundamentals under consideration to reduce the software design flaws. Now let's discuss the design flaws that should be avoided as much as possible.

The flaws in application design

The longer your code exists, the higher the probability that your code and design will change. The probability that it will change is directly proportional to the length of time the software exists. Even though Microsoft is releasing new versions and is pushing customers to move to the newer version, there are certain instances where upgrading is not that easy or feasible. So, we must take care of the following flaws to make the product easy to redesign and maintain.

The three flaws are as follows:

- **Generating and keeping design/code that isn't needed at that point of time**: You should not keep any part that is not needed at this point of time. This means that any part of code or design that is generated for future purposes should be eliminated. This not only help reduce the time for the development, but also prevents redundancy in the code. It also helps keep the design simple and to the point.

- **Not making the design/code easy to change**: The design and code written should be easy to modify and change as per the requirements. The design should be precise but it should be designed in such a way that, if the change request comes, then it should support that process with a minimal number of steps and without affecting the existing part. In the programming world, it is said that "design should be loosely coupled and highly cohesive". The aim of the design should be to make the application:
    - Less fragile
    - Easier to develop
    - Easier to maintain
    - Easier to add new features
- **Being too generic about the requirements**: You should not consider too many virtual use cases and design your application based on these assumptions. This does not mean that your design should be skeptical towards all other estimates. This means that if you are designing any section, then your design should be precisely focused on the given use case. You as a developer might not have a complete picture and the person who has provided you with the use case might have worked on this already. But if you stick to your work on the input provided, then there is a maximum probability that you will finish your work on time.

Design consideration

There are many considerations that we need take care of while designing a close-to-perfect design for Dynamics NAV. Every day we learn new stuff; the code written 2-3 years back sometimes looks stupid. The same is the case for design as well. You should just try to make your design more robust and efficient and always try to check the worst-case condition that might occur. The following are some aspects of design considerations that you can focus on for good software design:

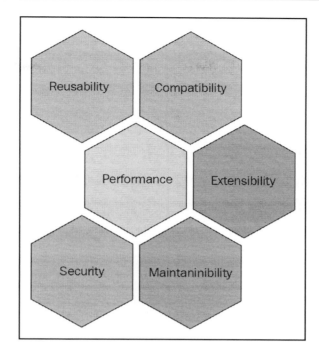

- **Compatibility**: The code you write should, of course, be compatible with the existing module and code. In Dynamics NAV, many of the modules might be using the same process flow, so if you are by any means writing code in those sections, make sure you use the compatible codes. Also, make sure you follow the design pattern followed by Dynamics NAV so that if the product is integrated with any third-party software or online services in future, then your design works like any other process of Dynamics NAV.

- **Extensibility**: Always make sure that you follow good design practice so that your design has the capability to add additional designs of modification without making a major change or altering the working of your designed system.

- **Maintainability**: Your design should produce a well-composed product that can be maintained easily along with other existing systems. Maintainability is one of the main aspects behind system acceptance and can highly affect the system life.

- **Reusability**: The design should be reusable. If other processes can use your design for certain processes, then the cost of the design also decreases and the effort behind the design get better paid off.

- **Security**: Your design should not risk the security of the Dynamics NAV system. This might create a legal issue for the developer and the Dynamics NAV vendor since the system protects valuable data and information. Make sure you do not design something that is prone to hacks and database injections.

Read more about security in `Chapter 8`, *Security in Dynamics NAV 2016.*

- **Performance**: Even if you fulfill all the earlier aspects properly but end up with a very slow system, then it is useless. No one will pay for a system that is not responsive or is slow to operate.

Read more about the P-NP problem of algorithm in `Chapter 7`, *Tuning Up the NAV System,* which will help you better understand how slow system design can be eliminated.

Development

After a proper design, you must be careful while implementing the design with the available datatype that is present in the Dynamics NAV. If you can use some of the specialized functions, then you can also keep the data flow pattern that is implemented in the Dynamics NAV system. Now Let's discuss some of the main concepts in the development of Dynamics NAV systems.

Some of the specialized functions in C/AL

There are special features that are already included, which can make life easier and allow us to follow the structure and design pattern and the coding standards of Dynamics NAV. Features such as **FlowFields**, **FlowFilter Fields**, and **SumIndexFields**, can be used to follow the pattern since you might want to get the updated value from a specific table each time your table is run:

Three kinds of specialized fields	• SumIndexFields • FlowFields • FlowFilter Fields

The CALCFIELDS function In order to keep the value of **FlowFields**, in C/AL programming, we use the CALCFIELDS function.A code example is as follows:[Ok :=] <Record>.CALCFIELDS(Field1, [Field2],…)

Database schema synchronisation

A schema is a blueprint of database design which should always kept in sync during the development process. In Microsoft Dynamics NAV, it can lead to different kind of errors if one misses to follow the synchronization pattern or keeps different levels of synchronization operation due. It is always best practice to keep the tables in sync to avoid errors and system crashes.

Table Compile:	• Now - with validation • Later • Force
Later: Sync. Schema for All Tables:	• Check Only • With Validation • Force

Database schema synchronisation can be achieved using **Flowfield** very easily. This might be very easy for expert NAV programmers, but I am mentioning this here just to give a reference of how you should understand the NAV system well before starting the development activity.

Table fundamentals

We should always understand the basics before we dive deep into the complexity. While understanding the table structure in depth, we should understand the different components of the table, as shown in the following figure. We should understand how triggers work and what the pattern they follow. You should also understand what the order of each trigger is. This will help you with high-level designs in order to accomplish complex issues:

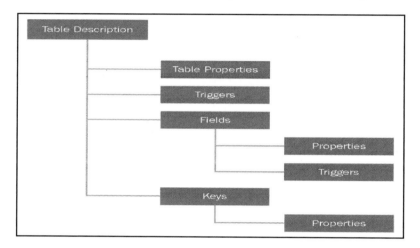

- **Table properties:** You can view or modify table properties from the **Properties** window, which is accessed from **Table Designer**. To view and modify table property, go to the blank line, which is the row after the last value in design mode of the table. Then, click on the **Property** icon on the top bar or use the shortcut *Shift + F4*.

- **The TableType property:** The first type is **Normal**, which, as the name specifies, is the normal type of Dynamics NAV table. The second type is the **external CRM table**. The third one is **ExternalSQL tables**.

  External tables are not managed by Microsoft Dynamics NAV. These tables use a different SQL Server connection than normal tables. These external tables are used when we want to connect external entities:

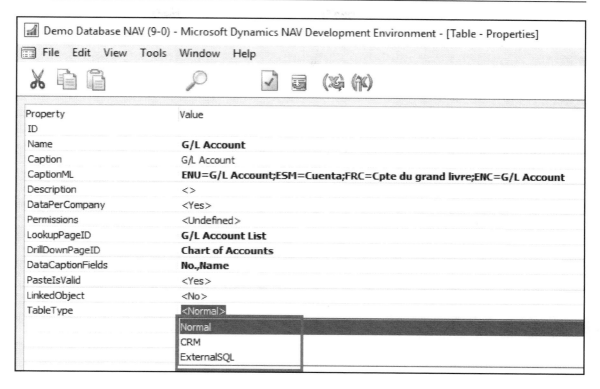

The description is explained in the following chart for clear understanding:

Value	Description
Normal	Specifies the table as a normal table in the Microsoft Dynamics NAV database. This is the default value.
CRM	Specifies the table as an integration table to integrate Microsoft Dynamics NAV with Microsoft Dynamics CRM. The table is typically based on an entity in Microsoft Dynamics CRM, such as the Accounts entity.
ExternalSQL	Specifies the table as a table or view in SQL Server that is not in the Microsoft Dynamics NAV database.

- **Table relationships**: There can be three different kinds of table relationships, which is, the standard for the database level of table relationships. Two different tables can share one-to-one, one-to-many, or many-to-many relationships.

  The three kinds of relationships are as shown in the following figure:

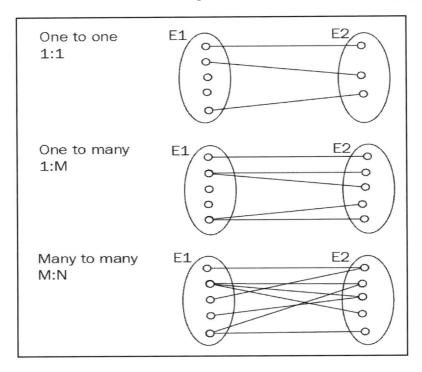

The examples in NAV can be between **Items** and **Order documents**, it is many to many relationships. One sales order can have many items and one item can be used in many different sales orders. Similarly, order to customer is a many to one relationship. One sales order can have just a single customer, but one customer can reference to many sales orders. You must understand these simple concepts while designing the table. The best practice is to use a table ER diagram and get approved by the customer.

Other important things that need to be kept in mind are as follows:

- The TableRelation property
- Filter Table Relation
- Conditional Table Relation

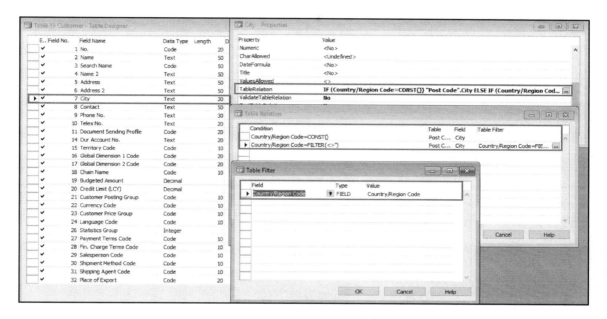

This is important to understand where we need a table and where we can use options for the field. I have seen many customizations where smart consultants have used option fields to accomplish the task of additional information. However, it is risky and not so cool when the requirement of the customer varies as per the time. Therefore, it is extremely important to design the system as per the requirement of the customer.

Conditional table relation

In the case of table relation, you can use the condition that is most impressive. You can filter the values based on the conditions:

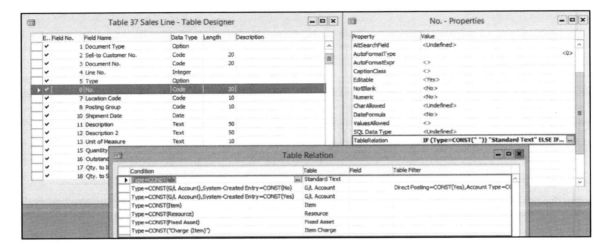

It is very important to get the condition right as it might lead to the wrong output.

Database schema synchronisation

Metadata is the identity information of any object, such as tables in dynamics NAV. When you create an object, its identity are created. Some of the important identities are ID and Name, which is also used for **indexing**. After we create a table, it must be created at the SQL level so that the information can be later transferred to the SQL DB. This is also called synchronization between NAV and SQL. In addition to the synchronization, while creating object, you must synchronize the business database table schema with the new or changed table definition so that the two are the same. So, every time you make a change to the schema at the NAV level, it must be passed to the SQL side as well. There are three options presented when you perform save operations on those modified or newly created objects in the NAV side:

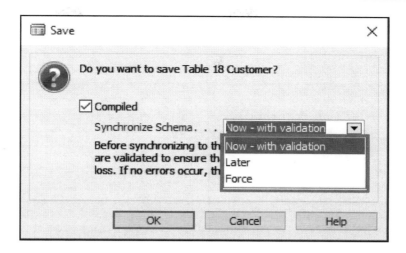

If you select Later, then you must sync all the schema for the tables before you want to run it. Sometimes, after you import the objects and you do not compile them, the errors related to metadata arise. The easiest way to resolve this issue is to compile the object with the error or compile metadata objects (**2000000000** range).

Page fundamentals

Page is the view object that should be as light as possible. You should avoid the habit of writing long codes in the code section. A better practice is to write code in the table and call it in the respective page if you need to do so. For long functions, always use codeunit as the best programming practice of Dynamics NAV.

Let's have a look at a different component Page object. Here in this object as well it is extremely important to understand the trigger hierarchy and properties. Page has an additional component called Action, which is nothing but the buttons and icons that allow you to carry out operations on the related data.

The following diagram illustrates different level of page triggers:

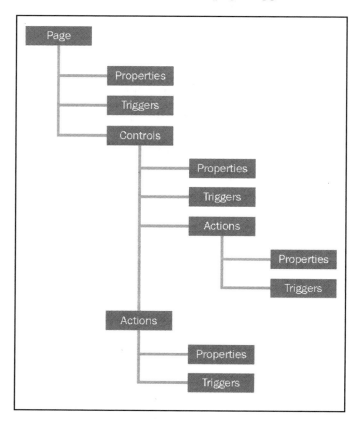

The trigger hierarchy is very important since it maintains the flow while page objects are in action. You also must be careful while setting the property of the page. If you want to set the property of the page, then you must go to the blank row that is below the last row. The **Delayed** insert property in some cases can be very useful in increasing the performance of the process. If you set the property of the **Delayed** insert as **YES**, then the value gets pushed to the DB after you go to the next line or after you leaves the record. This property is mainly used in the combination AutoSplitkey property. It allows complex new data record to be entered with all the necessary fields completed. This reduces the traffic to the DB. The following screenshot shows the page property windows where you can adjust some out of the box features:

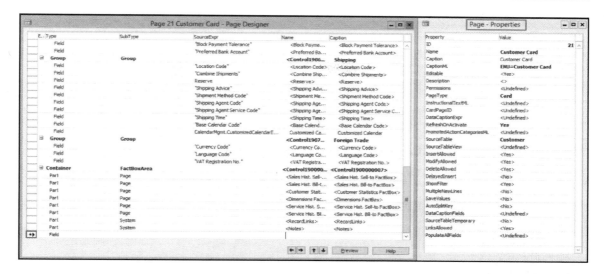

Some of the important properties of the page that need to be kept in mind while designing or redesigning page objects are listed here. Make sure you understand these properties with their combined effect as well. I have experienced that just understanding the accurate applications of these properties leads to saving time and money. These are also called out-of-the-box features, which can be altered to achieve greater objectives without extra code and modifications.

Important properties of the fields are as follows:

- ShowMandatory
- UpdatePropagation
- Scope

ShowMandatory

The ShowMandatory property is one of the latest additions to the NAV. It was added to the NAV in the 2015 release, which is mostly used in the web forms. It helps easily identify the mandatory fields and thus the entry and posting process can be carried out smoothly.

UpdatePropagation

UpdatePropagation is also one of the latest additions to the NAV system. It is only available on part controls. If you set **UpdatePropagation** to a subpage, then the update action updates the subpage:

```
CurrPage.UPDATE();
```

But if you set **Both**, then the same update action will update both the main page and the subpage. This is useful if you want to automatically update the values:

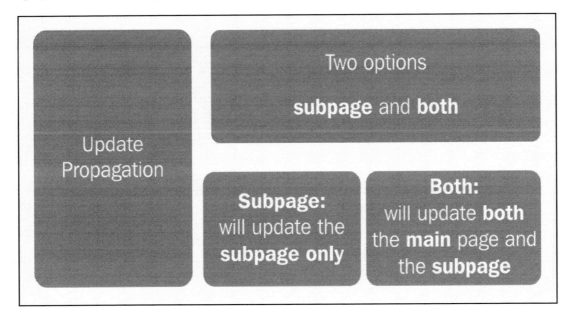

In order to achieve this property with customization, there will be at least 5-10 lines of code and it needs testing and maintenance and also makes the system slower if used in many places. Hence, using properties should be the first choice when you are approaching any solution.

Scope

Scope is the property used in the control section of the page. For this, follow these instructions:

1. Go to page controls.
2. Select the control.

3. Click on the property icon on the top.
4. Go to the **Scope** property.

After the last step, you will get two options, **Page** and **Repeater**, **Page** being the default option since the scope of any action is within the page where it is present by default. But the second option, **Repeater**, explains its main usage. The following figure explains how it can be better understood:

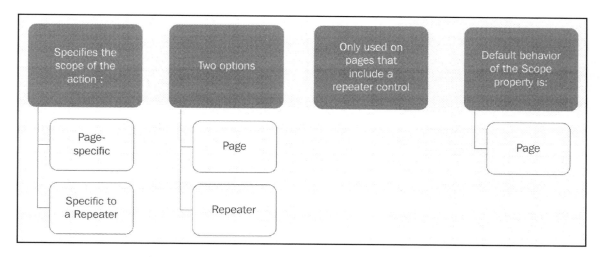

The **Scope** property has the following effects:

	Windows Client	Web Client	Tablet Client	Mobile Client
Page	No effect	The action will be shown in the ribbon.	The action will be shown in the page action menu.	The action will be shown in the page action menu
Repeater	No effect	The action will be shown in both the repeater control and in the ribbon.	The action is moved from the page action menu to the repeater control shortcut menu.	No Scenario

As explained in the preceding chart, this is the result of the **Scope** property on a different client environment.

Page controls

Controls can display data from the following sources:

- A database table field
- The value of a C/AL expression
- Bitmap pictures
- Static information, such as descriptive text
- Other pages
- Predefined system features, such as Outlook or Record Links

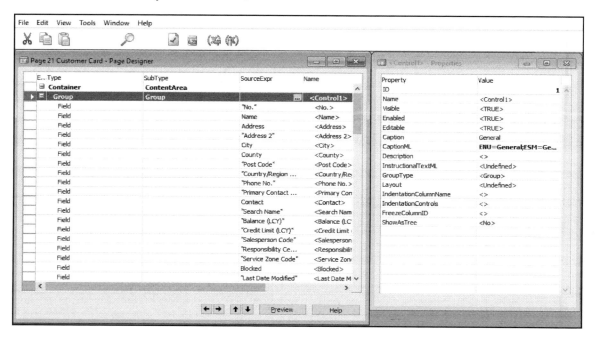

Expressions as property values

In Dynamics NAV page objects, you can use different expressions as values of different properties. It can be used in order to provide some level of dynamism in the page view. Following are some of the points explaining the same concept:

- Several control properties allow expressions as their value
- This enables the dynamic appearance of these controls depending on the value of the expression
- The default value of properties that accept the expression is **<TRUE>** instead of **<Yes>**
- Remember to use **IncludeInDataset**

Control trigger

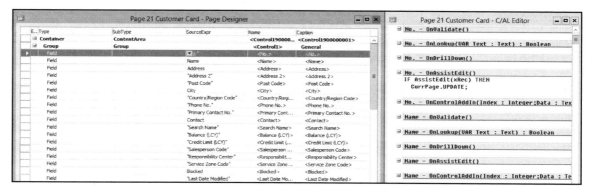

Now let's see how to create Filter Pages for filtering tables:

To create a filter page, you use C/AL code and the functions that are available for the **FILTERPAGEBUILDER** data type:

```
FilterPageBuilder.AddRecord('Item Table', Item);
FilterPagebuilder.Addfield('Item Table', Item."No.", '>100');
FilterPageBuilder.PageCaption := 'Item Filter Page';
FilterPagebuilder.RunModal;
Item.SetView( filterPagebuilder.Getview('Item Table'));
```

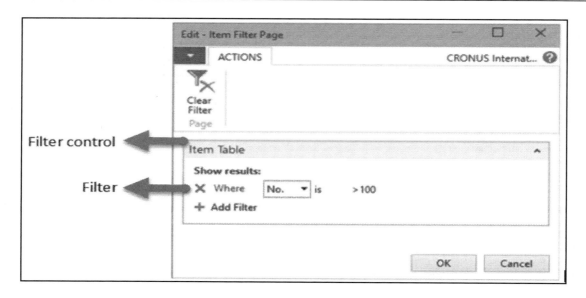

Object metadata virtual tables

In Microsoft Dynamics NAV virtual table contains the data or information sent by the system with response to the system. Basically, virtual tables behaves similar to that of normal tables but its information is not accessible to the user. The following image shows different types of virtual tables in Microsoft Dynamics NAV:

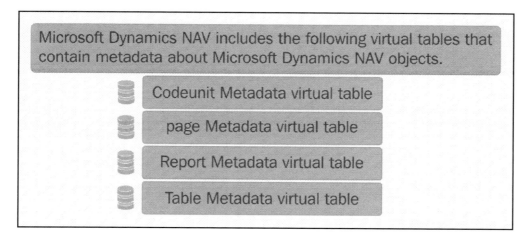

The following are the steps to create a page to view virtual table:

1. Open **Object Designer**. Select **Page Object** and then choose the **New** button.
2. Enter the page ID of the virtual table in the new **Page** window. In Dynamics NAV, virtual tables have IDs in the range **2000000001 to 2000000203**.
3. In the next step, create a blank page and click on **OK**.
4. Now it's time to create **Container**. In the first row of page designer, enter a name for the container, such as **VirtualTablePageContainer**. Make sure **Type** is **Container** and **SubType** is **ContentArea**.
5. In the same **Page Designer** window, go down to the second row in the **Type** column, choose **Group**, and in the **SubType** column, choose **Repeater**.
6. Now go to the third row. On the **View** menu, choose the **Field** menu.
7. In the **Field Menu** window, select all the fields in the virtual table that you want to display on the page.
8. Save the page designer and assign **Valid ID** and **Name**.
9. Now run the page and see the output.

The thing that you need to need to understand here is that virtual tables are not stored in the database. They have been designed in the NAV system to fulfill a special function. You cannot view them directly. You must create a list page that is based on the virtual table. The preceding steps will guide you in doing that.

In Microsoft Dynamics NAV, the metadata has been introduced as a special feature. These are read-only tables and have all the metadata information about the respective objects. The information that you can access in the previous version by looking at the properties (*Shift + F4*) of the object, you can now access all that information from these tables. You just need to create a List page and view the information.

You should always be careful while adding or removing the preexisting code. You should make sure you apply the proper version name and your name tag when you alter the section of code as shown in the following screenshot:

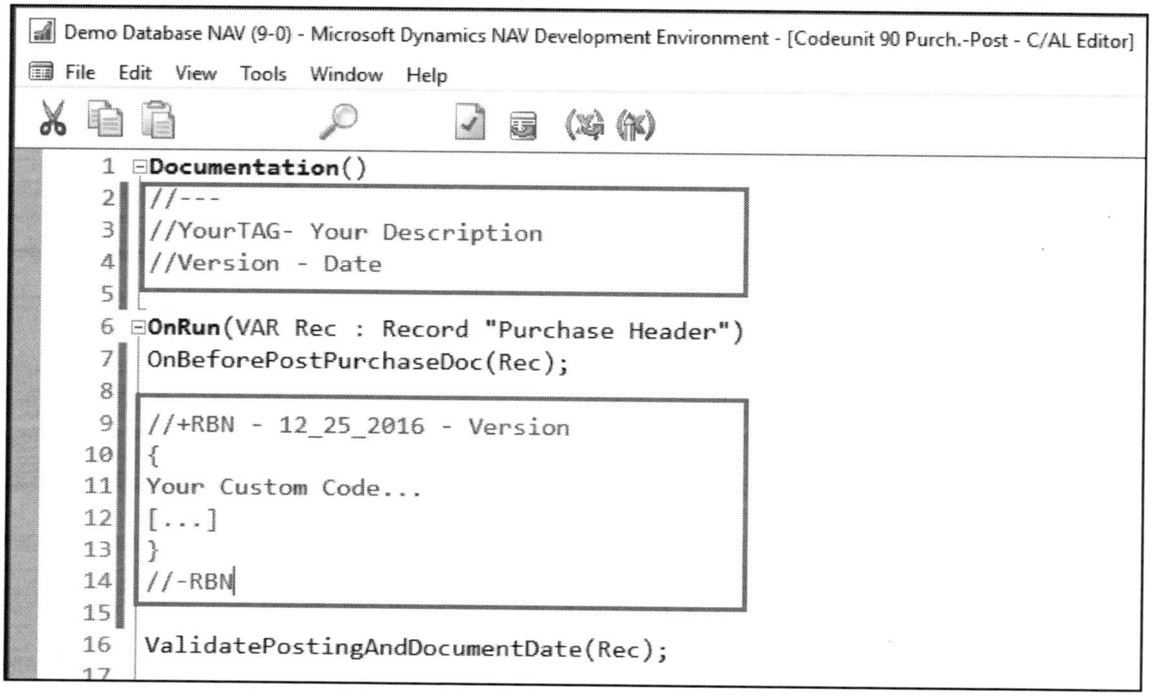

Design and development considerations for Report design

Reports are the most important aspect in Dynamics NAV System because of their ultimate usage. In most cases consultants face the situation where the client vary their requirement or time to time and ask for different kind of reports. I have also seen the projects where requirement involving custom reports constitute almost 60% of the overall development time. The Report design considerations can affect the overall duration of the project lifecycle. This is the main reason the design and development considerations for the Report design have been given greater importance in this chapter.

Object designer fundamentals

In this section, we are going to see the design fundamentals of the main objects in Dynamics NAV.

Team development features

unlock the objects. The four basic operations are as follows:

The locking and unlocking feature has been introduced to NAV in the 2009 version release. It is very useful in the case of Team Environments, where different developers are working together on the same module or process. Here, since they are working closely, to eliminate the risk of overwriting changes made by other users, you can use this feature to lock the objects, and once you are done with your process, you can easily unlock the objects. The four basic operations are as follows: Locking Unlocking

- Force unlocking
- Auto-locking on design

This is illustrated in the following screenshot:

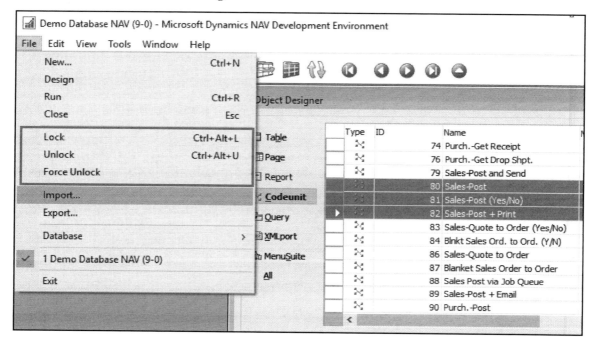

Locking

To lock the objects, follow these steps:

1. Select all the objects you want to lock for your process.
2. Select **File** and click on **Lock**. The shortcut is Ctrl + Alt + L.

Now since the object that you selected is locked, you can perform your operations on those objects.

During the object lock state, other developers will still be able to open the object and read the value in the **READ ONLY** mode. Imagine the object to be a page or table for ease of understanding.

Unlocking

To unlock the object, perform the following operations:

1. Select the object that you need to unlock.
2. Go to **File** and select the **Unlock** option. The shortcut is Ctrl + Alt + U.

Force Unlock

If you are a super user and you want to access the object that I locked by another developer but they forgot to unlock it, you can use the **Force Unlock** operation on the object to unlock it. To force unlock, follow these operations:

1. Select the object that you need to force unlock.
2. Go to **File** and select **Force Unlock**.

 Make sure the other developer is not using the object, or else you might end up destroying his or her work.

Auto-Lock

There is a fourth special operation available for the developers. With the help of this option, when developers select the design of an object, it will be locked automatically. For this, perform the following steps:

1. Go to **Tools** and click on **Options**.
2. Set the **Auto-Lock** option on the design option to **True**.

This will automatically lock the object when open in the design mode. This is for all objects:

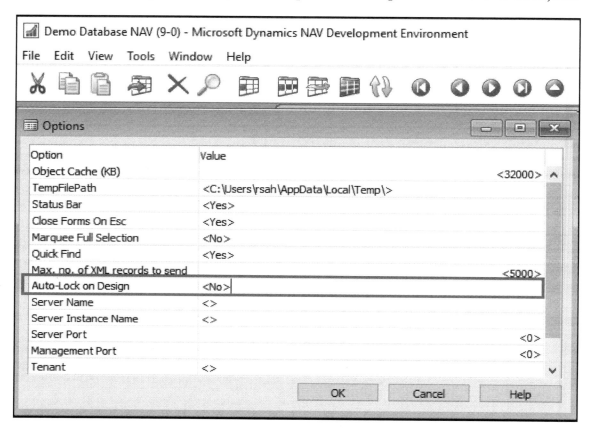

There is no function to unlock the object automatically. If you can use these functions carefully, then it is of great benefit in a team environment.

Physical and logical databases

It is important as a consultant to understand how the database is actually created. From the system side, when you access the database, you generally see only the logical database. Say, you have a NAV database of size 500 GB. Now in reality, it might not be a single stack of 500 GB. This can be because of different factors. As the database size increases, we do not replace the whole hardware because doing that can be an expensive and time-consuming task. So we end up adding extra memory physical disks to get the required storage capacity.

The following diagram illustrates how the logical space can be realized by using totally different physical hardware memory disks. The physical disks can also be in different places yet supporting the same logical database system:

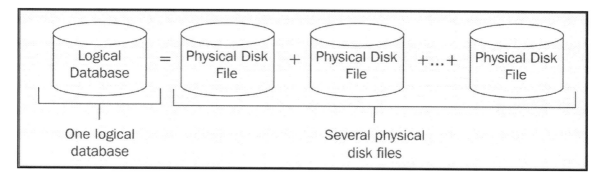

Besides this, there is logical structure inside the database as well. A logical divide means further categorization of the database so that we can place our record in a DB pattern. To achieve a logical structure of DB, we divide the database into the following categories:

- Fields
- Records
- Tables
- Companies

The database is divided into different companies and the companies are subdivided into different tables that hold records in the form of different field data. So we can say fields are the smallest logical division of the database. Fields hold a single piece of data, which can be of different types, such as decimal data, text data, date data, and other datatype data. The combination of fields makes records that are somewhat identical and are distinguished with the use of a certain field, which is called a primary key field.

This is done for indexing. The table holds many records and the combination of different tables and its relations constitutes a company. Refer to the following diagram for better understanding:

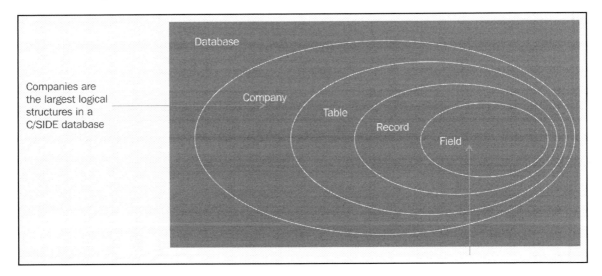

There is further detailed information on the databases such as how SQL manages to keep the data, how the data is stored on the hardware, and how the SQL manager manages a different physical memory device, all of this is out of the scope of this book.

Considerations while coding

All the considerations for coding cannot be covered in this chapter. I have tried to cover some of the interesting and most useful topics in this chapter.

The Try function

The Try function is the latest addition to the Dynamics NAV system. It is directly taken from the C# language and serves the purpose of catching the exceptions that were impossible to catch in previous versions. The first thing that a programmer wants in any language is to catch the exception because in other programming forms, it is the first thing that we write. To create a Try function, add a function in the C/AL code of an object. Then, set the **TryFunction** property to **Yes**.

A Try function has the following restrictions:

- In test and upgrade code units, you can only use a Try function on a normal function type
- The Try function cannot have a user-defined return value

 The details on how to create the Try function and implement it in your code are explained in `Chapter 3`, *The C/AL and VB Programming*. Make sure you start using this function as a base to good programming practices.

The CURRENTCLIENTTYPE function

In order to get the Microsoft Dynamics NAV client type that is running in the current session, we use the **CURRENTCLIENTTYPE** function in the C/AL code. It is a straight forward function call that returns values such as Windows, web, tablet, desktop, and phone. The following table lists the output of this function:

ClientType	CURRENTCLIENTTYPE
Windows	Microsoft Dynamics NAV Windows client
Web	Microsoft Dynamics NAV web client
Tablet	Microsoft Dynamics NAV Tablet client
Desktop	Microsoft Dynamics NAV web client running the app
Phone	Microsoft Dynamics NAV Phone client

An code example of the CURRENTCLIENTTYPE function is as follows:

```
IF CURRENTCLIENTTYPE = CLIENTTYPE::Windows THEN
    Message('The session is running the Microsoft Dynamics NAV
Windows client');
url := GETURL(CURRENTCLIENTTYPE);
MESSAGE('The URL is %1.', url);
```

The DefaultClientType function

In order to get the default Microsoft Dynamics NAV client that is configured for the Microsoft Dynamics NAV Server instance that is used by the current session, we use the **DEFAULTCLIENTTYPE** function. It is similar to the previous function, but the only difference is that the default value can be configured into Microsoft Dynamics NAV Server, and this function just returns the value configured there. The following code is an example for the DefaultClientType function:

```
[ClientType :=] DEFAULTCLIENTTYPE
  Example:
    IF CURRENTCLIENTTYPE = CLIENTTYPE::Windows THEN
      Message('The default client is Microsoft Dynamics NAV Windows
client');
    url := GETURL(DEFAULTCLIENTTYPE);
    MESSAGE('The URL is %1.', url);
```

Report fundamentals

Report is another very important object type in Dynamics NAV. Customers are only concerned with the page to enter the data and the reports to get the output in the form of documents and statistics. They do not really care about what goes on inside the system or the database. So, they are choosy about the look and feel of reports. You must be very careful while designing reports because it can be really time consuming and you might end up billing more hours just on the reports, and at the end of the day, the total cost of the project might be huge.

To avoid these conditions, you must understand what a person needs to consider while designing and developing a report in Dynamics NAV. The following is the description of the components of s report. It mainly consists of property, trigger, data item, labels, request page, and RDLS data:

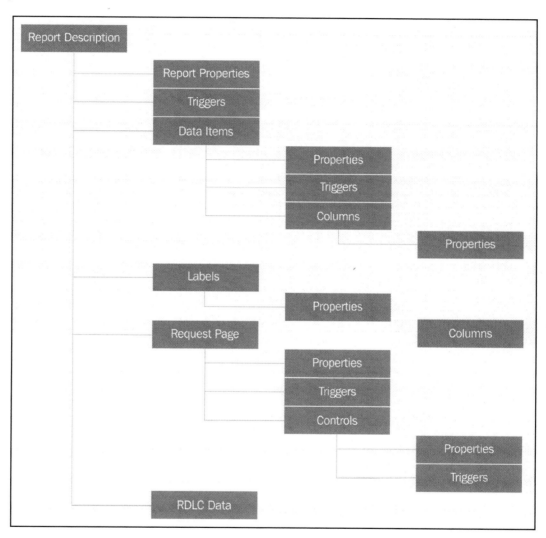

The Report design process is divided into two distinct phases that reflect the different aspects of creating a report:

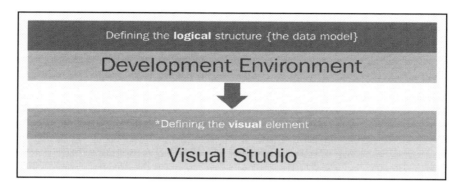

 The related steps on Report design are explained in `Chapter 3`, *The C/AL and VB Programming*. Here, we will just understand the considerations of the report design.

Grouping and totaling

It is very easy to assign the grouping in the **RDLC report** since it supports the grouping feature. Unlike classic reports, it present you with simple grouping options and more dynamic options. The following image aims to clear the concept of grouping and totaling:

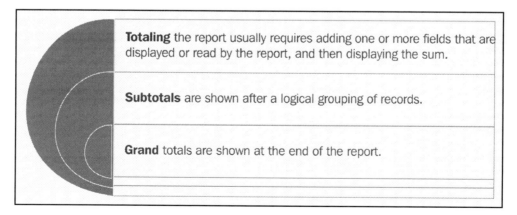

Totaling the report usually requires adding one or more fields that are displayed or read by the report, and then displaying the sum.

Subtotals are shown after a logical grouping of records.

Grand totals are shown at the end of the report.

Saving reports in other formats

There are some of the features in reports that needs to be understood so that while presenting certain report to the customer, you can get all the points and impress the client. Microsoft has been trying to integrate its other applications to Dynamics NAV and it can be seen in the Pages and Reports section. You can directly export the report into other Microsoft format, such as Excel, Word, and universal web forms, such as XML and PDF format. The following is a description of these features:

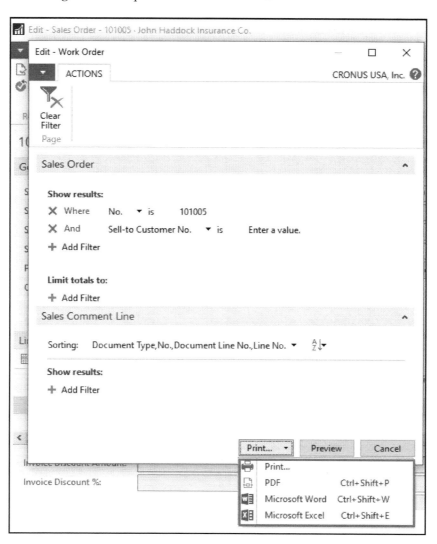

Therefore, using these inbuilt features, you can export reports in different formats.

Important Report functions

There are many functions to save reports in several formats available in Dynamcis NAV. These functions are presented as follows:

Function	Description
SAVEASXML	Saves a report as an .xml file on the computer that is running Microsoft Dynamics NAV Server: [Ok :=] Report.SAVEASXML(Number, FileName [,SystemPrinter][,Rec]) [Ok :=] Report.SAVEASXML(FileName)
WORDXMLPART	Returns the report data structure as structured XML that is compatible with Word custom XML parts: String := ReportVariable.WORDXMLPART([ExtendedFormat])
WORDLAYOUT	Gets the Word report layout that is used on a report and returns it as a data stream: [Ok :=] ReportVariable.WORDLAYOUT(InStream) [Ok :=] REPORT.WORDLAYOUT(Number, InStream)
RDLCLAYOUT	Gets the RDLC layout that is used on a report and returns it as a data stream: [Ok :=] ReportVariable.RDLCLAYOUT(InStream) [Ok :=] REPORT.RDLCLAYOUT(Number, InStream)
HASCUSTOMLAYOUT	A function in codeunit 1 that determines whether a report has an active custom Word layout or RDLC layout at runtime: HasCustomLayout(ObjectType : 'Report'; ObjectID : Integer) : Integer
MERGEDOCUMENT	A function in codeunit 1 that loads the custom Word layout that is active on the report and renders it in the targeted format, such as Word or PDF: MergeDocument(ObjectType : 'Report'; ObjectID : Integer;ReportAction : 'SaveAsPdf,SaveAsWord,SaveAsExcel,Preview,Print'; XmlData : Instream; FileName : Text)

REPORTGETCUSTOMRDLC	A function in codeunit 1 that loads the proper custom RDLC layout for a report at runtime and uses the layout to render the report: ReportGetCustomRdlc(ReportID : Integer) : Text

Codeunit

Codeunit is another main topic that needs to be discussed in this section. As you already know, writing code into codeunits makes the code a lot more manageable and efficient. It also helps smooths the upgrade process and makes the handover process a lot simpler. Let's look at how we can consider some of the basic points while implementing codeunits.

The user of a SingleInstance codeunit

Set the **SingleInstance** property of the codeunit to **YES** in order to use the same instance of variables for the codeunit. This lets developers create global variables. A single instance codeunit is instantiated when it is used for the first time.

The limitations of codeunit

Codeunits in C/SIDE environment has various limitations but is surely evolving with time. The following are some of the limitations of codeunit that we can experience:

- From other application objects, you cannot access the global variables and temporary tables; you can access these values using user-defined functions created in the codeunit.
- Another limitation of codeunit is that two or more user-defined functions cannot have the same name. which is unlike the constructor of C sharp.

.NET interoperability

Microsoft Dynamics NAV 2016 is very rich in .NET interoperability operations. Most of the variables and functions used in .NET are now available or are supported in the C/SIDE environment. This provides us the power of the .NET platform in a C/SIDE environment.

.NET Interoperability features include communication between client- and server-side objects and the introduction of the concept of constructors.

You can call .NET Framework types from C/AL code, which is pretty interesting. In addition to this, you can also call methods, properties, and constructors from C/AL code. It is a straight forward deal.

Follow these steps:

1. Define a **DotNet** type variable referring to the .NET Framework assembly type that contains the member:

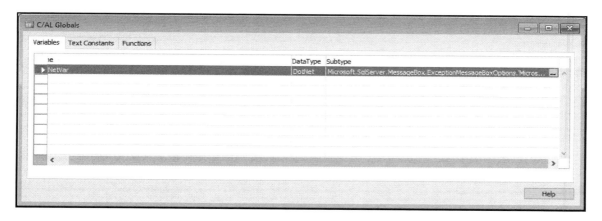

2. Define the subtype of the variable from the .NET assembly present:

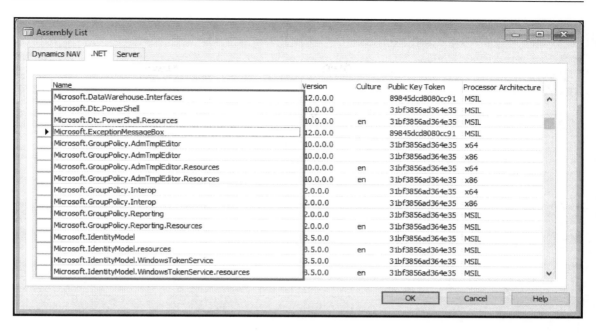

3. Call the variable as any other function variable in C/AL code:

```
Documentation()


OnRun()
//Calling .NET variable in C/AL
IF DotNetVar.Equals(DotNetVar2)
  THEN
  MESSAGE(|
                MESSAGE(String [, Value1] ,...)
```

4. By declaring a variable of the **DotNet** data type and subtyping it to a specific .NET Framework class, you can access all the functionality of the referenced class:

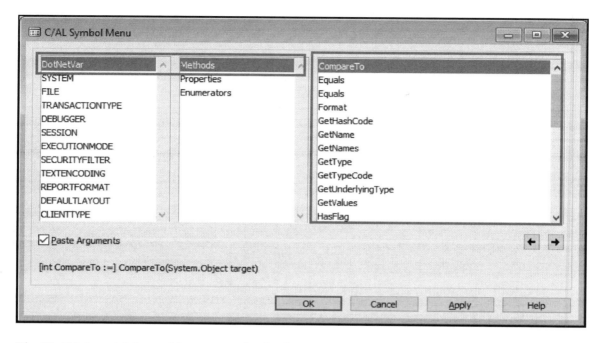

The **DotNet** variable enables you to do the following:

- Access a specific .NET Framework class and its members
- Respond to events that are raised by the referenced .NET Framework class
- Target the Microsoft Dynamics NAV server or the Role Tailored Client

 Hold your horses. We will discuss .NET in `Chapter 10`, *Interfacing NAV with Other Applications*.

Test posting

In this section, we will look into the new Posting Preview functionality. This will let you understand the posting process without affecting the posting table or disturbing the current data. This step can also be carried out on a live system for a certain level of testing before the actual posting process. I have found that most of the clients are now more confident with this feature because they can now see the posted documents and the outcome before actually posting the document.

Prior to posting a journal or document in Dynamics NAV, a user can use this feature. It also helps reduce errors during posting. The best thing about this functionality is that you do not need to configure it. It is ready to go. Let's look at this functionality with the help of an example.

Let's open a journal page with a default batch:

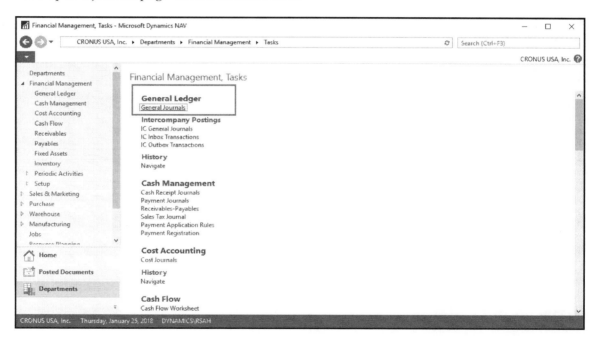

Open the journal page with default batch, for example, and enter just two kinds of transactions for testing purposes, **G/L Account** and **Bank Account**:

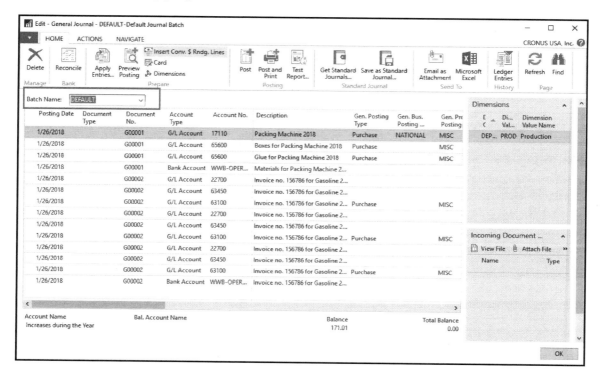

The Preview Posting code also runs the same validation code as the original posting process, so it can be used to check whether the journal and document are properly filled:

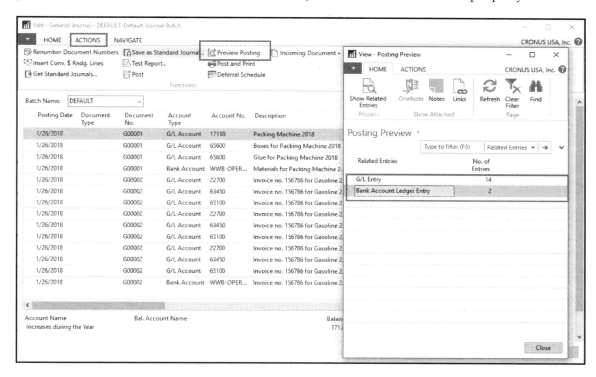

After you click on the **Post Preview** icon, it will open a page that is similar to the page that opens when we navigate the posted documents in Dynamics NAV. You can also click on **Related Entries** and see what values are posted into the posted table. For simplicity, I have just taken the example of **G/L Entry** and **Bank Account Ledger Entries**. If there are other types of entry in the journal, then all the relevent related entry links will be present in the **Posting Preview** page.

The posted table view is presented in following screenshot:

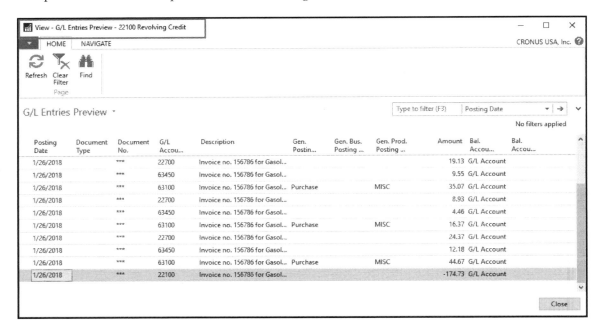

The same steps can be followed in the case of **Document Posting**, for example, **Purchase Order**. This is really a time-saving feature that increases productivity:

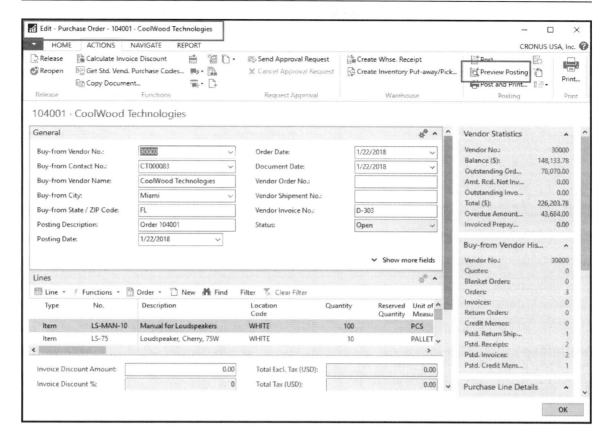

The best part of this functionality is that it runs on the exact same code and follows the exact same process flow as the original posting process. Therefore, it can be used to track the missing posting before the actual posting.

The magic behind this Preview Posting functionality is that rather than posting, it saves the record in a temporary table but using the current state of the system, presenting the precise values of the posted documents in the relevant tables.

This process can be taken as a workflow in NAV. It can be used to learn where the data gets posted into the system. It also explains the nature of the validations that take place in the system.

Summary

In this chapter, we learned about the design and development considerations of Microsoft Dynamics NAV. Most of the consultants do not understand the importance of design considerations and they end up generating weak design and eventually an inefficient system. This chapter was intended to provide a broader perspective on how to approach any design or design operation and how to convert that design into actual development. The chapter also clarified between the concept of customization and development. Finally, the chapter explained how we can understand the dataflow using a special feature called test posting.

In the next chapter, we will discuss one of the most interesting topics of this book, version control. Version control is the least discussed topic in the field of Dynamics NAV but has a greater importance. Many VAR companies with larger teams have developed their own style of version control to allow many developers to work in parallel. We will discuss the basic concept that is intended to help an organization move toward a version control environment.

6
Version Control and Code Management

In the last chapter, we explored different design and development considerations of Microsoft dynamics NAV. We discussed how important it is to understand the design considerations. We also realized how to avoid certain customization and development activities for better performance of the system and timely software completion. All of these concepts helped us understand the entire process of the Dynamics NAV system development aspect.

In this chapter, we are going to dig deep into the **version control** mechanism. Version control, being the least discussed topic among common consultants, created a huge gap between experts and average consultants. It also created a divide between the ways of implementation of the Dynamics NAV project by international certified partners and small silver partner organizations. But, fortunately for those who were not in the race, there is a way they can learn to handle the version, and in a way, control different versions of different phases of Dynamics NAV system development. It is intended to increase productivity and the sense of achievement among the team members. In addition to the functional benefit, version control can facilitate parallel development and thus the vendors can better utilize their resources. In this chapter, we are going to understand these concepts and try to look at the whole picture with the simplest of approaches.

At the end of this chapter, you should be able to implement a version control system for your project. It is just a matter of breaking the ice; once you understand the core process explained in this chapter, you should be able to explore on your own.

This chapter will cover the following topics:

- The basic concept of version control
- Version control setup (GitHub and Team Foundation Server)
- Different pattern for correct ways to implement the concept of version control

Version control

Version control systems are the third-party system that provides the service that tracks changes in the file and folders of the system. In this section, we will be discussing two popular version control systems for Microsoft Dynamics NAV. We are going to understand GitHub and team foundation server/service. Let's discuss why we actually need a version control in Microsoft Dynamics NAV through an example.

Let's assume, last week you added a field to a sales header table; today you added an additional field to that sales header table. Now, since we have modified the table twice, within NAV, you only have a current version; you will not have a history of these changes. In this simple example, you might argue that you can write comments on the table stating the version of these changes, but when it comes to more detailed and complex changes and keeping different levels of versions, it is almost impossible for the NAV system to do that. This is the main reason we are looking for a solution that can do that for us. Luckily, we can tweak a little bit of the steps and use solutions such as Team Foundation Server/Service, GitHub, and other version control services. In this chapter, we will discuss Team Foundation Service with Visual Studio and GitHub desktop and the online service for version control to solve the issue explained in the example. The general model of version control repository is shown in the following figure:

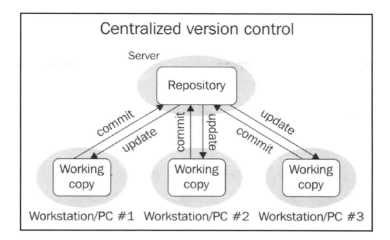

There is a main central repository that is often maintained over the cloud for easy access to all the developers, but it can also be maintained in the secured network in some special cases. The basic steps that one follows are:

1. Synchronize the local repository with the main repository.
2. Make changes to the code.
3. Stage for commit.
4. Commit to the local repository.
5. Push to the main repository.
6. Pull updates from the main repository.

 Stage is a technical term used in different version control systems which simply means to prepare the file for commit.

The best feature of the version control system is that you can always go back to the previous version. It also provides different developers working in the same team a chance to work independently while referring to their local repositories, yet being updated to the latest push (upload-modified objects) of other team members. It allows parallel work and often increases the productivity of the team.

The following image explains how different users might utilize the powerful technology of version control while working in parallel on the same project:

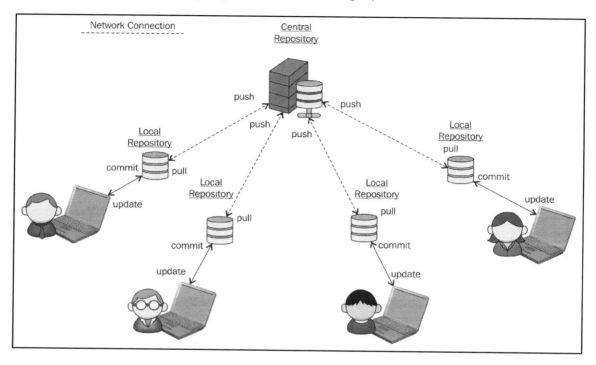

In the preceding figure, it can be better understood how different team members are working for a common project yet are totally isolated to their work. They just need to predetermine the object range which they will be working on and the rest of the things will be taken care of by the version control system.

GitHub

GitHub is a web-based Git repository hosting service (https://en.wikipedia.org/wiki/Internet_hosting_service) that is the best repository service for Dynamics NAV so far. By best, I mean the feature that it provides is best suited to our purpose, and it is also very easy to implement and maintain. Let's discuss how to implement GitHub for Dynamics NAV.

Setting up GitHub for Dynamics NAV

The first step is to sign up for GitHub. You can use any valid e-mail account to create an account in `https://github.com`. After you confirm your account from the e-mail, you should be able to access the online service of GitHub. You can also download the desktop version of GitHub, which is highly recommended. The following screenshot shows the desktop application of GitHub:

The preceding figure is the desktop version of GitHub, which allows you to take control of most of the activities locally. I would recommend that you take a look at the available features of GitHub desktop.

Here, we are not covering all the steps and features of GitHub operations because that is out of the scope of this chapter. But it will be very difficult to understand version control based on GitHub without understanding GitHub. So, I would recommend that you spend some time and understand GitHub and its basic features. Follow these links: `https://www.youtube.com/watch?v=w3jLJU7DT5E` `https://www.youtube.com/watch?v=EUvmCuPjHD4`

For the GitHub repository over the cloud, you can log in with your GitHub credentials. The screen will look like what is shown in the following screenshot:

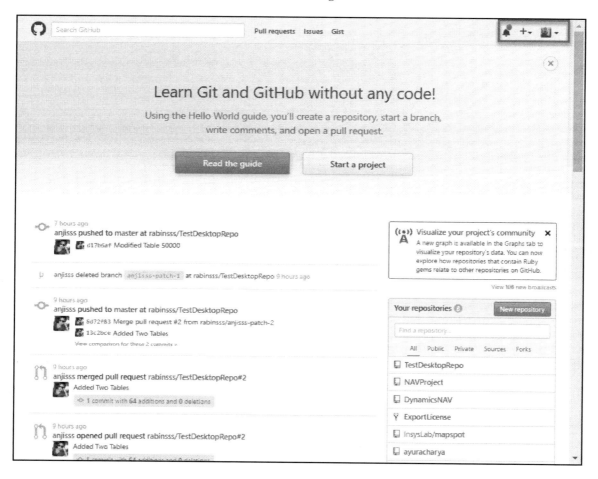

Now you can create a repository by following the simple steps explained at https://help.GitHub.com/articles/create-a-repo/. You just need the basic skills to do this on your own. It is as easy as accessing features on Facebook and LinkedIn.

Since you have already created a repository, the first stage of setup is finished. Now let's prepare our Dynamics NAV object to feed the central repository.

Preparing an object for the repository

Follow these basic steps to export an object for the repository:

1. Open the **Object designer** window of Microsoft Dynamics NAV Development Environment.
2. Open the database you want to use for the process.
3. Select **Table** and export it in **Text Format** to a temporary folder on your local computer:

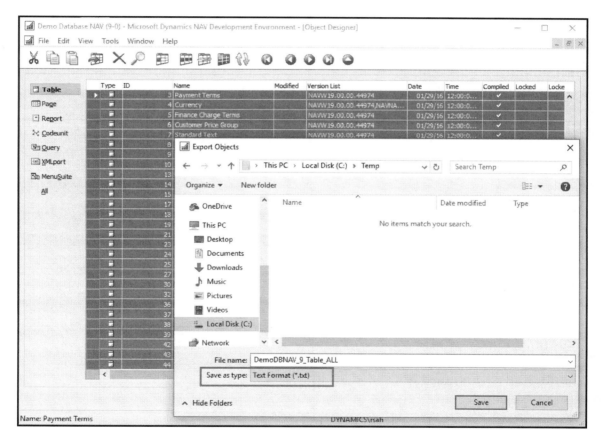

4. Now use the **Object Splitter** application, which you can find on Mibuso site.

   NAV Object Splitter
   (http://mibuso.com/downloads/nav-object-splitter-v3.0.0.0).

5. Download the application and open the `WinNavObjectSplitter.exe` file. In the **Source** section, locate the `DemoDBNAV_9_Table_ALL` file that you just exported to the temporary folder in Step 3 (choose your file). Take a look at the following screenshot:

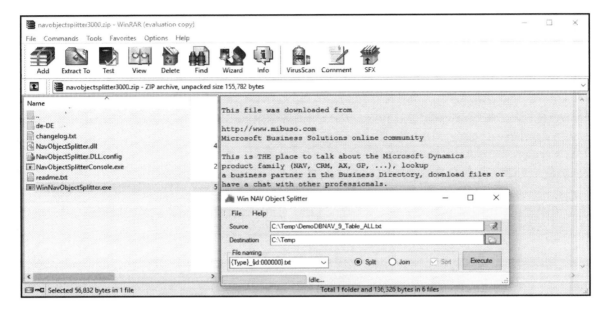

6. Also, enter the **Destination** folder, as `Temp` folder of C drive in my case. Click on the **Execute** button. Make sure the **Split** radio button is selected before you execute the code.

7. After all the objects are split, copy the objects and paste them into the
   `Repository` folder.

   You can directly put the folder into the cloud using GitHub online (drag and
   drop into the repository or use manual buttons).

   Or else, place it in your local repository folder and then click on **Commit** and
   then click on **Push** into the cloud, as shown here:

This is a one-time process when you set up your database in the main repository. After you have successfully imported the object, you will see something similar to what is shown in the following screenshot:

8. Add other team members as **Collaborators** to the repository, permitting them to access the online repository.

9. They will get an e-mail and after they accept the request, they can see the repository in their GitHub.

10. All **Contributors** must have valid credentials for GitHub and must use their own credentials in all the steps. Take a look at the following screenshot:

In the preceding screenshot, you can clearly see that another developer has been added as **Collaborator** to this repository as **TestDesktopRepo**. This concludes the repository setup, with the repository ready for use. You always have two options to push your objects into the repository, that is, use the online repository interface or use the desktop GitHub.

Now let's visualize the next step, which is how we actually commit and push the objects in a real scenario and how it affects the overall repository and other collaborators.

Basic operations in GitHub

In this example, we will set a scenario in which we are going to create three objects and push them into the repository using the Desktop GitHub application. We will then try to show how different users make changes to the same object and try to push their changes to the main repository and how GitHub keeps different versions.

GitHub needs detailed understanding and I highly recommend anyone who wants to use the concept of version control to first understand the basics of GitHub. Here, I have just tried to show you how to use GitHub; you always need to play with the product like this and find out how you can use it in your environment.

1. Create an object; here, we created three table object. This will be valid for every kind of object:

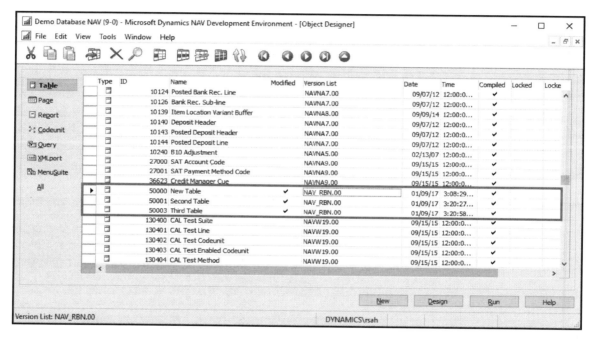

2. Export these objects in text format; here I exported `Tables.txt` to a folder called `TempRepository`. You can use any folder as an example.

3. Use the NAV Object Splitter, which is the same application we used in the previous example:

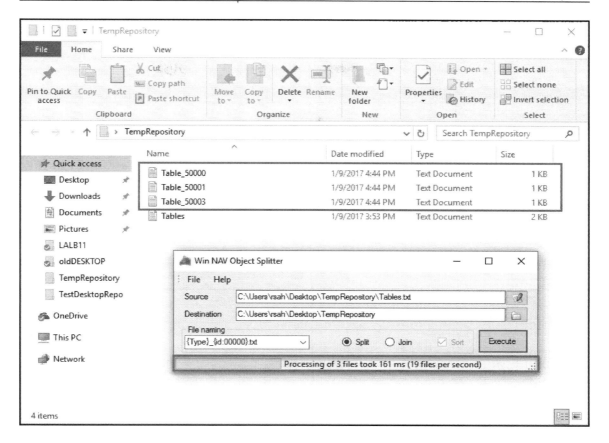

Since we exported three tables, it will split the object into three parts, each representing a separate table.

You can also export each object separately; in that case, you do not need to use this application. But if the object count is more, then exporting the object separately will be time consuming and frustrating, so you should use the Splitter app here.

4. Now you can either use the **Drag & Drop** feature of online GitHub or use the GitHub desktop to push these files into the main repository.

   Just do not forget to write comments each time you push something into the repository and make sure you write comments that explain your purpose.

5. Click on **Commit**.

6. Push the object.

You can also use the Command Console of GitHub, which is handy like PowerShell and is more powerful, but that is not in the scope of this chapter.

The following screenshot shows the steps that you can follow in order to sync your objects to the main repository. It is very important for everyone in a team to understand terms such as sync, commit, stage, pull, and so on:

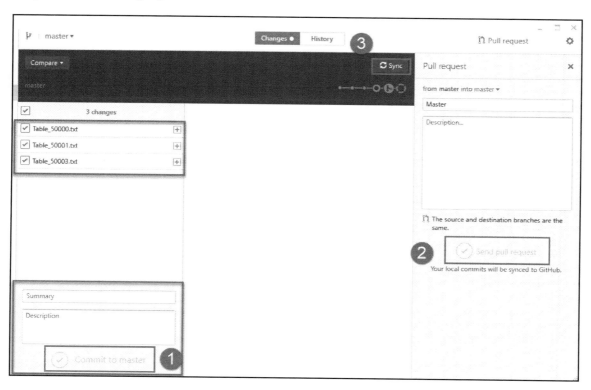

Make sure there is no error while committing and pushing; this will ensure your changes have been pushed into the main repository and all other collaborators can view your changes and pull them into their local repository in order to synchronize the development process.

You can confirm the changes in the online Git (main repository). Make sure all your active developers have been added as collaborators in the GitHub **Settings** section:

Here, you can see that the `Tables` folder was created in first example, and it is kept separate just to make the example more clear and easy to digest.

The main point to note from the preceding screenshot is this: try to create a folder hierarchy that is easy to manage and easy to understand and explain. Here, I have just created a folder called `Tables`, which contains all the tables; similarly, you can create `Pages`, `Reports`, `Query`, and other objects just to avoid confusion. Refer to the following screenshot:

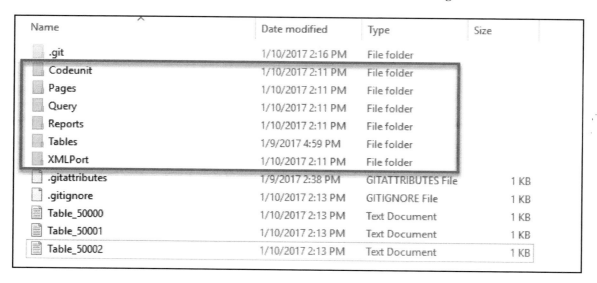

Now, since we already have three tables synchronized in the main repository and the local repository, let's assume an assigned developer made some changes to the table object 50000. Refer to the following screenshot:

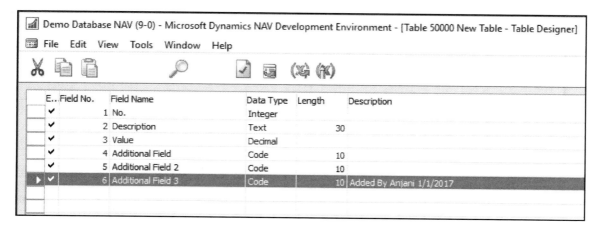

Anjani, the developer, added an extra field for **Process XYZ**. Now she needs to keep track of this change in her repository, and once the process is complete and tested, she wants to push it to the main repository. She follows the following steps to push her modifications:

1. Export the object in a text format. Since there is single object change here, Anjani chooses to do this manually.

   Now since she already has a file called `Table_50000.txt` in her synchronized local repository, she will have to replace it with the latest exported file.

2. Replace the pre-existing table object with the modified object.

   Make sure the object you export has the same name, or else it will create a new file in the repository:

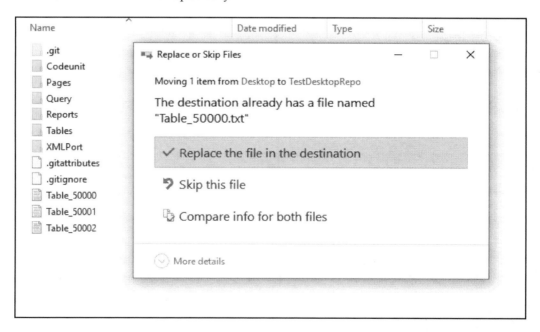

3. She prefers the drag and drop functionality of GitHub, so she logs into her GitHub repository and drags the modified file into the repository.

Assign **Description** to explain the process of push:

Finish the process with committing the changes using the **Commit changes** button.

4. Here, she can choose to create a separate branch, which will not affect the master directly; instead, it will keep its own branch for further push–it is all up to her, she will just select the option and commit the change.

To understand more about branching, refer to the last section, *Pros and cons of branching*, of this chapter.

5. The authorized person in the team will review the changes and push them into the repository in the final step.

6. After the objects get pushed into the repository, anyone who has access to the repository can see the changes that have been made to the object.

This is one of the impressive features where you can see significant changes in different colors. Here, since the developer who made the change is different from the one who actually created the object, there is a totally new object being pushed and the color is different as a whole. But if the creator makes the change to the object, only the changes are presented in a colored form in order to present the changes clearly:

Hence, all other users can see what has actually happened to the object and can eliminate extra meetings just to share each other's changes. In addition, the GitHub system also kept a record for future use.

The technology also helps in the tune-up process, which we will discuss in the next chapter.

This section provided some of the basic operations you need to know in order to start on your own. I would highly recommend that you learn the commands for Git; it will make life easy. Also, try to learn other functions of the application that might come handy.

Team Foundation Server/Services

The **Team Foundation Server** (**TFS**) is the same as GitHub in a sense but is comparatively less useful. It is a product of Microsoft for source code management. It also supports Visual Studio (even GitHub can be connected to Visual Studio).

I will not go in details on how to set up TFS on a server; instead, I will provide a link that you can easily Google,

`https://msdn.microsoft.com/en-us/library/hh561426(v=vs.120).aspx.`

And the link for the Setup Team Foundation Server on Visual Studio is

`https://www.visualstudio.com/en-us/docs/setup-admin/tfs/install/get-started.`

TFS setup for Dynamics NAV

These are straight forward steps, similar to those involved in installing any other Microsoft product. Now, I will assume that you have successfully set up the TFS in your Visual Studio system. You can follow the following steps for the setup of TFS for Dynamics NAV:

1. The first step after you have set up TFS is to create a folder structure, a bit similar to what we did for GitHub; this will eliminate confusion later on.

Folder structures are also called the skeleton of the system, which allows you to locate files and eliminate confusion when the count of the object increases. Try to create a simple structure that fits your requirements.

2. Now log in to `https://www.visualstudio.com/` with your Microsoft e-mail account and select **Visual Studio Team Services**:

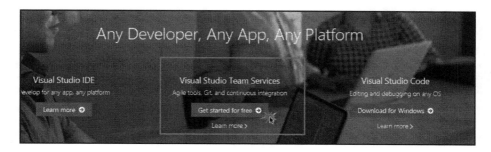

3. It will take you to the page where you can create your own projects for Visual Studio on the cloud. This is the screenshot of the same page in my case. Your page should also look similar to it:

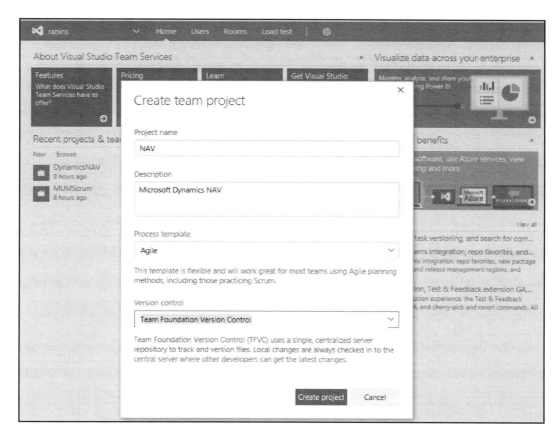

4. Create a new project for NAV project; call it NAV. Select **Agile** as a process template and **Team Foundation Version Control** as a version control option:

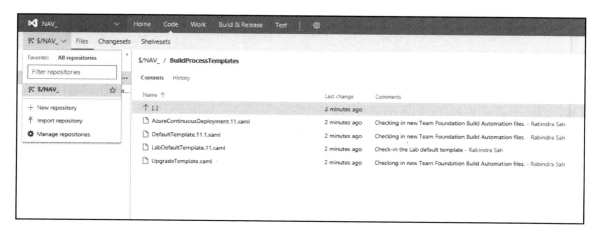

5. Here, you can import a preexisting repository or create a new one; I will create a new repository. You can also create a folder structure and then import it. It all depends on what you prefer:

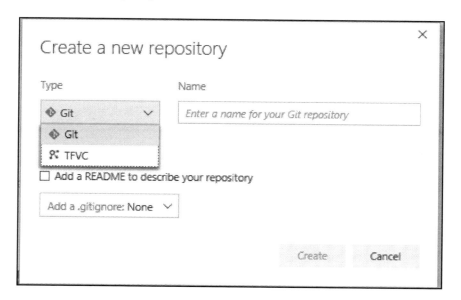

When you want to create a new repository, you can select two types, which also includes **Git**. But here I will select **TFS** and click on **Create**.

6. You are done with the repository. Now let's connect TFS to the Visual Studio **Source Control Explorer**:

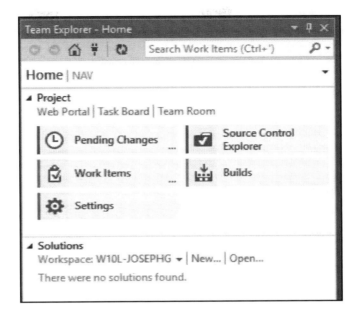

It will automatically pull the repository structure and information to the **Source Expression** side bar. Here, you can also manually create a folder to make the structure more suitable for you to understand:

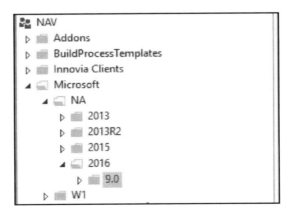

In the preceding screenshot, you can see that there is a repository. Also, take a look at how the folder structure is arranged. It allows smooth navigation and supports good manual indexing.

Never add stuff to the root of the directory. There should be only main, or here in our case Just NAV:

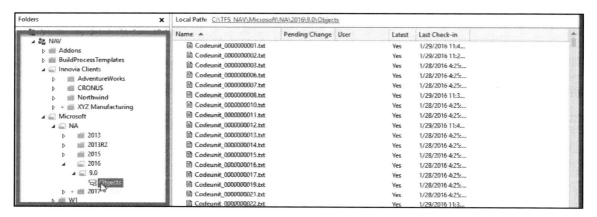

We basically created different branches for different purposes. For example, **Dev Team** will work on its own common branch, which will be isolated from the main and release branches.

In the next section, we will see how the branching mechanism works.

Now let's look at a real-life example of how **TFS** can be successfully implemented in a project:

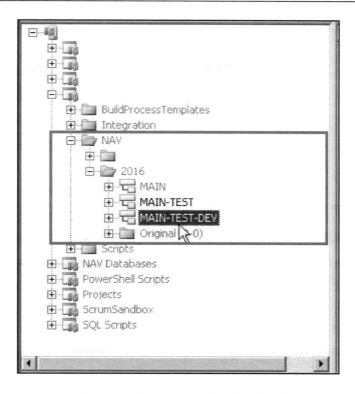

Here, we have three branch databases. You can easily identify the branch with its symbol. **MAIN-TEST-DEV** is a branch database that contains the database where developers dump their development objects. After the developers are done with their level of testing, professional consultants pull the objects into the **MAIN-TEST** branch database and then carry out their level of testing. After their testing is successful, they provide a green signal to the system administrator to move it to the **MAIN** branch, which can also be the main repository, and then the **GO LIVE** process starts. This is a highly standardized process in NAV, and certified companies use this pattern for system development.

Version control can also work as a technical documentation in some cases.

In TFS, all of the functionality is similar to that of GitHub. So, I assume you can learn this on your own. I have just tried to cover the ground and provide a base on which you can build different ideas on your own.

Pros and cons of branching

Always make sure you create a branch if it is required. With proper branching, developers can work more freely and in parallell on different issues. Developers can also roll out small fixes quickly without extensively testing the latest development version of the code.

On the other hand, having too many branches can create more complex issues than having a single branch. It can create problems while merging code. Always make sure you keep on pulling the changes at regular intervals, or your branch might lead to extra time and effort just to merge, resulting in delay of the project.

So, make sure that branching is needed and educate your developers enough before implementing it in your department.

 If your team members have a programming background, then you must expect them to know this pattern. This might be something new to NAV, but it is widely used in other programming languages when developing software with a large team.

The following are some of the branching patterns used, and it is important to understand them before you make a decision about branching.

Branching for a big modification project

If a single group of developers is working, then it can still create a single branch for development. This modification can also be an add-on to projects for Dynamics NAV or third-party integration processes, in which case the branch needs to keep pulling the changes made in the NAV system at a certain interval of time to make sure the synchronization process is smooth.

In most of the Dynamics NAV projects, this is the scenario:

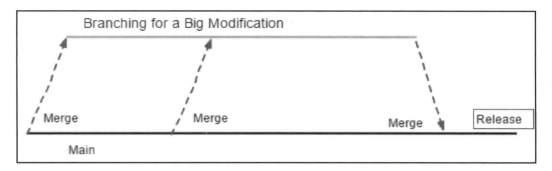

Branching for small isolated modifications

In these types of projects, we have different features to be developed; we can also say that we are able to separate the process in order to assign different groups at the same time. These processes require branching similar to what is shown in the following figure:

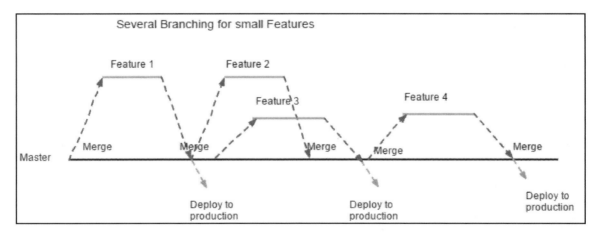

This model works well if your feature sets are very independent of each other, which means that if the developers are assigned modifications sets that are not dependent on each other with a separate set of object ranges, then this is highly efficient. When the object ranges overlap, then we deploy the solution to the master branch only after the completion of both dependent branches.

Branching for mixed type modification

"Mixed type" branching can be considered to be the most practical one since in a real-life scenario, most of the cases are mixed with certain modifications that require segregated branches, while some are lengthy ones. We need to make sure we use the proper push and pull operations in this case, allowing minimum error at the time of final merge. The following image explains mixed type branching with practical illustrations:

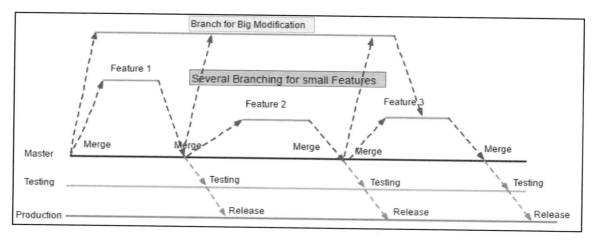

Let's assume different developers are assigned different features with their own branch. But in parallel, some senior developers are working on something big which will span the length of almost all the development of small features. In that case, what we can do is this: after the end of each **sprint** (sprint is the time period assigned for specific work to make it ready to review), the developers working on the big modification pull the modifications done by the team working on **Feature 1**. This allows them to be in track with the changes, and less energy needs to be wasted while merging the changes at the end.

On the other hand, after the end of each sprint (features), the code and process is passed to the testing department, to be forwarded for release. If small bugs appear, then they can easily be fixed in this stage, allowing a smooth production process. At the end of all the sprints, one final level of testing is carried out, which ensures that all the processes in the modification package are working fine. This is generally handled by the test codes that we discussed in Chapter 4, *Testing and Debugging*.

Always make sure you write the test code for your part so that at the end, it can be utilized while testing the whole process flow.

Summary

In this chapter, we learned the entirely new concept of version control. For most experienced consultants and developers who have strong C# and other programming experience, this concept might not be that new. But those who have always worked with an NAV system might perceive this as a new one. We learned the most basic ways to harvest some of the functionality of version control in dynamics NAV. For some, it might look like a lengthy process to implement, but once you understand the core concept, you will love it and implement it in team projects in particular. We also understood the pattern to use while branching and how it can be of great importance.

In the next chapter, we will discuss the tune-up process of the Microsoft Dynamics NAV system. When a project gets implemented with unorganized patterns and without any proper planning, it can be unacceptable to clients in terms of time and memory. In these cases, clients often hire experts to tune up the system to optimize the resource, which costs money. We will be discussing these concepts in the next chapter.

7
Tuning Up the NAV System

In the previous chapter, we discussed version control techniques that can be implemented in Microsoft Dynamics NAV projects. We discussed GitHub and TFS as the two version control services. We also discussed what difference it can make to the overall project life cycle if the proper code and version are preserved. As this is the latest trend in Microsoft Dynamics NAV, one must pay added attention to the chapter.

In this chapter, we are going to understand different techniques and considerations to boost the performance of different components of Microsoft Dynamics NAV. It is very essential that one understands the basic operations while developing the system; in the absence of a broader picture of the system, one might develop a solution with low performance, so in this chapter, we will be learning how to avoid bad practices that might lead to a low performing system, and at the same time, we will understand how a slow performing system can be detected and turned into an acceptable one.

At the end of this chapter, you should have an idea of how to detect slow systems, how to carry out testing operations, and how to eliminate them. You also should be able to develop a system with good performance. In the last section, the chapter is intended to provide core knowledge for good programming practices.

This chapter will cover the following topics:

- Optimization technique
- The core of system components
- Detecting and resolving performance issues
- Algorithm and good programming practices

Tuning up the NAV environment

Performance tuning is mostly a difficult section of software engineering. This is similar to redesigning the solution and for which you always need to investigate the problems and inefficient units of the existing system. Tuning up processes are mostly carried out by experienced professionals with some serious experience with the system. Here in this section we will focus on some of the major aspects of system tune up which are more generic to all kinds of system tune up processes. We will start from the root level, which is always the database, and will look into other different sections that usually contribute to an inefficient system.

Optimizing SQL Server performance

There can be several factors that contribute to the slow performance of a system. In this section, we are trying to focus on some of the basic elements.

Data access

In Microsoft Dynamics NAV Version 2009 and earlier, Dynamics NAV was used for **Open Database Connectivity (ODBC)** as an API to connect to the database. But thereafter, it has implemented the ADO.NET API to interface with the SQL Server. There are many advantages of using ADO.NET over ODBC. We shall discuss them briefly.

ADO.NET and ODBC are both Microsoft Standard Application programming interfaces. ADO.NET is quicker and gives flexibility in its setup in comparison to its counterpart, ODBC. Here are some of the benefits of using ADO.NET over ODBC:

- Simple setup
- Better compatibility with the Windows server
- Resource-efficient
- Better caching
- Better performance

Database information

We can make changes to the existing database by going to **File** | **Database** | **Alter** from the development environment.

Collation setting

Collation determines the character set and sort order of the files in a database. This is important to understand since it might affect your queries with the order by syntax in the where clause as well as the structure of underlying indexes. Collations are set at the server, database, and column level:

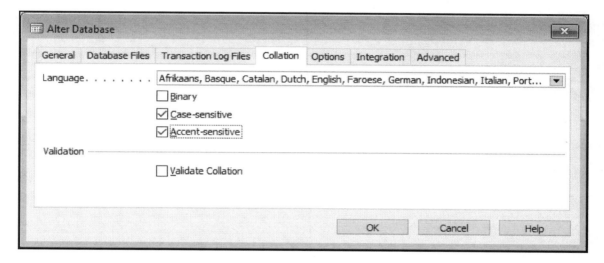

Collations are used to define the rules of the language, character set, region, and so on. The **Binary** option is case-sensitive and is the fastest sort order, but it cannot be used concurrently with the **Case-sensitive** and **Accent-sensitive** options.

Database and log files

It is highly recommended that you keep database and log files separate. This optimizes the performance of the database. Try to keep the MDF and NDF data file in two different physical drives; this can be crucial during the disaster recovery process.

The following screenshot shows where you can find this information:

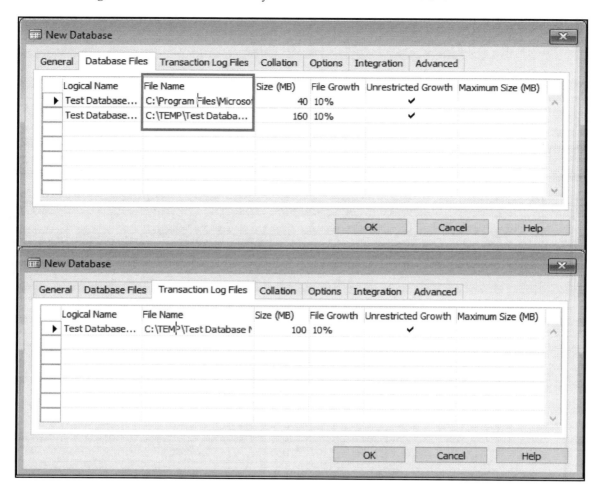

In the example, I have kept them in different folders since I have just a single drive in this system.

The relationship between tables

Defining table relations is very crucial in systems such as Dynamics NAV. If you fail to define an efficient relationship, then you might end up creating an inefficient system. There are three basic relationships between tables:

- One-to-one relationship
- One-to-many relationship
- Many-to-many relationship

One-to-one relationship is very simple and is rarely used in NAV. We mostly use one-to-many relationships. There might be situations where you use many-to-many relationships, but you must understand the consequence of using such relationships in the system. The best solution is to break down many-to-many into two or more one-to-many relationships.

Table keys and performance

Keys in the database are the most important unit. They actually provide concrete meaning to the database where the data is systematically placed and can be retrieved once requested. That being said, if proper planning is not done while creating keys for any table, it might lead to a huge performance-related problem, causing disturbance to the business logic of the system. It is the same as designing a skyscraper without proper planning of the lift and numbering of the apartments.

The performance of the system crumbles when the time taken by the system to search a subset is too large; if not possible, then you should be ready to define a key. To maximize the system performance, you must define the keys that support your code in the table. You must then specify these keys correctly in your code.

For example, to search the entries of a specific customer, a filter to the **Customer No.** field should be applied in the **Cust. Ledger Entry** table. To run the code efficiently, you must define a key in the **Customer** table or the table that contains the customer record. Also, make sure the keys are set as primary.

The table should have these keys:

- **Entry No.**
- **Customer No.**
- **Posting Date**

The code that uses these keys looks like this:

```
SETRANGE("Customer No.",'1000');
IF FIND('-') THEN
REPEAT
//Your Operation on the Customer record here
UNTIL NEXT = 0;
```

 If you want to use other keys in your code, then use SETCURRENTKEY(key/s…) before your code; this function will set the key you passed as the parameter to the function to be the current key.

Bulk insert

Imagine a condition where on every **CRUD (Create/Read/Update/Delete)** operation on the data, the Dynamics NAV system has to interact with the SQL database layer. It will create huge traffic when the operation (such as multiline posting) and the number of users increases. To overcome this, Microsoft Dynamics NAV has a feature of caching information before sending it to the DB. This reduces the number of calls, ultimately improving the performance, which is somewhat similar to the browser caching while surfing the Internet.

Try to use bulk insert as much as you can. In order to construct a system with maximum DB interaction in the form of bulk insert, try to avoid using the following functions:

- The COMMIT function
- The MODIFY function in the table level
- The DELETE function in the table level
- The FIND or CALC methods on the table level

All these functions, if called in their respective levels, send information directly to the SQL DB.

In addition, if you are inserting a record of a table that contains the BLOB datatype or contains fields with the AutoIncrement property set to Yes, then these operations are not buffered. If the application is using the return value from an INSERT call, for example, IF (GLEntry.INSERT) THEN, even then the record is not buffered.

Let's examine an example that shows what changes can be made in your code in order to make it compatible with Bulk insert:

No Buffered Insert	Buffered Insert
| ```
IF (JnlLine.FIND('-')) THEN BEGINGLEntry.LOCKTABLE;
 REPEAT
IF (GLEntry.FINDLAST) THEN        GLEntry.NEXT :=
GLEntry."Entry No." + 1
ELSE
 GLEntry.NEXT := 1;
 // The FIND call will flush the buffered records.
GLEntry."Entry No." := GLEntry.NEXT ;
GLEntry.INSERT;
 UNTIL (JnlLine.FIND('>') = 0)
END;
COMMIT;
``` | ```
IF (JnlLine.FIND('-')) THEN BEGIN
 GLEntry.LOCKTABLE;
 IF (GLEntry.FINDLAST) THEN
 GLEntry.Next := GLEntry."Entry No."
+ 1
 ELSE
 GLEntry.Next := 1;
 REPEAT
 GLEntry."Entry No.":= GLEntry.Next;
 GLEntry.Next := GLEntry."Entry No."
+ 1;
 GLEntry.INSERT;
 UNTIL (JnlLine.FIND('>') = 0)
END;
COMMIT; // The inserts are
performed here.
``` |

The code on the left-hand side uses the FIND call on the G/LEntry table within the loop [IF (GLEntry.FINDLAST)], so it is not buffered. If we can tweak the code just by shifting the loop down, then it can be buffered easily.

SumIndexfields functionality

SumIndexfields are a special feature of Dynamics NAV that give it the power to calculate FlowFields on a large scale. It is a decimal field that can be assigned in the **Key** section, as shown in the following screenshot:

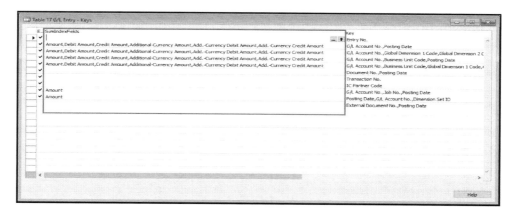

SumIndexfields has always been a part of Dynamics NAV, which gives it a unique capability that, if calculated with a normal approach, is generally inefficient.

As has been said, *too much sugar leads to diabetes*. Similarly, excessive use of keys or SIFT fields can negatively affect the system's performance. The two main performance issues are:

- The index maintenance processing load
- The table locking interference

The table locking interference occurs when multiple threads request update access to a set of records that affect the SIFT values.

On the other hand, lack of necessary keys or SIFT definitions can also cause severe performance issues.

Performance tuning in reports

Reports are the ultimate truth in the ERP system. The processes that are carried out inside the business logic and algorithms to calculate different values does not matter much to the user, all they need in the end is the report or document which provides the understanding of the data they feed the system. All they care about is fast running, good-looking reports. Even most projects heavily rely on the addition of many custom reports and/or the customization of existing reports to adjust to the needs of the client.

In reality, you must understand how bad reports with large runtime can affect the overall performance of the system. Let's discuss how we can tune up reports in Microsoft Dynamics NAV.

Creating new reports

While creating a report, you might have noticed that there are two major phases:

- Construction of dataset
- Creation of report layout

All other operations can be included in these two major phases. It is essential to understand the importance of understanding the report standard and perceive how reports are constructed, since it can help you understand how standard reports can be altered with standard approaches.

Dataset considerations

In a dataset, you can make certain changes in order to improve the performance of the report. This is not always applicable for all reports; it depends on the nature of the problem, and you should spend time analyzing the problem before fixing it. The following are some of the basic considerations that you should keep in mind when dealing with datasets in NAV reports:

- Try to avoid the creation of dataset lines if possible; create variables instead
- Try to reduce the number of rows and columns
- Apply filters to the request page
- For slow reports with higher runtime, use the job queue to generate the report in the server
- Use text constants for the caption, if needed
- Try to avoid **Include Caption** for a column with no need for captions

The following screenshot shows where you can implement the **Include Caption** option in the report design:

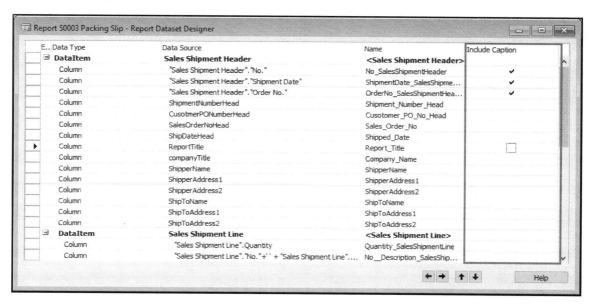

When you are updating a report from an older version, then all captions, by default, are in the dataset. Try to move these captions to the parameters of the report (using include captions and labels). This will automatically remove the caption fields from the dataset at runtime and improve the performance of the report.

Optimize the usage of the BLOB datatype in your report. When you are adding an image to your report, then a BLOB datatype can hold up to 2 GB of memory. Put the BLOB field in only one row in the dataset. You can use Integer dataitem, filtered on one row. Or, you can leave the dataset as it is and add some code to the trigger in order to clear the BLOB field after it has been added to the dataset after the first iteration. Use the Clear() function to clear the field.

Let's take an example of **Report 1306 Mini Sales – Invoice**.

In the **OnPreDataItem()** trigger of the header data item, you can see the following code as seen in the screenshot:

```
FirstLineHasBeenOutput := FALSE;
```

The following screenshot explains the location of the code in the code section of the report:

```
Report 1306 Mini Sales - Invoice - C/AL Editor
    4  GLSetup.GET;
    5  CompanyInfo.GET;
    6  SalesSetup.GET;
    7  CompanyInfo.VerifyAndSetPaymentInfo;
    8
    9  OnPreReport()
   10  IF Header.GETFILTERS = '' THEN
   11     ERROR(NoFilterSetErr);
   12
   13  IF NOT CurrReport.USEREQUESTPAGE THEN
   14     InitLogInteraction;
   15
   16  CompanyLogoPosition := SalesSetup."Logo Position on Documents";
   17
   18  OnPostReport()
   19
   20  Header - OnPreDataItem()
   21  FirstLineHasBeenOutput := FALSE;
   22
   23  Header - OnAfterGetRecord()
   24  IF NOT CurrReport.PREVIEW THEN
   25     CODEUNIT.RUN(CODEUNIT::"Sales Inv.-Printed",Header);
   26
   27  CurrReport.LANGUAGE := Language.GetLanguageID("Language Code");
   28  IF RespCenter.GET("Responsibility Center") THEN BEGIN
91 %
```

Then, in the **OnPreDataItem()** trigger, there is this code:

```
FirstLineHasBeenOutput := FALSE;
CompanyInfo.CALCFIELDS(Picture);
```

Basically, this code calculates the BLOB field and picture.

Next, in the **OnAfterGetRecord()** trigger of the line data item, you will notice the following code:

```
IF FirstLineHasBeenOutput THEN
CLEAR(CompanyInfo.Picture);
FirstLineHasBeenOutput := TRUE;
```

For the first time in the dataset, the variable is false, but after that, the variable is set to true and the BLOB field is cleared, saving the space and time required to do that. The following screenshot explains the concept better:

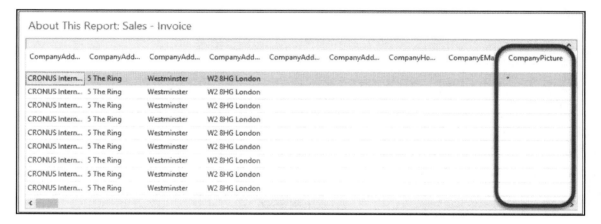

The output makes it even more clear that this bunch of code can make life easier for the consultant working on the tune up process for slow reports.

Try not to insert the BLOB datatype in common tables, such as vendor, customer, and so on. This can make the Select * query expensive, which is abundantly used in the reports.

Use of the Temporary table

The use of the **Temporary** table might sound like extra work, but in some cases, it can be worth investing time in doing so. The use of the **Temporary** table can decrease the time and size of the report, ultimately boosting the performance of the report. An example can be seen in the following **1306: Mini Sales – Invoice** report:

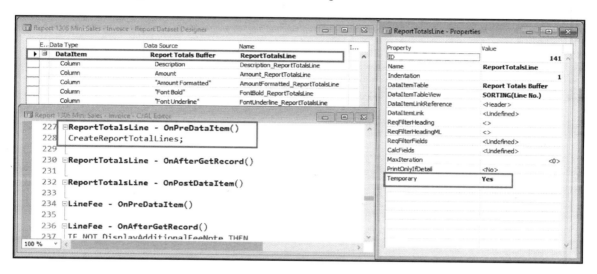

Here, the **Temporary** property of the **ReportTotalsLine** dataset is set to **YES**, making the table temporary; it is calling the **CreateReportTotalLines** function:

```
ReportTotalsLine.DELETEALL;
IF (TotalInvDiscAmount <> 0) OR (TotalAmountVAT <> 0) THEN
ReportTotalsLine.Add(SubtotalLbl,TotalSubTotal,TRUE,FALSE, FALSE);
IF TotalInvDiscAmount <> 0 THEN BEGIN
ReportTotalsLine.Add(InvDiscountAmtLbl,TotalInvDiscAmount,
FALSE,FALSE,FALSE);IF TotalAmountVAT <> 0 THEN
ReportTotalsLine.Add(TotalExclVATText,TotalAmount,TRUE,FALSE, FALSE);
END;
IF TotalAmountVAT <> 0 THEN
ReportTotalsLine.Add(VATAmountLine.VATAmountText,TotalAmountVAT,
FALSE,TRUE,FALSE);
```

This is a very efficient way to do totaling in NAV reports. The function just adds a line to the temporary table for every total that needs to be displayed in the report. You can use the temporary table in many other ways since it gives you the flexibility to delete and create the grouping of your records, and it can be utilized for many other purposes as well.

Number formatting

You might have noticed that every time you create a decimal field dataset of a report, you get a format type dataset for free. Imagine that there is a report that contains 50 decimal fields, and you have to create all 50 fields/variables in the dataset; here, you might need to avoid an extra formatting option that will consume extra memory while running the report. Fortunately, there is a way to avoid this. In order to eliminate the format dataset, apply the **Format(...)** function, as shown in the following screenshot:

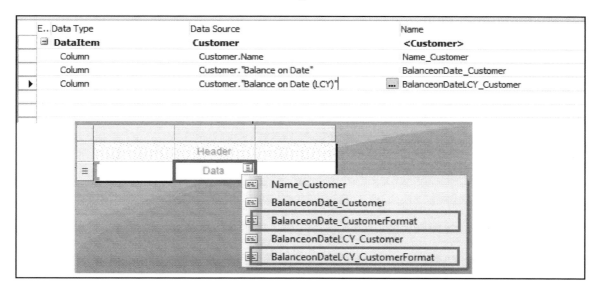

After adding **Format(...)** to the data source, **Formatdataset** is gone. This not only makes it easy for the designer to choose from the dataset, but also reduces the internal memory consumption during the runtime of the report:

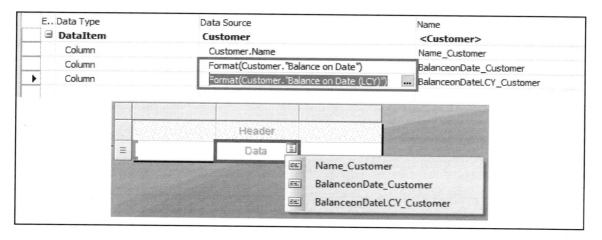

Hence, this small tweak can bring a big change to the performance.

Looking at layout considerations

After you have managed the dataset properly, it's time to dive into the layout considerations that can help make the performance of the report easier. I have explained the basic VB concept in Chapter 3, *The C/AL and VB Programming*, which can be taken as the foundation for this concept.

As layout is directly related to the clients, always try to ask for the template from the user first. Try to arrange a meeting to finalize the layout provided by them and only then should you start the layout design phase of the report.

In many cases, I have seen that even after generating a standard report layout, the report fails to meet the expectations of the customer. Almost all users want to keep the best part of their previously used system, and if we decide to create a totally different layout, then they might not be able to adjust to the change.

Disabling Print Preview

You might have experienced that the **Print Preview** option is default but is not used much generally. If the client always sees the report by exporting it into the PDF format or in the print format, then you might choose to disable **Print Preview**, which will save you memory at the time of running the report:

Property	Value
ID	
Name	**Sales - Invoice**
Caption	Sales - Invoice
CaptionML	**ENU=Sales - Invoice;ESM=Ventas - Factura;F**
Description	< >
UseRequestPage	<Yes>
UseSystemPrinter	<No>
EnableExternalImages	<No>
EnableHyperlinks	<No>
EnableExternalAssemblies	<No>
ProcessingOnly	<No>
ShowPrintStatus	<Yes>
TransactionType	<UpdateNoLocks>
Permissions	**TableData Sales Shipment Buffer=rimd**
PaperSourceFirstPage	<Undefined>
PaperSourceDefaultPage	<Undefined>
PaperSourceLastPage	<Undefined>
PreviewMode	PrintLayout
DefaultLayout	Normal
WordMergeDataItem	PrintLayout
PDFFontEmbedding	<Default>

Go to the report property and change **PreviewMode** to **PrintLayout**. It is as simple as that. Microsoft Dynamics NAV has done this for most standard reports as well. If you are designing a new report and if your customer does not bother about the preview, then this can be handy.

Avoiding conditional visibility

In Dynamics NAV, report items such as columns, rows, tables, textboxes, and so on, all have visibility properties. You can always set the condition to show and hide these report items. A calculation is performed every time you click on the toggle item, and this consumes memory. If dataitem is bigger, then the calculation will be longer and thus the memory consumption will be higher. Hence, it is not recommended that you apply conditional visibility on the big dataset.

 In addition to these considerations, it is always recommended that you keep reading whitepapers and authorized blogs of MVPs. Since this is an evolutionary process, you cannot build a perfect system with 100% efficiency; it's always better to keep note of the best practices and try to implement most of the good stuff into your project.

In the next section, we are going to understand how to carry out load testing on the system in order to determine the performance of the system.

Load testing

Load testing is a very interesting technique to test the load of the system process. Basically, we carry out a load test on the following operations:

- **Open Page**
- **Enter Data**
- **Click Action**

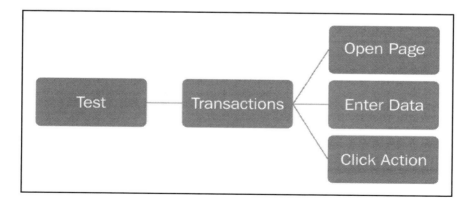

This constitutes the total transaction. We measure the start and end of each transaction and then compare it with the standard time and look at the difference in the measurement.

Here, running the `LoadTest` project requires a basic level of Visual Studio knowledge. You need to download the already created project and run it in the system that contains the Dynamics NAV system or the system that is linked with it.

The basic steps required for load testing are as follows:

1. Create a `NAVLoadTest` project in Visual Studio online.
2. Set up the `NAVLoadTest` project to run tests in Visual Studio online.
3. Run the load test using Visual Studio online.
4. Compare the result.

Here, we are going to use a GitHub repository called `NAVLoadTest`, which has all the code that you need for this load test. The link for the repository is `https://github.com/NAVPERF/NAV2016-Sample`, and you can also find the load test for the other version of Microsoft Dynamics NAV by switching to the root, that is, `NAVPERF`:

Just clone the project into Visual Studio, and you are ready to go. You can also download the ZIP file and open the project into your Visual Studio:

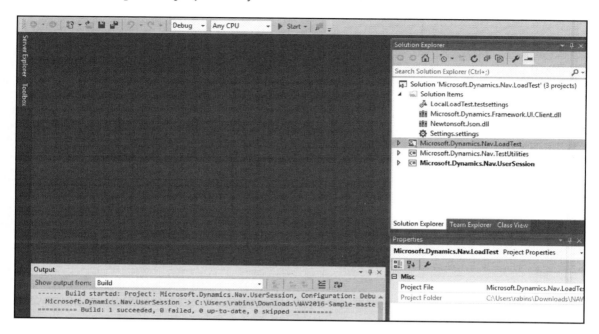

Just follow the instructions in the readme file of the project, and you will be good to run the project.

After you have cloned the project (you can also download and run the project from your local directory), on Microsoft Dynamics NAV 2016 CTP DVD, you will find a folder called `Test Assemblies`. This folder contains one DLL, which is needed for the running of load tests, `Microsoft.Dynamics.Framework.UI.Client.dll`. Following are the dependencies for this solution.

The solution requires the NAV client framework libraries from Microsoft, which are available with Microsoft Dynamics NAV Cumulative Updates. The required assembly name is `Microsoft.Dynamics.Framework.UI.Client.dll`.

Building and running load tests requires the `Microsoft.VisualStudio.TestTools.LoadTesting` library and the load testing tools in Visual Studio. The load testing tools are currently only available in Visual Studio Enterprise Edition. It is recommended that you carry out this process on a secure server.

The prerequisite to run the load test on Visual Studio is the basic idea of creating and running of VS projects. Here, you just need to open the project, do the configuration, and run the project. It will present you with the load test output in a graphical form. Always make sure that you use the Enterprise version of Visual Studio for this purpose.

Algorithm

It is very important to understand the time and memory/space complexity of the code you write. Most programmers lack the knowledge to do that. It is essential that you figure out the methods to analyze the time and space complexity of the code you write; also, while tuning up the system, you should be able to figure out the so-called non-efficient code and replace it with code that can perform better in the same given parameters.

 An algorithm is a step-by-step procedure to solve a problem in a finite amount of time. Some familiar problems solved with algorithms include sorting an array of numbers, finding a specific string in a list, computing the shortest path between two locations, and finding prime factors of a given integer.

In this section of the chapter, we are going to examine the following questions:

- How can we determine whether an algorithm is efficient?
- What is the correctness of code?

Given two algorithms that achieve the same goal, how can we do the following:

- Decide which one is better?
- Make our analysis independent of a particular configuration of system?
- Express the steps of an algorithm without depending on a particular implementation?

Let's dive deeper into the patterns that we should master in order to tune up the code we write.

Natural things to ask

In the day-to-day life of programmers, they generally work on instincts while writing code. They will pick up their favorite patterns with their favorite statement (for loop, while loop, and so on) and use their own style of programming. But in this section, you are going to learn how to compare two different ways of programming and how to decide whether one has been written with the most efficient form of code accomplishing some given solution.

A framework to analyze the given algorithm

We will specify the following in this section:

- A simple, neutral language to describe algorithms
- A simple, general computational model in which algorithms execute
- Procedures to measure running time
- A classification system that will allow us to categorize algorithms (a precise way of saying fast, slow, medium, and so on)
- Techniques to prove the correctness of an algorithm

We are going to analyze the time complexity of a written code first.

Time complexity

The running time of a set of code (algorithm) is our main point of concern here. Most algorithms transform input objects into output objects. The running time of an algorithm typically grows with the input size. The average case time is often difficult to determine:

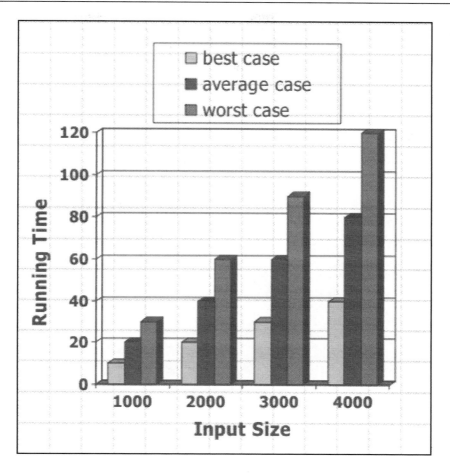

Often, we focus on the worst case running time because of the following factors:

- It's easier to analyze
- It's crucial to applications such as ERP, CRM, and other engineering calculations

The following screenshot shows the difference between the runtime of two different code snippets:

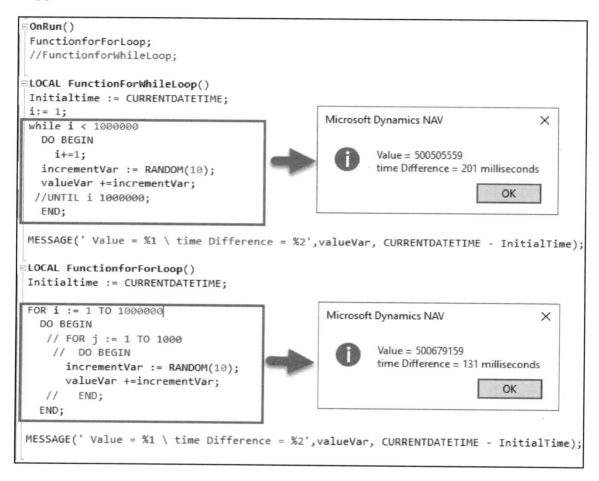

If the same code is run on different systems, it will have a different runtime that is directly proportional to the amount of processing throughput of the current system.

But in real life, the calculation can have more details and more levels of complexity, such as nested loops and a combination of different loops, and there is always a possibility of a large amount of data if you are using the same algorithm in the case of ERP systems such as Dynamics NAV.

It is obvious that the runtime of the algorithm is directly proportional to the amount of data that is being passed for processing. So here, it is important to analyze the size of the business that is going to implement the particular ERP system.

Determining the time complexity of the algorithm

In computer science, we use big oh, big omega, and big theta notations to denote worst case, average case, and best case scenarios (respectively) of the time required to process the code.

In general, we use Big-oh -> O(n) since we are not bothered about the best case here. We just want to see what the worst case of the code that we write can be so that we can see the lower bound of our code and then try to push it to make it more efficient.

Writing pseudocode

The following algorithm is a general type of algorithm for operation XYZ, which takes certain parameters and input and is intended to generate some output. In order to make it easy to understand, I have just used the `IF-ELSEIF-ELSE` statement because in C/AL, we mostly expect to use something like this:

```
Algorithm(Parameters...)
Input[. . .]
Output[. . .]

Condition
Begin[document]
Begin[algorithmic]
  IF[some condition is true]
    STATE do some processing
  ELSIF[some other condition is true]
    STATE do some different processing
  ELSIF[some even more bizarre condition is met]
    STATE do something else
  ELSE
    STATE do the default actions
  ENDIF
End[algorithmic]
End[document]
```

Pseudocodes are high-level descriptions of an algorithm. They are more structured than English prose but less detailed than a program. They are the preferred notation for describing algorithms to hide program design issues.

After we have written the pseudocode, it's time to analyze the time complexity of the code. We will follow the following steps:

- Calculate the number of primitive operations
- Find the highest order of primate operations
- Find the big-oh notation depending on the highest order of primitive operations

After you have found the Big oh notation, try to match it with the table of time complexity. Try to come up with alternative ways to solve the same problem and repeat the steps mentioned earlier and finally choose the algorithm with the minimum time complexity.

Counting primitive operations

By inspecting the pseudocode, we can determine the maximum number of primitive operations executed by an algorithm as a function of the input size:

Algorithm *arrayMax(A, n)*	# operations
currentMax $\leftarrow A[0]$	2
m $\leftarrow n - 1$	2
for $i \leftarrow 1$ **to** *m* **do**	$1 + n$
if $A[i] >$ *currentMax* **then**	$2(n - 1)$
currentMax $\leftarrow A[i]$	$2(n - 1)$
{ increment counter *i* }	$2(n - 1)$
return *currentMax*	1
Total	$7n$

The `arrayMax` algorithm executes 7n primitive operations in the worst case. This is the definition:

- a – time taken by the fastest primitive operation
- b – time taken by the slowest primitive operation

Let $T(n)$ be worst case time of `arrayMax`. Then, this is the result:

$a (7n) <= T(n) <= b(7n)$

Hence, the running time $T(n)$ is bounded by two linear functions.

The examples are as shown in the following table:

Pseudocode	Calculation of the number of primitives

`sum <- 0`
`  for i <- 0 to n-1 do`
`  sum <- sum + 1`
	assignment = 1
	assignment = 1
	comparison = n + 1
	summation = 2n
	increment = 2n

	Total = 5n + 3

`sum <- 0`
`for i <- 0 to n-1 do`
`for j <- 0 to n-1 do`
`sum <-sum + 1`
	assignment = 1
	assignment = 1
	comparison = n + 1
	inner loop = n(5n + 2) (from problem A)
	increment = 2n

	Total = 5n2 + 5n + 3

Though the example here is simple, we can easily understand the logic behind why you should choose algorithm A in place of B if both fulfill the same cause.

The Big Oh notation

For algorithm A, since the higher order n term is 2, we have O(n) and the Big Oh notation of algorithm B is O(n2). Using the chart, we can determine the best solution to be algorithm A in our case. Let's look at the following chart:

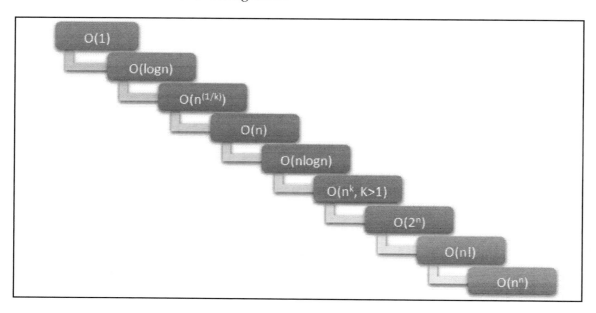

From the diagram, it is clear that the Big Oh notation is increasing as we go right and the code becomes heavier and consumes more time. In NAV, we might not need to understand them all, but it is essential to understand them all since there are many extensions that use .NET extensions and third-party integrations, and they might be using some complex logic that is eventually slowing down your overall process.

The diagram can be rewritten as follows: *O(1)< O(logn)< O(n(1/k))< O(n)< O(nlogn) < O(nk, K>1)< O(2n)< O(n!)< O(nn)* Here, the code gets O(1) as a Big Oh notation when it consumes one unit of time. If the code uses a `for` loop for an example that goes from 0 to n, then it gets O(n) and if there is a for loop nesting, then n operation gets nested with another n operation, so nxn leads to O(n2). Try to avoid higher order code. This is one of the reasons why we should divide bug chunks of code into small functions.

In case of conflict, use common sense and use constant factors to determine the best solution. By constant factors, I mean that if algorithm A and algorithm B, which are written to solve operation XYZ, have the same Big Oh notation, then we will try to find the constant factors that are determined by the number of basic operations, as follows:

- Performing an arithmetic operation (+, *, and so on)
- Comparing two numbers
- Assigning a value to a variable
- Indexing in an array
- Calling a method
- Returning from a method
- Following an object reference

These operations can be taken as one operation each. We calculate the number of operations like these in the pseudocode, and the one with least values of constant factors wins the race and should be used as the ultimate solution.

Let's summarize the best way we can write a good algorithm:

- Analyze the operation for which you are writing code
- Write the pseudocode before writing the actual code
- Analyze the time complexity of the code
- Analyze the space complexity of the code
- Try to find the best solution that reduces the time and space complexity
- Write the code
- Test the code

The same thing can be applied to a case where you are supposed to tune up the already written code.

Basic rules for computing asymptotic running time

There are some rules which can help you understand how the asymptotic running time of an algorithm is calculated.

Rule 1: For loops

The running time of a for loop is, at most, the running time of the statements inside the loop (including tests) into the number of iterations.

Rule 2: Nested loops

Analyze from inside out. The total running time of a statement inside a group of nested loops is the running time of the statement into the sizes of all the loops:

```
for i <- 0 to n-1 do
for j <-0 to n-1 do
k <- i + j
```

(Runs in O(n2))

Rule 3: Consecutive statements

The running time of consecutive statements should be added in order to compute the running time on the whole:

```
for i <- 0 to n-1 do
a[i] <- 0
for i <- 0 to n-1 do BEGIN
for j <- 0 to i do
a[i] <- a[i] + i + j
END
```

(Running time is O(n) + O(n2). By an exercise, this is O(n2))

Rule 4: If/else

Take a look at this fragment:

```
if condition then
S1
else
S2
```

Here, the running time is never more than the running time of the condition plus the larger running time of S1 and S2.

For purposes of examining, analyzing, and comparing algorithms, a neutral algorithm language is used, independent of the particularities of programming languages, operating systems, and system hardware. Doing this makes it possible to study the inherent performance attributes of algorithms, which are present regardless of implementation details. This is done in order to take a broader perspective of the runtime to write the code that can run in near optimal conditions regardless of slight changes in the hardware configuration.

Summary

In this chapter, we learned how we can avoid designing low performing systems, and we looked at how we can optimize low performing systems. It is essential to understand the core of the system and its performance in standard given conditions so that we can easily sense any slowdown in the system. This concept was presented in this chapter just to make you aware of the so-called small operations that might accumulate and lead to a greater problem. We also learned about the best practices in C/AL programming.

In the next chapter, we will be discussing the upgrade, migration, and implementation concept in Microsoft Dynamics NAV, especially for the Dynamics NAV 2016 version. The chapter will include the steps and processes on how we can upgrade the older version into the newer version, and it will also cover parts such as migrating data and implementation processes. This is a standard chapter that will provide the standard approaches in each step.

8

Security in Dynamics NAV 2016

This principle suggests that access decisions should be based on permissions rather thanThis principle suggests that access decisions should be based on permissions rather than

In the last chapter, we fathomed out the upgrades and changing nature of Microsoft Dynamics NAV. Over the year, Microsoft has made many appreciable changes to the system allowing the user to better harvest the solution. We also looked at the importance of the latest features, which make the system more competitive in the market and fulfill user expectations.

Now, in this chapter, we are going to examine the security aspect of Microsoft Dynamics NAV 2016 in particular. We will see how Microsoft is trying to develop all of its projects to a common security standard. This is also important when we are about to encounter the interconnectivity of different platforms and different solutions on the way. Security is the most important chunk of concern, since at the end of the day, all we need is to keep our data safe and keep the safe state buttoned up. This chapter is equally important for consultants, administrators, and implementers. Even the end user should understand some of the basics of software and system security to make sure he/she keeps his end intact.

At the end of this chapter, we will understand the different kinds of threats and concerns related to system and data security. We will also understand about the policies and protocols for prevention of security attacks. In addition, you will find out the different mechanisms used by Microsoft Dynamics NAV and operating system to secure the system, and take a look at how security measures are acknowledged by cloud services.

This chapter will cover the following points:

- Software design principles related to security
- Authentication and access control mechanismS
- On-premise and cloud security and firewall concepts
- Virus and other malicious logics
- Network security strategies and certificates

Software design principles

In the software world, all software either fulfills some or all of the design principles. These principles help eliminate security risks, and support better performance at the time of maintenance. They also reduce the chances of conflict in security policies while integrating with other software or services. Specific design principles directly control the design and implementation of mechanisms for supporting security policies. These principles are built on the ideas of simplicity and restriction. Simple designs are always easy to understand and they support redesign if needed. It can also be understood and explained easily, which reduces the cost and time. In addition, with simple designs the chances of errors are also minimal. It also makes the interconnection process smooth and simple since it is always easy to track different connections with another system if the design is kept simple and transparent. The following figure representation clearly points out different criteria for a good security protocol:

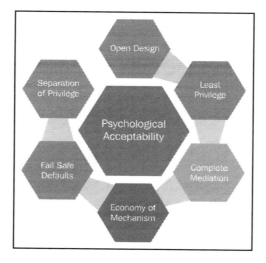

Software design principles

In the later part we will keep our discussion close to the Microsoft Dynamics NAV system and see how the NAV system fulfills the criteria for good security protocols.

Open design

This principle states that the design of a system should not be a secret. The mechanism should not depend on the ignorance of potential attackers; instead, it should depend on the possession of specific, more easily protected keys or passwords. Microsoft Dynamics NAV 2016 follows this design principle. We can understand the design of the system, and can modify and alter it. It also helps the developer integrate the system with other products.

Least privilege

The least privilege design principle states that each and every program and user of the system must follow the listed set of privileges it is required to complete the job which is pre-assigned to it. In Microsoft Dynamics NAV, we can see this as the permission set that we allow to the user so that he/she can operate any task. However, we should only provide specific roles so as to keep the system secure.

Complete mediation

In Microsoft Dynamics NAV, the system passes you through the license authorization whenever we try to access any object or any data within the object, and if you are allowed to access it, only then can you access that particular resource. This ensures that an unauthorized user does not access any object. Whenever any object tries to access any resource, the access should only be given after checking the authority which is granted to the object. This operation should be exclusive.

Economy of mechanism

Microsoft Dynamics NAV has improved a lot since it was first created in 1987-88. The main focus of the system developers was to keep the design simple so that the processing time and complexity can be reduced. This also helps consultants like us to easily understand the logic, and customize it as per need. It is vital that system design is kept simple enough. This well-known principle applies to any aspect of a system.

Fail-safe defaults

This principle suggests that access decisions should be based on permissions rather than exclusion. In default situations, there is not even a single access granted to the system; access is permitted by the protection scheme when needed. It is similar to the ticket granting service where a ticket is provided to a client system only when it needs to access any resources.

Separation of privilege

This principle suggests that multiple keys, which work together in order to access the resources, can be created to better protect data or system access. For example, a protection mechanism that requires two keys to unlock it is more robust and flexible than one which allows access with a single key. This can also be seen when we are transferring data. In Microsoft Dynamics NAV, we can see this principle in the form of login. If a document is sent by user 1 to user 2, then user 1 needs to log in in order to send the document in the first place, and after the file has been sent, user 2 must log in with his credentials and permission set to access the document and then approve it. This ensures that the document and system remain under the separation of privilege protocol.

Psychological acceptability

This is a very important principle from the user's perspective. It is always essential that the user interface be designed so as to make it easy to use for all kinds of users. It ensures that the user automatically applies the protection mechanisms correctly. With the help of this principle, changes of mistakes and vulnerability from the user's side can be minimized drastically.

Security policy

A security policy is a statement that partitions the states of a system into a set of authorized and a set of unauthorized states, that is, the state of secure states or non-secure states.

Let us take an example of three states during the permission granting process for posting a document inside the Microsoft Dynamics NAV system, where state 1 (**S1**) and state 2 (**S2**) are secure states, whereas state 3 (**S3**) is an unsecure state. This is depicted in the following diagram:

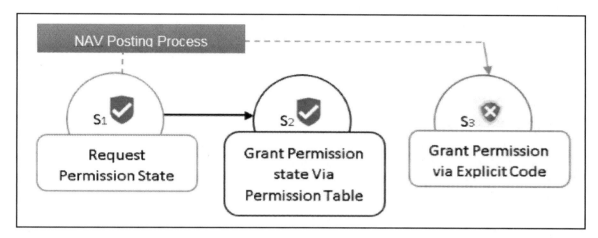

Secure and non-secure state example in Microsoft Dynamics NAV

In Microsoft Dynamics NAV, let us assume a condition where, for a posting process, a process requires permission to write data to a particular table. In this particular instance, NAV uses the setup table design pattern, where it first reads the data field in the permission table, which is based on the security policy. From the permission table, the system grants permission, and then the process completes the posting process. So here, the system refers to the value of the permission set, and acts accordingly. If the user is not assigned with the permission to write to a particular table, then there is a warning/error message. Hence, we can say that system stayed in safe state.

Let us imagine we wrote a codeunit that explicitly bypasses the permission table logic, and grants the right to access the table. In this case, we can say that the system compromises the policy. This has many different types of consequences, one of them being security of data.

Security policy goals

Following are the goals of a security policy:

- Keep sensitive information (such as company plans, new product data, and so on) confidential, on a need-to-know basis
- Only employees who handle purchases can access customer data
- Releasing sensitive data should require the consent of the company's officials and lawyers

Access Control Matrix

An **Access Control Matrix (ACM)** is a way of specifying policy. A simple example is shown in the following table. Here, two processes, Process 1 and Process 2, have been granted different levels of policy, which is shown in a matrix form. This is the most common way of representing policies among administrators:

	File 1	File 2	File 3	File 4
Process 1	Read Write Own	Read	Read Write Execute Own	Write
Process 2	Append	Read Own	Read	Read Write Execute Own

Let us take the example of a system of a specific company which uses Microsoft Dynamics NAV 2016, and where the security admin has to define specific policies for different classes of users. The organization can be divided into three internal divisions depending on the access policy of the resources.

 You should not be confuse access control of computer security with different types of operations on the database. There are basically five types of access controls: read, write, own, execute, and append. On the other hand, there are four kinds of operations: create, read, update/modify, and delete, which generally take place during database-related operations.

Internal organizations

The internal organization of users can be divided into three different categories, namely **Customer Service Group (CSG)**, **Development Group (DG)**, and **Corporate Group (CG)**. The roles of each are given as follows:

- Customer Service Group
  - This maintains customer data
  - It acts as an interface between clients and other internal. organizations
- Development Group
  - This develops, modifies, and maintains products
  - It relies on CSG for customer feedback
- Corporate Group
  - This handles patents, lawsuits, and others

The security policy describes the way information flows between these three groups. It minimizes the threat of data being leaked to unauthorized entities.

Data classes

In general, data can be divided into the following main five classes. This classification helps us understand better how to draw the matrix diagram. It is strongly recommended that you understand these concepts before implementing the Microsoft Dynamics NAV system.

Public data

Public data is the data that we generally pull from the NAV database to the website for all our clients to view. It might be outgrown statistics, or customer information, or a list of items that we manufacture or sell as a company.

It is available to all.

Development data for existing products

These can be codes, designs, objects, and any data related to development resources.

It is available to the corporate group and development group only.

Development data for future products

This data can be related to the **Research and Development (R&D)** department for future products like integration, extensions, or any specific module that is being planned for.

It is available to DG only.

Corporate data

Corporate data is vital to the organization. It has a permanent or lasting nature, and is related to the organization's mandate.

It is available to CG only.

Customer data

Customer data is available to CSG only.

 All these terms might look confusing, but in our day-to-day lives, we all actually use these terms. All these terminologies, if implemented in day-to-day practice, will give a standardization to your administration and implementation skills. I would recommend you visualize these terms with real case information.

User classes

Furthermore, users of the system can be categorized into the following four categories:

- **Outsiders**: Members of the public
    - Have access to public data
    - Can also order, download drivers, send e-mails to the company
- **Developers**: Have access to DDEP and DDFP
    - Cannot alter development data for existing products
- **Corporate executives**: Have access to CD
    - Can read development data for existing products, development data for future products, and customer data, but not alter them
    - Sometimes, can make sensitive data public
- **Employees**: Have access to customer data only

Now, having learnt all the categories, we will draw an Access Control Matrix table for the given conditions. We will understand how this process eliminates the possibility of poor security policy implementations:

	Outsiders	Developers	Corporate executives	Employees
Public data	Read	Read	Read	Read
Development data for existing products		Read	Read	
Development data for future products		Read, Write	Read	
Corporate data			Read, Write	
Customer data	Write		Read	Read, Write

Authentication

Authentication is the process of identifying an individual, usually based on credentials like a username and password. Authentication is a fundamental aspect of system security, and is used to confirm the identity of any user trying to log on to a domain or to access network resources. Passwords provide the first line of defense against unauthorized access to the domain and local computers.

 The weakest link in most authentication systems is the user's password.

The following screenshot shows the window which is presented to the user to get their secure authentication information for the sign in operation:

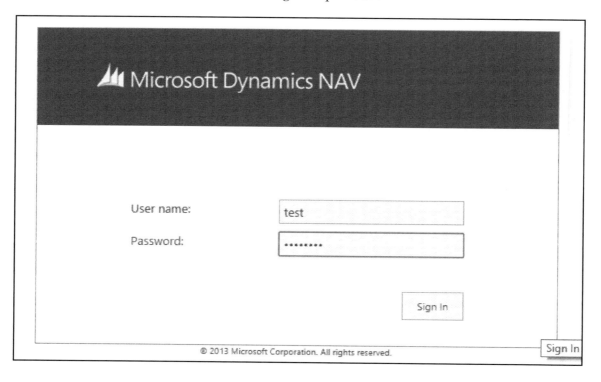

Strong password

This is important to all, including the end user of Microsoft Dynamics NAV. The user must follow some guidelines to ensure that his/her password is a strong one.

Best practices for creating a strong password are as follows:

- Always use strong passwords; strong password means a password with a complex combination of letters, symbols, and numbers:

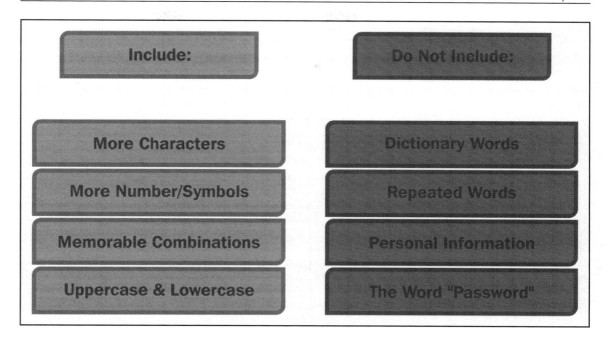

- Try to avoid writing the password on paper; in case you need to do so, erase or destroy it when it is no longer needed
- Never ever share passwords with anyone
- Use different passwords for all user accounts
- Be careful about where passwords are saved on computers
- Change passwords at regular intervals

The role that passwords play in securing an organization's network is often underestimated and overlooked. As mentioned earlier, passwords provide the first line of defense against unauthorized access to your network. You should therefore instruct your employees to use strong passwords and follow the guidelines presented in this section.

Defining the password policy

Password policy is another major point where we should spend some time. When you define your password policy, be sure to create a policy that requires all user accounts to have strong passwords. This ensures that the minimum criteria is fulfilled. This can be done using the **Group Policy Management Editor** window as shown in the following screenshot:

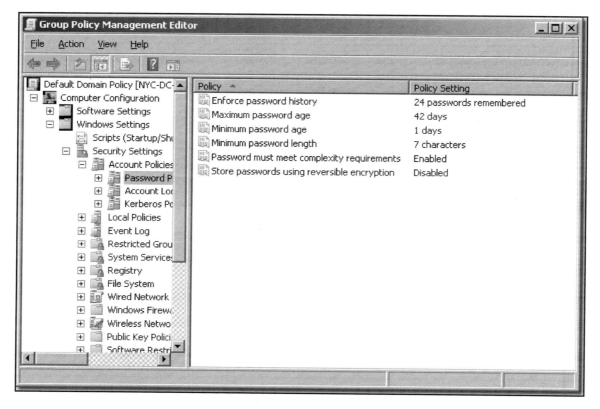

Following are the guidelines for password policies:

- Define the **Enforce password history** policy setting so that several previous passwords are remembered
- Define the **Maximum password age** policy setting so that passwords expire as often as necessary for the client's environment
- Define the **Minimum password age** policy setting so that passwords cannot be changed until they are more than a certain number of days old

- Define a **Minimum password length** policy setting so that passwords must consist of at least a specified number of characters
- Enable the **Password must meet complexity requirements** policy setting

Defining an account lockout policy

You always have to be very cautious while defining the account lockout policy. The account lockout policy should never be set in a small business, as it is also highly likely to lock out authorized users, and this can be very costly.

If you decide to apply an account lockout policy, set the **Account lockout threshold** policy setting to a high number so that authorized users are not locked out of their user accounts simply because they mistyped their password several times:

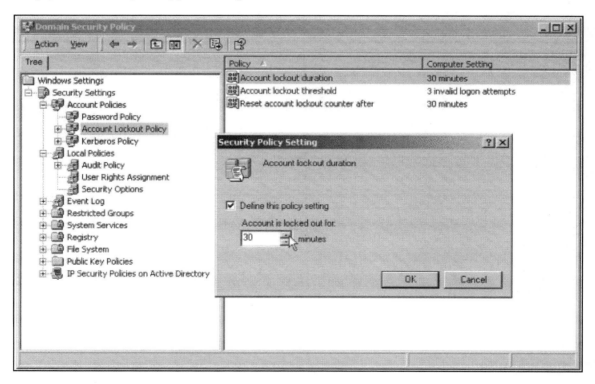

Access control

In general, Microsoft Dynamics NAV and computer resources can be secured by considering what rights the users, groups of users, and other computers have on the network. You can secure a computer or multiple computers by granting users or groups specific user rights. You can secure an object, such as a file or folder, by assigning permissions that allow users or groups to perform specific actions on that object.

Following are the key components of access control:

- Roles and permissions
- Ownership of objects
- Inheritance of permissions
- User rights
- Object auditing

Roles and permissions

The Microsoft Dynamics NAV security system provides extensive security and access control options. It helps you specify direct and indirect permissions even up to table-level security. It also provides records-level security for the MS SQL Server option.

A role in Microsoft Dynamics NAV is nothing but a set of permissions for various objects present in the system.

Permissions define the type of access granted to a user or group for an object or object property such as files, folders, and registry objects. Permissions are applied to any secured object such as files or registry objects. Permissions can be granted to any user, group, or computer system.

 It is a good practice to assign permissions to groups. It is also recommended that if you want to modify the pre-existing permission set by deleting or altering the default lines of the existing permission set, then start with copying the pre-existing set, and alter the new one.

Ownership of objects

In Microsoft Dynamics NAV, an owner is assigned to an object when that object is created. Every object has an owner, and by default, in Windows Server, the owner is the creator of the object. The owner controls how permissions are set on the object, and to whom permissions are granted. An administrator who needs to repair or change permissions on a file must begin by taking ownership of the file.

Ownership can be taken in three possible ways by different levels of users, which are as follows:

- **Administrator**: By default, the administrators group is given the **Take ownership of files or other objects user** right.
- **User or group**: Ownership can be taken by any one user or a group of users who has the **Take Ownership** permission on the object. If not, then the administrator can be requested for permission.
- **A normal user with direct right**: The ownership of an object can be taken by a normal user who has the **Restore files and directories** user right.

Inheritance of permissions

Inherited permissions simply propagate to an object from a parent object. Inherited permissions ease the task of managing permissions and ensure consistency of permissions among all objects within a given container. However, it can result in some serious complexity if not handled properly. Inheritance allows administrators to easily assign and manage permissions. This feature automatically causes objects within a container to inherit all the inheritable permissions of that container. For example, when you create files within a folder, they inherit the permissions of the folder. Only the permissions marked to be inherited are inherited.

 Explicit permissions take precedence over inherited permissions, even the inherited deny permissions.

User rights

User rights grant specific privileges and logon rights to users and groups in your computing environment. Microsoft has defined user rights under the following two categories:

- **Login right**: This right is directly assigned to a user, and specifies the ways in which a user can log on to a system, for example, the right to log in to the system using VPN.
- **Privilege right**: A privilege right can be assigned to a user, and specifies allowable actions on the system. This comes secondary, since the user must have a login right before he has the privilege to carry out some action. An example is the right to shut down a system.

Virus protection

A computer virus is a program that inserts itself into one or more files and performs some action. There are generally these two different phases of a virus:

- Insertion phase, when it inserts itself into a file
- Execution phase, when it performs some (possibly null) action

Viruses are often rewritten and adjusted so that they cannot be detected. Viruses are generally sent as e-mail attachments, for example, like a Word file. Antivirus programs must be updated continuously to look for new and modified viruses.

Microsoft strongly recommends you use antivirus software on all your computers. Antivirus software is usually installed at each of these three places: user workstations, servers, and the network.

Best practices for virus protection

Following are some of the best practices you can follow in order to avoid virus infection:

- You should always install a virus protection solution which scans incoming messages from the internet for viruses before the messages pass the router.
- You should use a virus-scanning software to detect and remove macro viruses. Virus scanning software can detect, and often remove, macro viruses from documents.

- Do not open a file unless they are from someone you know.
- Use the Microsoft Office macro virus protection.

Network security strategies

In the security strategy of networks, the firewall has become a key ingredient in safeguarding network integrity. A firewall is the default security module that prevents data packets from either entering or leaving a specified network. It can be hardware as well as software-based. It monitors and controls the incoming and outgoing network traffic based on predetermined security rules. It basically acts as a barrier between a trusted, secure internal network and another outside network. The perimeter network protects your intranet or enterprise **local area network (LAN)** from intrusion by controlling access from the Internet or other large networks. A perimeter network is sometimes referred to as the **demilitarized zone (DMZ)**. The following diagram clearly illustrates the concept of network security:

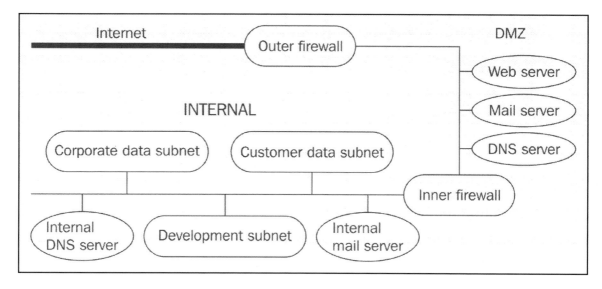

DMZ is a portion of a network separating a purely internal network from the external network. It allows control of access to some trusted systems inside the corporate perimeter. Even if the DMZ system is breached, the internal systems remain safe. It can perform different types of checks at the boundary between the internal and DMZ networks, and between the DMZ and Internet network.

Proxy is an intermediate agent or server acting on behalf of each endpoint without allowing a direct connection between the two endpoints. So each endpoint talks to the proxy, thinking it is talking to the other endpoint. Proxy decides whether to forward messages, and whether to alter them.

The following diagram shows a perimeter network, bounded by firewalls and placed between a private network and the Internet in order to secure the private network:

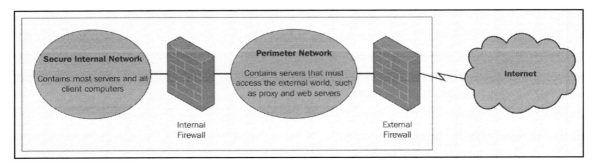

You can use different technological feathers provided by a modern firewall depending on the nature of implementation and requirements. Following are some of the implementations that you can utilize:

- IP packet filtering
- Application gateways
- Circuit gateways
- Proxy servers

IP packet filtering offers weak security, is inconvenient to manage, and is easily breached. Application gateways are more immune than packet filters and easier to manage, because they affect only a few specific applications, such as a particular e-mail system. Circuit gateways are most effective when the user of a network application is more important than the data. The proxy server includes an application gateway, safe access for anonymous users, and other services.

Wireless networks

Wireless networks are most vulnerable to a malicious outsider gaining access. This is because of the default settings on some wireless hardware, the accessibility that wireless networks offer. There are configuration options and tools that can protect against eavesdropping, but keep in mind that they do nothing to protect the computers from hackers and viruses that enter through the Internet connection. Hence, it is very important to include a firewall to protect the computers from unwanted intruders on the Internet.

 Eavesdropping is generally the illegal process of secretly listening to the private conversation of others without their permission.

Cryptography and certificates

Cryptography is a technique for secure communication in the presence of third parties called adversaries. An adversary is an entity which is generally malicious in nature, and aims to steal or damage secret data being communicated through a public channel. The theft might be in the form of corrupting data, spoofing the identity of the sender and receiver, disrupting the sending process, injecting their logic into the communicating process, and so on. We can use cryptography in order to achieve a secure communication experience, as shown in the following figure. Here, the sender encrypts the plain text message using the recipient's public key, and then forwards the message to the unsecure channel. On the arrival of the encrypted data, the recipient decrypts the data using its private key.

This is also the basis of cryptography, which is widely used in the modern data transportation system:

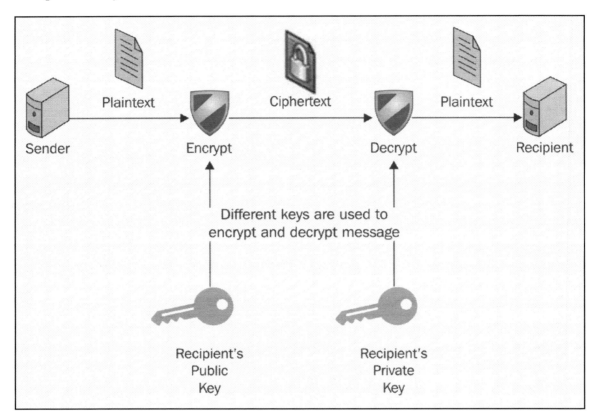

 A key is a piece of information that is generated by the cryptographic algorithm for securing the data transportation process over the channel.

A certificate is nothing but a token that binds an identity to a cryptographic key.

 Microsoft Management Console (**MMC**) is a presentation service for management applications in the Microsoft Windows environment. It is a part of the **independent software vendor** (**ISV**) extensible service, that is, it provides a common integrated environment for snap-ins, provided by Microsoft and third-party software vendors.

Certificate authority

A **certification authority (CA)** is an entity that issues certificates. If all certificates have a common issuer, then the issuer's public key can be distributed out of band:

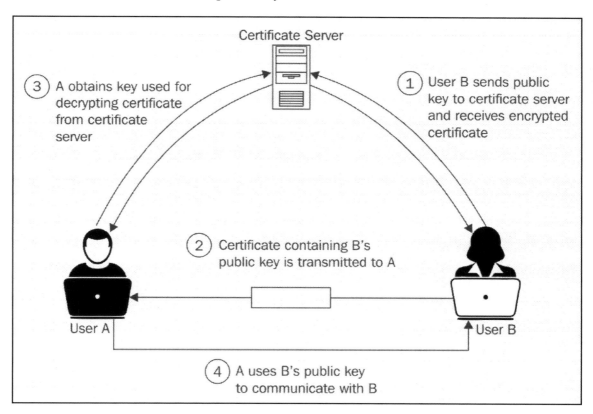

In the preceding diagram, the certificate server (also called CA) is the third party, which has a secure relationship with both the parties that want to communicate. CA is connected to both parties through a secure channel. **User B** sends a copy of his public key to the CA. Then the CA encrypts the public key of **User B** using a different key. Two files are created because of this trigger: the first is an encrypted package, which is nothing but the certificate, and the second is the digital signature of the certificate server. The certificate server returns the certificate to user B. Now **User A** asks for the certificate from **User B**. **User B** sends the copy of its public key to **User A**. This is again done using a secure communication channel. **User A** decrypts the certificate using the key obtained from the certificate server, and extracts the public key of **User B**. **User A** also checks the digital signature of the certificate server to ensure that the certificate is authentic.

Here, whatever data is encrypted using the public key of **User B**, can only be decrypted using the private key of **User B**, which is only present with **User B** and not with any of the intruders over the Internet. So only **User B** can decrypt and read the content sent by **User A**.

Once the keys are transferred, **User A** can communicate with **User B**. In case **User B** wants to send data to **User A**, then **User B** would need the public key of **User A**, which will be again granted by CA.

 Certificates are issued to a principal. The Issuance policy specifies the principals to which the CA will issue certificates.

The certification authority does not need to be online to check the validity of the certificate. It can be present in a server of a locked room. It is only consulted when a principal needs a certificate. Certificates are a way of associating an identity with a public key and distinguished name.

Authentication policy for CA

The authentication policy defines the way principals prove their identities. Each CA has its own requirements constrained by contractual requirements such as with **Primary Certification Authority (PCA)**:

- PCA issues certificates to CA
- CA issues certificates to individuals and organizations

All rely on non-electronic proofs of identity, such as biometric (fingerprints), documents (drivers license or passport), or personal knowledge.

A specific authentication policy can be determined by checking the policy of the CA that signed the certificate.

Kinds of certificates

There are at least four kinds of certificates, which are as follows:

- Site certificates (for example, `www.msdn.microsoft.com`).
- Personal certificates (used if the server wants to authenticate the client). You can install a personal certificate in your browser.

- Software vendor certificates (used when software is installed). Often, when you run a program, a dialog box appears warning that **The publisher could not be verified. Are you sure you want to run this software?** This is caused either because the software does not have a software vendor certificate, or because you do not trust the CA who signed the software vendor certificate.
- Anonymous certificates (used by a whistle blower to indicate that the same person sent a sequence of messages, but doesn't know who that person is).

 Other types of certificates Certificates can also be based on a principal's association with an organization (such as Microsoft (MSDN)), where the principal lives, or the role played in an organization (such as the comptroller).

Security updates

In this complex world of software engineering, it is essential that software works reliably and does not compromise the security or stability of the IT environment. When it comes to big programs like operating systems and Microsoft Dynamics NAV, it is even more important that the coordination between the developers is precise. To minimize any problems, programs are tested thoroughly in different phases of code and integrations testing before release. However, attackers continually strive to find weaknesses in software, so anticipating all future attacks is not always possible.

Whatever the nature and size of the organization, from large scale to small-sized ones, it is vital to have a good update management strategy, even if the organization does not yet have an effective change and configuration management in place. The vast majority of successful attacks against computer systems occur against those systems where security updates have not been installed or have not been installed properly. It is the duty of administrators and security admins to understand the seriousness of this fact at the time of installation of the system and during the upgrade process.

In the Microsoft Dynamics NAV 2016 environment, you must ensure that your clients have the most recent security updates installed into their system. Make sure the client uses one of the technologies that Microsoft has made available. These include the following:

- Microsoft Security Notification Service
- Microsoft Automatic Updates

- Microsoft Security Bulletin Search Tool
- Microsoft Baseline Security Analyzer
- Microsoft Systems Management Server Software Update Services Feature Pack

You should always consider adopting each of these tools. It is very crucial that security issues are addressed as immediately as possible while maintaining the stability of the environment.

 It is recommended to use a checklist while carrying out these activities. Always check the tasks finished and forward the checklist, once done, to the client administrators. This is part of good security administration practice.

SQL Server security settings

Microsoft Dynamics NAV 2016 can run on the SQL Server, and smaller installations can also run on SQL Server Express. It is vital to understand the requirements of the client in the first place. It is recommended to use the following steps to help increase SQL Server security:

- Always make sure that the latest operating system and SQL Server service packs and updates are installed.
- For filesystem-level security, make sure all SQL Server data and system files are installed on NTFS partitions. Also make sure to make the files accessible only to administrative or system-level users through NTFS permissions. It safeguards against users trying to access those files when the MSSQLSERVER service is not running.
- Use a low-privilege domain account such as NT AuthorityNetwork Service (recommended), or the local system account for the SQL Server service (MSSQLSERVER or SQLEXPRESS). This account should have only local user-level permissions in the domain.
- Most editions of SQL Server are installed with some default databases. They should not be deployed within a production environment. Delete these sample databases if you find those in the production environment.
- Auditing of the SQL Server system is disabled by default. Enable auditing of failed logins. This is done to prevent it from attackers, and to carry out smooth intrusion detection process.

AZURE security setting

We will now look at Azure Security Center, a new service that helps you tap into Microsoft's real-time intelligence on the threat landscape including how it can help you get a centralized security monitoring set policy and provide deep security to your Azure resources, and get advanced threat detection with machine learning.

Let's look at it from the IT and information security perspective.

If your organization has a lot of resources deployed in Azure, it probably will look like this:

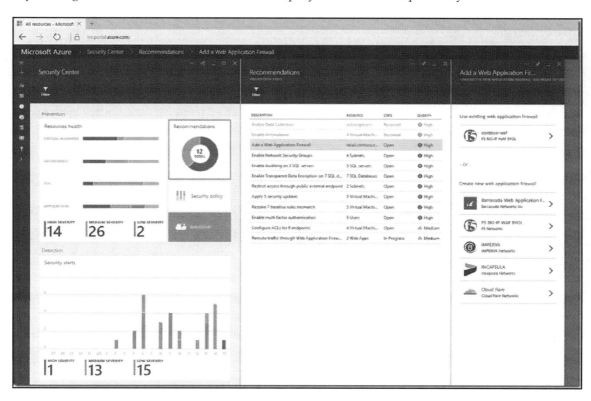

And if you are not the operational owner of those resources, it is difficult to get all the visibility you need into their state of security. And if you are the security administrator, then you are definitely going to be accountable for the security state of all these resources. The Azure Security center gives you that visibility where you can define policies for how these resources get protected against attack and how data is made secure.

You can also separate the policies on the basis of subscription, for example, if you do not want to give the production unit and the development and test resources the same policy.

Summary

In this chapter, you learnt about the security aspects of Microsoft Dynamics NAV design. We also looked into some of the important contents of a security system. We studied how we can prevent our system from different malicious logics, and how to cut down the risks of security failures. It is highly recommended for everyone, especially administrators, to understand the concepts of this chapter in order to provide a robust defensive environment to Microsoft Dynamics NAV.

In the next chapter, we will go into detail on customization, development, and implementation considerations for Microsoft Dynamics NAV 2016. The chapter will provide you with the core knowledge of the best practices that one should follow while developing and customizing a solution. It will also cover the implementation considerations that an implementer should follow in order to achieve the best result.

9
Upgrade and Migration

In the previous chapter, we became familiar with the different security elements of Microsoft Dynamics NAV. We examined the security aspect of Microsoft Dynamics NAV 2016 and understood how Microsoft has managed to keep security its major concern while redesigning the Dynamics NAV system. The chapter provided us with a better idea when it comes to the interconnectivity of different platforms and different solutions with Dynamics NAV. We also discussed different security policies and measures to keep the system secure.

In this chapter, we are going to dig deep into the technicality of the upgrade process. This chapter has some prerequisites, which are simple upgrade knowledge using simple or no tool. The chapter will basically try to focus on the benefits of implementing automated processes, such as the use of PowerShell-like tools, allowing you to optimize your effort while conducting an upgrade process. The chapter also includes in-depth knowledge of different phases and constraints of upgrade projects.

At the end of this chapter, you should know the most efficient ways of carrying out the upgrade projects. This will hit the technical aspect, as doing that can increase the productivity of the team and reduce the project duration. The chapter will provide you with a deep understanding of the core upgrade process.

This chapter will cover the following points:

- The basic concepts of software upgrade and the upgrade workflow
- Upgrade estimation and planning
- Different toolkits and testing methodologies

The need for upgrade

As Microsoft keeps investing in Microsoft Dynamics NAV, they encourage their users to keep taking advantage of the enhancements and innovations. It is essential for every software user to keep up with the changes, very much like how you keep up with changes in the latest fashion and latest gadgets. Once you are up to date with the latest release of Microsoft Dynamics NAV, you will get better security features, your productivity is expected to grow, you can reduce the effort for certain operations, reduce the cost of hardware maintenance, and many more. It will also give the company the upper hand while they are competing with other companies.

Microsoft has been evolving, and with every release, it is trying to deliver strong and more robust products to its valuable customers. These are the list of additions if you want to upgrade to version 2016:

- Posting preview
- Deferrals
- Document sending profiles
- Microsoft Dynamics CRM integration
- Improvement in the web client
- Microsoft social engagement
- Control add-ins on Microsoft Dynamics NAV phone client

There are many more optimized features.

For more details on the features of Dynamics NAV 2016, refer to `Chapter 2`, *Upgraded Features and Configurations in Dynamics NAV 2016*.

Upgrade considerations

An upgrade is an opportunity to streamline your NAV Solution. It either reduces the degree of customizations or uses new features to address new changes into an organization. Different consultants approach their upgrade projects differently, and there is not a single standard on how to approach the upgrade. However, there are certain best practices that are considered efficient. Let's discuss these considerations, which can save energy and help the smooth upgrade transition process:

- The source and destination system
- The system size
- Upgrade codeunits
- Company name
- Name of the variable
- System table with non-English names
- Deprecated or redesigned functionality
- Testing
- Tune-up

Here, we will be discussing the upgrade process of Dynamics NAV System from 2015 or 2013, but if you ended up on this chapter expecting to read about the upgrade from the old version, such as 2009, then you must be very sure about what you are trying to achieve. The Microsoft Dynamics NAV system has been through a huge amount of redesigning, and it is not possible to change it directly from the older version to the 2016 release. But you can follow the two-step process, that is, upgrade from version 2009 to 2013, and then from 2013, you can upgrade to 2016. For the first part, consult the older books from Packt.

Custom object review

After you have found the custom code that you need to carry into the upgraded system, you must dip into the details of the code and determine exactly which custom objects need to be implemented. This is very important to address initially, and before doing so, always make sure you know about the full features of the destination system because there might be some additional features that eliminate most of the custom code from the previous version. There can be three possible results of customer object review:

- **Merge**: If the custom code and object can be directly merged and upgraded into the destination system.
- **Re-implement**: If the custom code and object cannot be directly upgraded, then it needs to be re-implemented as a new customization and should be passed to the relevant team.
- **Use customization**: If the customer-specific objects exist in the destination system, then you can use the objects, but in most of the cases, you might need customization techniques to totally retrieve the functionality of the old feature. For example, you might need to develop new reports, page views, and so on.

Customization upgrade analysis

In this phase, you should make sure that you eliminate most of the useless stuff in order to make the upgrade process more efficient. There are many cases where customizations might not need to be carried forward into the upgraded destination system:

- Older customization is no longer needed
- The same feature is built into the standard NAV
- The solution is already present in the market at an affordable price
- New customization is preferred because of the poor quality of the older customized system

There can be other cases where you want to dump the idea of upgrading the custom code and/or object. The main idea is to filter those cases and only then move forward.

Business process analysis

This is similar to the requirement analysis of the software development life cycle process. Here, you can sit with the stakeholders and decide on the amount of customization to be done. This should be done because throughout the time, most of the customization requirement process could have changed and the company is no longer using the feature, making the whole sense of upgrading that particular section of the system useless and expensive. So it is recommended that you treat this step very carefully and, if possible, product designers should also take part in this meeting in order to grant better perspective toward the business process of the system to be upgraded.

Reviewing your dimension structure

Basically, this process should be carried out together with business process analysis. But here, the concerned department should be more streamlined into the nature of dimension structure. It has been observed that over time, people who are using the system might have realized the flaws of using too many dimensions and they want to upgrade the structure of the system, but since the system dimension structure should not be modified in the middle of transactions, it is hard to do it at some other time. Upgrade is the perfect time to tighten up and streamline dimensions to simplify data entry and improve reporting for your users. It is also recommended that you generate some financial reporting and check whether the change that you are proposing does not affect the reports and key performance indicators.

Upgrading from older versions

It is very important to have the development environment of Dynamics NAV 2013 when you are trying to upgrade the much older version of NAV since 2013 can be considered the bridge between the older and modern Dynamics NAV product. There are many changes that should not be attempted for upgrading manually. The Microsoft Dynamics NAV Upgrade toolkit can be downloaded from the Microsoft Partner source, and most of the installation DVD already contains these tools for the upgrade. The following figure explains how Dynamics NAV 2013 links the upgrade process:

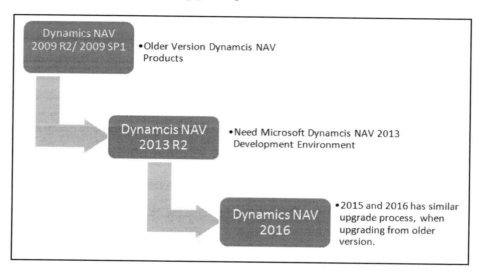

It is also important that you break down the steps into two different substeps in order to minimize the confusion while upgrading. The first process, that is, upgrading from a much older version to version 2013, should be the first one, and then the 2013 version should be changed into 2015 release with the help of a different set of upgrade toolkit.

Technical upgrade

Technical upgrade is the least used upgrade process, which is when you are making one version upgrade at a time i.e. from Version 2009 to Version 2013 or Version 2013 to Version 2015. So, when you are planning to jump multiple versions at the same time, then technical upgrade might not be the perfect option to choose. It can be efficient when there are minimal changes in the source database objects, that is, fewer customizations. It can also be considered an efficient choice when the business requirement from the product is still the same or has very less significant changes.

The upgrade workflow

Different phases that constitute the upgrade process are as follows:

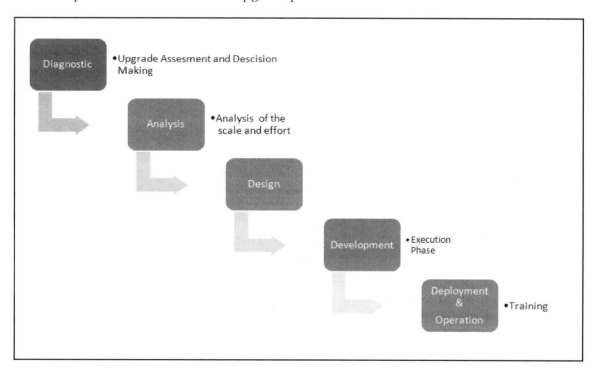

When you are going to start the upgrade process in Dynamics NAV, there is a specific workflow that you need to follow. This workflow helps you quickly complete the workflow with maximum output.

Each of these phases have different tasks and responsibilities, and one must be very careful while changing the phase. It is very important that you have the necessary output in that you have extracted from the previous phase in order to provide that material as the input to the next phase. This is the reason you should not neglect any phase.

Diagnostic phase

Diagnostic phase is the first phase that can be taken as the nontechnical phase, but the person carrying out the steps of this phase should have a good technical background. Only a good technical expert can diagnose the expectation of the given case. This phase starts during the sales process of the project. This starts with a meeting between the stakeholders to decide the nature of the project. The second step of this phase is to collect enough information from the existing system in order to draw an idea of the project. Here, we define the scope of the project. The diagnostic process ends with providing some deliverables. You as a consultant are responsible for creating a proposal document and present the high-level project charter. The technical documentation at this stage is also called **Statement of Work (SOW)**. It all depends on what your style of documentation is.

After the documentation is finalized and you and your client agree on the proposal, you move forward with the next phase of the project.

Analysis phase

This is the second phase of the project upgrade process, where we can determine how we are going to approach the whole upgrade project. We start the phase by creating a project plan. Here, we go deeper into the scope of the project, which is also called **scope analysis** in software engineering terminology. In scope analysis, we filter out the stuff that we will be working on and the remaining stuff that we will not be work on. In a sense, this creates a clear-cut understanding on our scope that we will be working on until the time of project implementation.

Here, we conduct the **Fit Gap analysis** operation, where we analyze whether there is any additional customization work present in the existing system that needs extra attention. Another key feature of this phase is to start the development of the upgrade testing strategy that will explain how we are going to test everything at the end of the upgrade process. This is done to ensure the quality of the upgrade project. In addition to this, you should also start a different environment, such as development environment, pre-production environment, and test environment.

Always keep in mind the proper versioning you learned in Chapter 6, *Version Control and Code Management*. Since you have different teams working on different environments, you all should be clear about the responsibility for your own versioning. Also, make sure you keep the versioning of different documentations and change the request that might come during the project life time.

The data upgrade preparation process should also be started in the analysis phase of the project. This is critical since the only valuable information the customer want to keep intact is their data, so you should provide enough time to get it ready.

The main point of this phase can be summarized in the following points:

- Project planning
- Working on detailed scope
- Fit Gap analysis
- Developing an upgrade testing strategy
- Setting up non-production environments
- Planning for version control
- Initial data upgrade preparation

Design phase

While developing a solution, the design phase is a crucial phase in the whole project, and it requires a specialist with a huge amount of designing experience. Some of the big vendor companies keep a system architect especially for this phase, where he or she is supposed to design the best solution to satisfy the need of the client. If the design can be kept simple and close to the original structure of the system, then you can save much of your work, and it guarantees the success of the project.

But since we are just talking about the upgrade project here, it's a lot easier through a critical phase. Here, you should define the implementation of the upgrade. Microsoft provides the data upgrade checklist, which is nothing but a standard procedure to carry out the upgrade process. We are going to follow this process:

- Reviewing the data upgrade checklist
- Reviewing the existing code of the system
- Reviewing the existing integration of the system and interfaces
- Reviewing the user experience

In practical life, some of the upgrade projects might bring up some development work; you must be very careful with those chances to the system and follow the standard customization and development guidelines.

Development phase

Design phase is followed by the development phase, where you will be executing the application upgrade process. Here, you upgrade different application modules. The customization of the code is also upgraded and two levels of testing are performed. The main reason for performing unit testing and integrating testing is to ensure that every part is in synchronization with each other while meeting its requirement. Here, you should set up a new production environment and upgrade the integration of all interfaces that were shortlisted in the phase of analysis for operation. The final operation of this phase is to verify and benchmark your data arguments of the upgraded solution. Development phase is also sometimes called the execution phase since the major execution of the operation takes place in this phase.

The major operations of this phase can be summarized in the following points:

- Upgrading application modules
- Upgrading customizations
- Conducting unit testing and integration testing
- Setting up a production environment
- Upgrading integrations and interfaces
- Verifying data from the production environment

Deployment and operation phase

This is the last phase of the upgrade project. Since most of the technical aspects of the project are already being carried out in the development phase, all we need to do in this phase is verify the changes from the user side. We need to conduct various levels of training if there are significant changes in the system or if a new feature of Dynamics NAV is added in the new version. This phase also includes the UAT process, which is the user level of testing. The user is supposed to test the system as per the process flow provided to them. After the user provides the green signal with UAT, you might need to perform a final data upgrade or data migration process into the production environment. And you are all set for Go-Live. Once the users start using the system, you can call for a successful end to the project and start the support and maintenance process if needed.

The major operations of this phase can be summarized in the following points:

- Conducting user training
- User acceptance testing
- Final data upgrade to the production environment
- Go-Live
- Transition solution to support

Upgrading estimates

In this section, we are going to look at the core components that are responsible for the estimates of the upgrade process. The components that are to be considered while estimating for the upgrade process are as follows:

- Code upgrade
- Object transformation
- Data upgrade
- Testing and implementation

Code upgrade

The best method to estimate the code upgrade is to use a file compare tool. It helps us compare the file, folder, version control, conflicts and resolution, automatic intelligent merging, in-place editing of files, track changes, and code analysis.

> You can use third-party tools for this. Or, you can use a version control system such as GitHub to compare files. Refer to Chapter 6, *Version Control and Code Management.*

You can also design your own compare tool if you want, for example, take two version of the same object, take two versions of Customer table. Open them in Notepad and check line by line whether there is any difference in the line, and then get that line value and show it as a log. You can achieve this via C# or any programming language. This should run for each object in two versions of the NAV system and provide you with the statistics of the amount of changes:

```
CustomerTableVersion9.0.txt - Notepad                    —    □    ×

File  Edit  Format  View  Help
OBJECT Table 18 Customer
{
  OBJECT-PROPERTIES
  {
    Date=12/30/16;
    Time=[ 1:06:44 PM];
    Modified=Yes;
    Version List=NAVNA9.00.00.44974;
  }
  PROPERTIES
  {
    Permissions=TableData 21=r;
    DataCaptionFields=No.,Name;
    OnInsert=BEGIN
             IF "No." = '' THEN BEGIN
                SalesSetup.GET;
```

```
CustomerTableVersion8.0.txt - Notepad                    —    □    ×

File  Edit  Format  View  Help
OBJECT Table 18 Customer
{
  OBJECT-PROPERTIES
  {
    Date=12/30/16;
    Time=[ 1:06:44 PM];
    Modified=Yes;
    Version List=NAVNA8.0;
  }
  PROPERTIES
  {
    Permissions=TableData 21=r;
    DataCaptionFields=No.,Name;
    OnInsert=BEGIN
             IF "No." = '' THEN BEGIN
                SalesSetup.GET;
```

This can be really handy when it comes to the point of estimation for the code changes. You can also do it manually if the number of objects is less.

It is recommended that one must use the Microsoft Dynamics Sure Step methodology while carrying out any upgrade projects. Dynamics Sure step is a full life cycle methodology tool which is designed to provide a discipline and best practice to upgrade, migrate, configure and deploy Microsoft Dynamics NAV Solution.

Object transformation

We must take a close look in the case of some objects that are not directly upgraded. As, for example, if your source database reports are in the classic version or early RTC version, it might not be feasible to transform them into the latest reports because of the huge technological gap between the reports. In these cases, you must be very careful while estimating for these upgrades. For example, **TransHeader** and **TransFooter** and other categorizations that are present in classic reports are hard to map directly into Dynamics NAV 2016 reports. We might have to develop our own logic to achieve these grouping values, which might take some additional time. So, always treat this section as a customization instead of upgrade. Mostly, Microsoft partner vendors keep this section separate and, in most of the cases, separate resources are assigned to do that for parallel work environments.

Reports can also have word layouts that should also be considered during the estimates.

Data upgrade

We perform a number of distinct steps while upgrading data. You must consider the time for each section in the data upgrade process in order to correctly estimate the time for it.

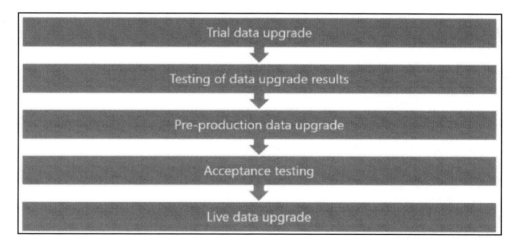

The first thing that we do is a trial data upgrade process. This allows us to analyze different aspects, such as, to see how long it takes; if data upgrade process works or not; and will it allow us to test the results of this trial data upgrade. Once we are done with the trial data upgrade, we might need to do it a number of times before it works. Then, we can do a preproduction data upgrade because since the moment we started our analyses and development, the production data might have changed, so we also need to do a preproduction run to also have a closer estimate of the time windows that we have available when we are going to do the real implementation. Acceptance testing is also a very important phase. Once you have done the data upgrade, you need the end users or key users to confirm that our data has been converted correctly. And then you are ready to perform the live data upgrade. So all of these different phases in the data upgrade will also require some time. The amount of time will also depend on the size of the database or the version that you are starting from. So, this gives you an overview of the different pillars that are important to estimate how much time it might take to prepare and analyze the updates project.

Testing and implementation

Testing is a very important phase, and you must estimate it wisely. If the gap between source and destination systems is large, as for example, from 2009 to 2016, then in those cases, the testing time should be larger ,as most of the logic that is implemented in older versions is drastically enhanced in order to optimize the performance of the system, and the testing team should test each and every process meticulously.

One of the good aspects of testing in Dynamics NAV 2016 is that you can design your own test cases and write code for them. It also filters out most of the bugs before you actually go for UAT. Microsoft Dynamics NAV Installation DVD also contains the test codeunits.

 For more details on how the testing process can be optimized using the test code units, refer to `Chapter 4`, *Testing and Debugging*. I highly recommend the use of these features of Dynamics NAV. It not only reduces the cost of upgrade, but it also ensures the performance of the final system.

There are two categorizations in testing, UI testing and functional testing:

- User interface testing
    - Depends on the number of new and modified objects
- Functional testing
    - Creating user guides and manuals
    - Test scripts and cases that are provided by customer/partner

Upgrade tools

There are various tools you can use in order to assist your Microsoft Dynamics NAV upgrade. The following is the list of tools that we will discuss in this section:

- Dynamics NAV Upgrade toolkits
- Application test toolsets
- PowerShell cmdlets

Dynamics NAV upgrade toolkits

Dynamics NAV upgrade toolkits contain data conversion tools and upgrade guides:

- Data conversion tools
- Upgrade guide

Many VARs and other partner companies have developed their own ways of upgrade tools since they have their own upgrade standards, and most of them also want to keep the versions of objects while upgrading.

For version control strategy, refer to Chapter 6, *Version Control and Code Management*.

Data conversion tools

Microsoft provides you with data conversion tools in the Installation DVD. We also talked briefly about different folders and their functions in the first chapter of this book. Here, we will understand what FOB files inside the data conversion tools mean and how we can use them.

The location of the folder where you can find the FOB file is at **NAV.9.0.44974.NA.DVD** | **UpgradeToolKit** | **Data Conversion Tools**.

Here, **NAV. 9.0.44974.NA.DVD** is my DVD folder:

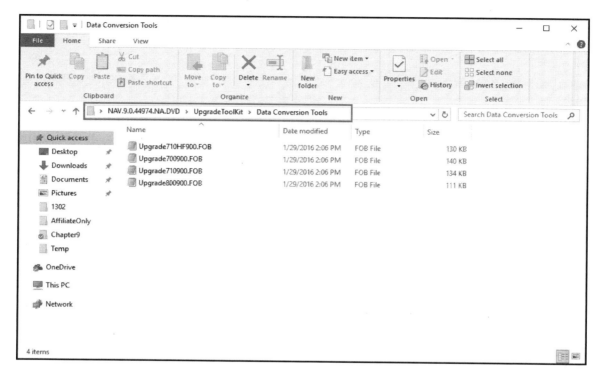

From the preceding screenshot, you can clearly see that there is a certain number assigned to the FOB file, for example, the second file has the name `Upgrade700900.FOB`, which is to signify that this FOB file is to be used when you are upgrading your system from version 7 to version 9, that is, Microsoft Dynamics NAV 2013 to Microsoft Dynamics NAV 2016. Similarly, the `Upgrade710900.FOB` file is for NAV 2013 R2 to NAV 2016 and `Upgrade800900.FOB` is for Dynamics NAV 2015 to Dynamics NAV 2016.

The FOB file

The FOB file contains the objects that can assist you in the upgrade process. Whenever you import these objects into your Dynamics NAV system, it will create a bunch of table objects and a code unit that basically assists all the operations required for data upgrade:

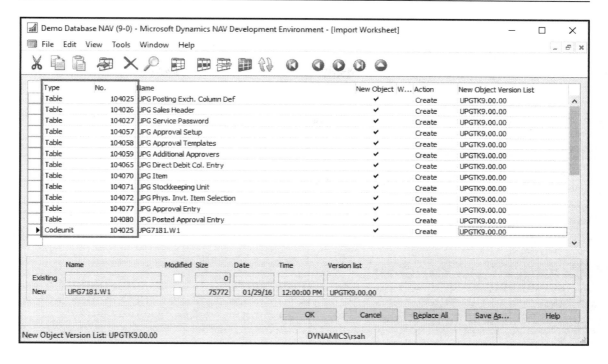

Upgrade guide

Refer to the MSDN link for the upgrade guide: `https://msdn.microsoft.com/en-us/library/dn271649(v=nav.90).aspx`

Application test toolset

Application test tool sets for Microsoft Dynamics NAV have been completely rewritten for Microsoft Dynamics NAV 2016. It is actually a test tool that you can use to execute tests that are normally performed by end users; you can use these tools to automate these tests and you can use the tools to select which test you would like to perform. You can use the application test toolset for the following purposes:

- The test tool used to execute tests
- The test selection feature to filter relevant tests
- The code coverage tool to measure code coverage

- Code coverage means analyzing and monitoring which code is executed, depending on what process you are going to run.

- Contains between 6000 and 9000 of regression tests depending on the country/region version.

In addition to these points, you can use the test toolsets to automate your tests; your test scripts usually work during the end of the upgrade process to determine whether everything is still working as it should be. You can also use the application test tool suite to perform a test and to perform, for example, stress tests and performance tests on the database itself.

PowerShell cmdlets

PowerShell is a very powerful scripting tool that we can use for different administrative operations. In addition to administrative operations, it can be used in a number of development tasks. It can be used to automate the upgrade process, resulting in cutting time and the dedicated resource for the overall upgrade process. It also helps minimize human interface errors:

- Sample scripts for code upgrade:
  - **WindowsPowerShellScripts | ApplicationMergeUtilities**
- Sample scripts for data upgrade:
  - **WindowsPowerShellScripts | Upgrade**
  - HowTo-UpgradeNAVDatabase.ps1
  - Set-PartnerSettings.ps1
  - Example.ps1

You should always refer to the installation DVD, where Microsoft has tried to include all the cmdlets that will be needed. The location of cmdlets is as follows:

NAV.9.0.44974.NA.DVD | WindowsPowerShellScripts | Upgrade:

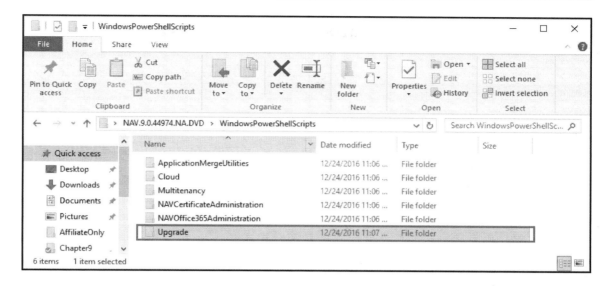

Inside the upgrade folder, you can find these:

- Cmdlets
- HowTo
- Example.ps1
- Set-PartnerSettings.ps1
- Set-PowerShellEnvironment.ps1

The WindowsPowerShellScripts folder also contains ApplicationMergeUtilities, which contains scripts and demo data to assist and help us in, for example, the process of merging and comparing all objects.

The idea here is actually to upgrade our database to Dynamics NAV 2016, but in order to do that, we need to upgrade the application code, and then we need to upgrade the data, and these two processes can require a lot of time. What we can do is that we can automate both of these parts using PowerShell. There are a number of sample scripts that we can use. You can modify these sample scripts to automate these two steps, but you can also use them to test, for example, the steps before we actually apply them in a real production environment. It is very interesting that by automating the upgrade process, you can also time how much each of these steps is going to take, so we can use this information to determine the time gap or the time window you will have available if you have to do, for example, the upgrade of a real-live database, so you can communicate to your customer what the offline time of that process will be.

So when you are upgrading your code, there are a number of sample scripts that you can use. First, we need to compare a number of different versions of our object. We have the original version, we have our custom version, and we have the target version-actually, the virgin version of the object of the database that we'd like to migrate to the end of code compare process.

There are a number of sample scripts available that can help you to automate this process, so let's start with where we can find these scripts. we can find them on the installation DVD of NAV 2016, and you can see a Windows PowerShell script folder with a subfolder application merge utility:

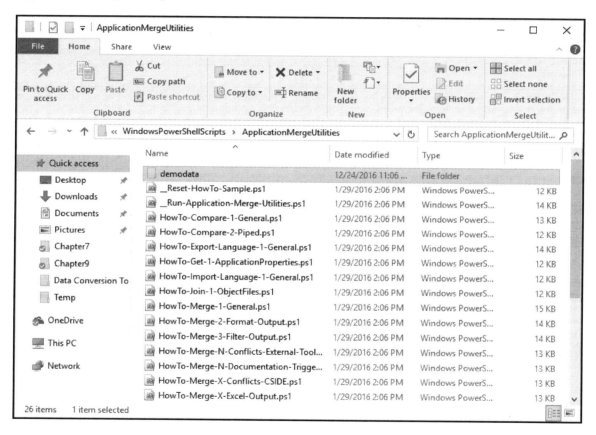

You can find some scripts you need in the the Dynamics NAV development shell, or you can run your PowerShell ISE or your integrating scripted environment. There are a number of application merge scripts that we can follow. You can find them in the merge utilities folder. There are four subfolders in there that you can use as an example to put your objects. We have the original, modified, and target folder:

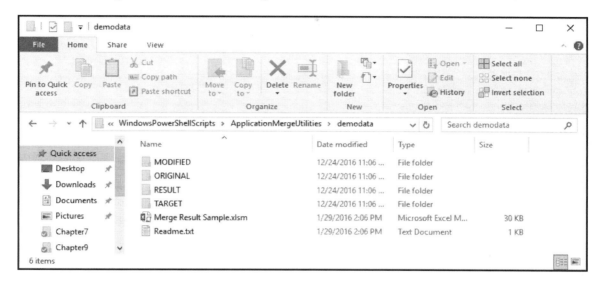

In these folders, you can already find some sample files that have been used by these sample scripts. There's also demonstration data in these folders that you can use, so we can immediately run the script, and it basically starts with `Run Application merge utilities.ps1` script.

Now, you can run that script or you take a look at that script to see how it's working. Basically, if you want to automate the process, the first thing that you need to do is import the Nav Model Tools module. Once it has been imported, you can then, for example, run the how-to-merge N conflicts external tools script. You can take a look at how to start the import, how to run the application merge, and how to reset the sample script, so we can actually re-execute your object merge.

Scripts for code upgrade

Let's take a look at the application at these scripts. In the application, I have my product DVD open, and we have the Windows PowerShell scripts there. As a subfolder, I also have the application merge utilities, and there you will also find a subfolder with some demo data. Below the demo data, you have the modified, the original, the result, and the target folder, which basically contains some objects so you can get started. If you have a look at the application merge utilities, there are some scripts in there. You can open them with your ISE:

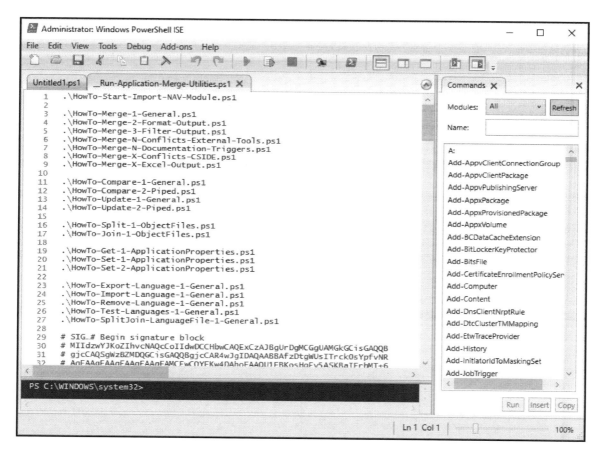

The first script that we will be discussing is the Run application merge utilities script. What you see in there is that from within this script, in the same folder, other scripts are will be executed in a specific order. So first, we need to import the module, and then we are going to take a look at the general merge settings, explore how we need to format and filter our output, learn about what kind of conflicts we can have, what needs to be done with documentation, and so on; we can see some merge scripts, and we can also see scripts that we can use to compare objects and to update and create your delta files. We can also find some examples on how we can split your object file into multiple files and how we can join them back again into one file, and then we can take a look at some scripts that you can use, for example, to work with application properties to import and export languages and test them.

You can see a description of the script and how you can use it, and the script basically writes something as a result, and then it will use the compare Nav application object script, for example, between the original and the modified files, and based on these two, it's going to create the delta file:

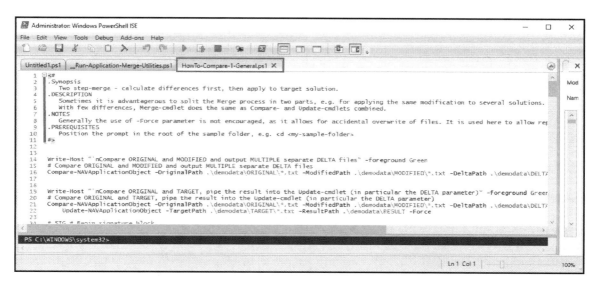

Afterwards, this delta information will be used in the update Nav application object on the target to create the result files. The following script can be used for this purpose:

```
Write-Host "`nCompare ORIGINAL and MODIFIED and output MULTIPLE  separate
DELTA files" –foreground Green# Compare ORIGINAL and MODIFIED and output
MULTIPLE separate DELTA  filesCompare-NAVApplicationObject -OriginalPath
.\demodata\ORIGINAL\*.txt -ModifiedPath .\demodata\MODIFIED\*.txt  -
DeltaPath .\demodata\DELTA -ForceWrite-Host "`nCompare ORIGINAL and TARGET,
pipe the result into  the Update-cmdlet (in particular the DELTA
```

```
parameter)" -foreground  Green# Compare ORIGINAL and TARGET, pipe the
result into the Update- cmdlet (in particular the DELTA parameter)Compare-
NAVApplicationObject -OriginalPath .\demodata\ORIGINAL\*.txt -ModifiedPath
.\demodata\MODIFIED\*.txt  -DeltaPath .\demodata\DELTA -Force -PassThru |
Update-NAVApplicationObject -TargetPath .\demodata\TARGET\*.txt  -
ResultPath .\demodata\RESULT -Force
```

There's another script to merge your conflicts, so if, for example, there are any conflicts that are found, the system uses Notepad and opens them, or you can also modify the script to use your own merge and file compare tools:

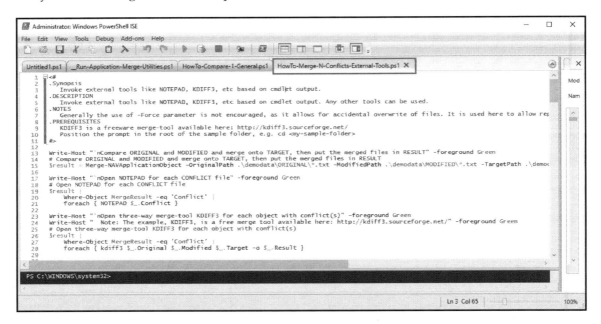

There are lots and lots of scripts in (**NAV.9.0.44974.NA.DVD** |
WindowsPowerShellScripts | **ApplicationMergeUtilities**), which you can use and take a look at and understand. It is pretty straight forward. Most of the commands have a proper description. There is also a reset script that you can use to go back to the original settings. I would advise that you take a look at these scripts that can really help and assist you.

Script for data upgrade

For data upgrade, you have a number of sample scripts available. You can also find them in the product DVD in the `Windows PowerShell scripts` folder, but now we have to go into the `Upgrade` subfolder.

The first thing or script that you will use is how to upgrade an `NAV database` script as shows in screenshot below which can be found on the following link:

NAV.9.0.44974.NA.DVD | WindowsPowerShellScripts | Upgrade | HowTo | HowTo-UpgradeNAVDatabase.ps1

Here as shown in the screenshot, it contains number of scripts with proper documentation:

If you can read the comments section (starting with # symbol) properly, it can basically guides you through the complete process. You need to run these scripts with the correct license file. You can use your partner license. You can also use your customer license file because we are upgrading data; we are not modifying objects. In the partner settings parameters, there are a number of important parameters that you need to set:

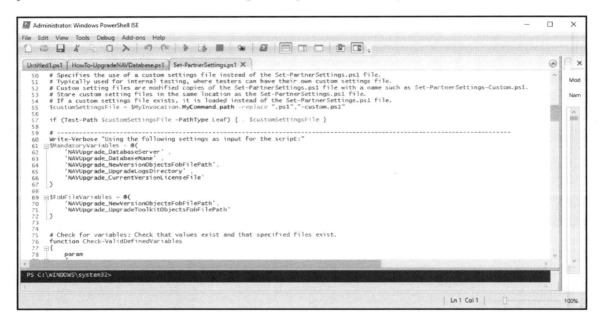

The first thing the code is doing it upgrading the data. Data comes from a database. You need to know what is a database you would like to upgrade.

I would also like to recommend that before you start the process, you might benefit from creating a backup of that database. Then, you also need a folder where your license file is stored. The script is going to use that license file automatically, and of course, you also need the location with the FOB file that contains the upgraded application object that is the result of the previous process.

Now you can take a look at the example script. In the example script, you can find an example of how to perform the upgrade.

The script always starts by the following:

- Loading the partner settings file and importing the required modules to be able to work with these scripts in the ISE
- It then saves the license file depending on the version of NAV that you are running, using, or upgrading
- The next thing in the steps is to use example scripts that will create a backup of your database for which you would like to upgrade the code
- It then converts that database into NAV 2016
- The next process it does is connect a server instance to your converted database and import the license file and synchronize the table schema

This is a very important step in order to keep the database synced to avoid fetal database errors. All these steps are explained by the following diagram:

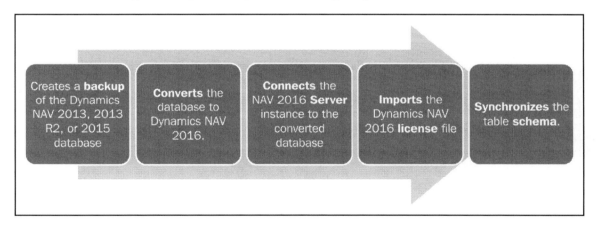

After the sync operation is finished, our application import will happen from our application objects, the file that you actually create, and also the object file or the FOB file that contains the upgrade tool kit, which is actually the code unit or the upgrade code units that you need in order to be able to upgrade the data. After the import of these objects, the table schema is synchronized again so that our SQL Server database is kept in sync with the objects that you have imported. Now, if some data might be lost or needs to be migrated, the upgrade code units do that automatically, so the synchronization process will make sure that the data is saved in the upgrade or archive tables. The following are the steps that will take place:

1. It executes the `Start-NavDataUpgrade` cmdlet, which performs the actual data upgrade.

2. It verifies the preconditions.

3. It also starts the transfer of the data.

Next, the obsolete tables will be deleted (tables that are no longer required), which also includes the upgrade toolkit objects.

Finally, your companies will be initialized in the database, which now contains the upgraded data.

The sample script returns the statistics of the upgrade tasks; if a task failed, you will be able to see it. You can see the error messages and the stack trays to help identify a problem:

```powershell
# Import settings
. (Join-Path $PSScriptRoot 'Set-PartnerSettings.ps1')
. (Join-Path $PSScriptRoot 'Set-PowerShellEnvironment.ps1')

try
{
($UpgradeTasksStatistics = HowTo-UpgradeNAVDatabase `
        -NAVServerInstance $NAVUpgrade_NAVServerInstance `
        -DatabaseServer $NAVUpgrade_DatabaseServer `
        -DatabaseInstance $NAVUpgrade_DatabaseInstance `
        -DatabaseToUpgradeBakFile $NAVUpgrade_DatabaseToUpgradeBakFile `
        -NewVersionObjects $NAVUpgrade_NewVersionObjectsFobFilePath `
        -UpgradeToolkitObjects $NAVUpgrade_UpgradeToolkitObjectsFobFilePath `
        -DatabaseName $NAVUpgrade_DatabaseName `
        -UpgradeLogsDirectory $NAVUpgrade_UpgradeLogsDirectory `
        -RapidStartPackageFile $NAVUpgrade_RapidStartPackageFile `
        -CurrentVersionLicenseFile $NAVUpgrade_CurrentVersionLicenseFile `
        -UpgradeObjectsFilter $NAVUpgrade_UpgradeObjectsFilter) `
        | %{ if($_.Status -eq 'Failed') { Write-Error $_."Error" } }
}
finally
{
    # Uncomment the following line in order to have a better rendered view, in a separate
    # $UpgradeTasksStatistics | Out-GridView
    $UpgradeTasksStatistics | ft
}
```

In that upgrade folder, there is an `example` script and a `partner settings` file. In the example scripts, the system first imports the settings, and then it imports the modules that are actually stored in the second script. All you need to do is remove the to-dos so they become active in the `set-Partnersetting` file. And once you have removed the to-dos, you must then provide the values for these parameters; in this case, it was the name of your server instance, which account you are using, where is your SQL, where is your development environment, and so on. So, you have to provide values for all of these parameters. Once that is done, then the system actually uses that file, and it stores your upgrade statistics there.

There are also a number of how-to scripts that you can use. So, the how to upgrade your NAV database script actually contains a number of parameters. First, you'll find some descriptions about all of the parameters that the script will use. You can also see that the script will execute the complete data upgrade. If you execute the script, you can see that in your Command Prompt, you will get some comments so you can exactly follow what's happening. and you can also see the complete script of all of the different steps and tasks that are performed. You can see in comments, for example, what is a task that's currently being executed. The script also uses the same parameters:

```powershell
# Import settings
. (Join-Path $PSScriptRoot 'Set-PartnerSettings.ps1')
. (Join-Path $PSScriptRoot 'Set-PowerShellEnvironment.ps1')

try
{
($UpgradeTasksStatistics = HowTo-UpgradeNAVDatabase `
        -NAVServerInstance $NAVUpgrade_NAVServerInstance `
        -DatabaseServer $NAVUpgrade_DatabaseServer `
        -DatabaseInstance $NAVUpgrade_DatabaseInstance `
        -DatabaseToUpgradeBakFile $NAVUpgrade_DatabaseToUpgradeBakFile `
        -NewVersionObjects $NAVUpgrade_NewVersionObjectsFobFilePath `
        -UpgradeToolkitObjects $NAVUpgrade_UpgradeToolkitObjectsFobFilePath `
        -DatabaseName $NAVUpgrade_DatabaseName `
        -UpgradeLogsDirectory $NAVUpgrade_UpgradeLogsDirectory `
        -RapidStartPackageFile $NAVUpgrade_RapidStartPackageFile `
        -CurrentVersionLicenseFile $NAVUpgrade_CurrentVersionLicenseFile `
        -UpgradeObjectsFilter $NAVUpgrade_UpgradeObjectsFilter) `
        | %{ if($_.Status -eq 'Failed') { Write-Error $_."Error" } }
}
finally
{
    # Uncomment the following line in order to have a better rendered view, in a separate
    # $UpgradeTasksStatistics | Out-GridView
    $UpgradeTasksStatistics | ft
}
```

This is how upgrading an NAV database script works. I highly recommend that you use that, so first, update your partner settings file with the correct parameters and then just run the how to upgrade script, which performs the upgrade tasks. What you can see is that after running that script, you can see some information that will be generated regarding the statistics of each of these phases.

In addition to these, you also have some different cmdlets that you can use. There is a miscellaneous folder, where you can find some smaller scripts that explain, for example, how can you import my modules, how can you get temp file parts, and so on. There are some other NAV scripts that you can use, so can you import a license file, for example, for how can you invoke rapid start package, and there are also some SQL scripts available there. You have the following stuff that is noteworthy:

- Cmdlets
- How-to scripts
- Partner settings file
- Example script

Here, you have all of the information available that you need in order to be able to automate our upgrade process. What I would recommend you to do is take a copy of this folder. You can copy the complete `Windows PowerShell scripts` folder or only the upgrade folder to a local drive, and there, you can change the settings and execute the scripts. You can use your ISE to do that. Remember, if you run your ISE, run it as an administrator.

Summary

In this chapter, we learned about the modern upgrade process. We discussed the most optimal and efficient ways of upgrading a process that involved automating the processes, analyzing the time and effort, and understanding the core concept behind the upgrade project. We also tried to understand the difference between the upgrade process if carried out on different versions and how that might affect the project duration. We discussed the problems that might arise while working on a project and how to tackle them with the standard approach.

In the next chapter, we will discuss the interfacing possibilities for the Dynamics NAV system with other applications. This chapter will provide a technical depth of the process, keeping the functional aspect at the edge, allowing the consultants understand the why and how factors of the integration. The chapter is intended for techno-functional consultants, developers, and administrators.

10
Interfacing NAV with Other Applications

In the previous chapter, we studied Microsoft Upgrade and migration methodologies. We understood how the best practices can be implemented into the project upgrade processes. We also explored how the use of different toolkits can be beneficial in the process of Microsoft Dynamics NAV system's upgrade.

In this chapter, we are going to understand the different interfacing services provided by Microsoft Dynamics NAV. We will also be looking at how selecting a proper web service can make life easier for different API terminals. We are going to learn about the architecture of the web service in the Microsoft Dynamics NAV system.

At the end of this chapter, you should be able to use web services such as SOAP and ODATA to harvest the data outside the Dynamics NAV system through an external programming interface. You also should be able to select the right web service for the given task, allowing the best performance for the integration system.

This chapter will cover the following topics:

- Architecture and the concept of web services
- Working with web services in NAV
- SOAP and ODATA web services

Web services

Web services are application components that are basically used to publish business logic. They allow us to communicate using well-documented and open protocols, so we can use web services to, for example, communicate with other applications, and we can also use them to reuse or publish our business logic.

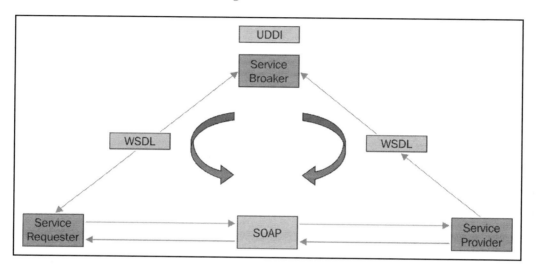

In the preceding diagram, **UDDI (Universal Description, Discovery, and Integration)** defines which system is which, respective to its specific data. First, the system to be contacted is discovered, and then contact is established using the SOAP web service.

The service provider system validates the request by referring to the **WSDL (Web Services Description Language)** file, processing the request, and sending the data using the SOAP protocol.

Web services are self-contained and self-describing, which means that, if you publish your business logic via a web service, it happens via some specific protocols that describe exactly how external components or applications can make use of our web services. Web services can be discovered via UDDI, or the universal discovery language for our web services. We create some documents that are automatically created, and they also describe how we can make use of our web services, for example, the methods and properties that our web services are exposing. Web services can then be used by other applications. For example, in our Microsoft Dynamics NAV application and development environment, we have a lot of business logic, and via web services we can publish this business logic so that it can be used by other applications.

There is also the other way around; there might be some business logic or some other applications out there in the cloud that contain very interesting business logic that you would like to reuse or make use of inside our development environment. We will discuss this in the later part of this chapter.

 HTTP and XML are the basis for web services, so you can publish them via the Web. If you would like to exchange information, we can also do that by exchanging it in an XML format or by making use of XML documents.

Web service as a reusable unit

Web services can also be seen as reusable application components, which means that we can offer the Dynamics NAV business logic and valuable data to the outside world. We can also consume the external business logic into the Dynamics NAV system.

 Examples of external business logic that we can implement into the Dynamics NAV system can be currency conversion, weather reports, language translation services, price calculations, and so on.

If we want to connect to the existing software outside the Dynamics NAV system, then the web service of Dynamics NAV can help us solve the interoperability problem by giving applications a new way and protocol to link their data. This concept can be extremely important when you want to connect other value-added products to the NAV system.

Web services in Microsoft Dynamics NAV

Let's take a look at the web services architecture in Dynamics NAV. Microsoft Dynamcis NAV 2016 uses two types of web service: SOAP web services and OData web services:

	ODATA	SOAP
Page	Yes	Yes
Query	Yes	No
Codeunit	No	Yes

The main difference between the two in Microsoft Dynamics NAV is that, with SOAP web services, you can publish and reuse business logic, and with OData web services, you can change data in external applications.

 Since the query objects read information from our database, the OData web services for queries will allow us to read information. They will be read-only web services.

The architecture of web services

The architecture of web services in Dynamics NAV is hard to understand since most of the unit of the architecture is either automated or hidden. In this section, we are going to understand some general architectural concepts of web services in the Dynamics NAV system in particular. We will discuss the SAOP and ODATA architecture in the next section.

The transaction and state of web services can be understood with the following key points:

- No server state is preserved between the calls
- No variables or single instance codeunits are remembered
- No session is maintained
- Each separate web service call is a single and independent transaction

In Microsoft Dynamics NAV, none of the service states are preserved, which explains the nature and relationship between two web service calls. Each web service call is distinct and the systems do not bother about keeping the state. This makes the web service run faster, and less memory is required, which also makes it implement easily. This also means that no variables or single instance codeunits are remembered by the system. There's no session that will be maintained, which means that each separate web service call that is performed is always a single independent transaction.

Security is a very important aspect when we are interacting with an external system using web services. The web service process must start with authentication. We can also implement different levels of authentication for different tiers:

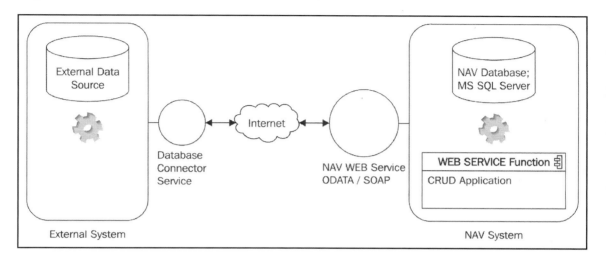

 For more information on security, refer to `Chapter 8`, *Security in Dynamics NAV 2016*.

Furthermore, we can make use of SSL, or secure socket layer, to encrypt the information that we exchange. It is really important to make the exchange of data and information secure and reliable, especially if you are exchanging information with third-party systems.

Publishing a web service

Publishing a web service in Dynamics NAV is really easy. You just need to figure out the object that you are want to link to the web service and publish it. These are the steps you can follow to publish the objects:

1. Figure out the objects that you want to publish. Remember that Page objects can be used in both SOAP and ODATA web services, Query can be used only in ODATA, whereas codeunits can be used with SOAP.

2. From the Role Tailored Client environment of the Dynamics NAV, search for web services or navigate to **Departments | Administration | IT Administrations | Services | Web Services**:

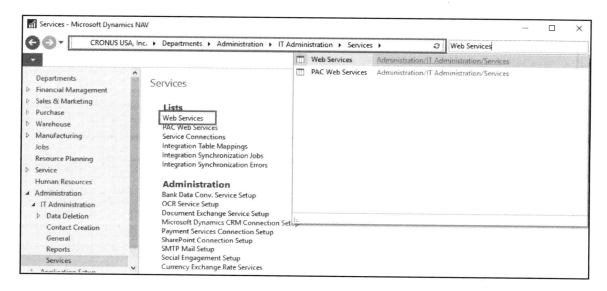

3. Fill in **Object ID** and enter **Service Name**:

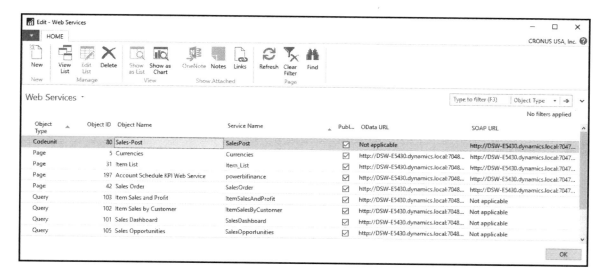

4. Click on the **Publish Boolean** button and you will see the **Relevant Service** link.

Now you can use Internet Explorer to view XML information contained in that link:

```xml
<?xml version="1.0"?>
- <definitions xmlns:tns="urn:microsoft-dynamics-schemas/page/itemlist"
  xmlns="http://schemas.xmlsoap.org/wsdl/" targetNamespace="urn:microsoft-dynamics-
  schemas/page/itemlist">
  - <types>
    - <xsd:schema targetNamespace="urn:microsoft-dynamics-schemas/page/itemlist"
      xmlns:xsd="http://www.w3.org/2001/XMLSchema" elementFormDefault="qualified">
      - <xsd:simpleType name="Costing_Method">
        - <xsd:restriction base="xsd:string">
          <xsd:enumeration value="FIFO"/>
          <xsd:enumeration value="LIFO"/>
          <xsd:enumeration value="Specific"/>
          <xsd:enumeration value="Average"/>
          <xsd:enumeration value="Standard"/>
        </xsd:restriction>
      </xsd:simpleType>
      - <xsd:simpleType name="Price_Profit_Calculation">
        - <xsd:restriction base="xsd:string">
          <xsd:enumeration value="Profit_x003D_Price_Cost"/>
          <xsd:enumeration value="Price_x003D_Cost_x002B_Profit"/>
          <xsd:enumeration value="No_Relationship"/>
        </xsd:restriction>
      </xsd:simpleType>
      - <xsd:simpleType name="Replenishment_System">
```

We can manage all of this from within the application. Web services will be published automatically.

SOAP web services

To display all published SOAP web services, you can use a URI of the following type:

`http://://WS//services`

To view the schema for a particular service, use a URI of the following type:

`http://://WS//Page/`

System services are services that are published automatically by the system. We don't have to do this manually. We can make use of the system service to get a list of all the companies that are contained in our database. The use of system services can make the overall process dynamic.

If you do not specify a company name in the URI, then the system takes the Default company by default.

Basic page operations

The operations that we can perform actually match the actions a user can also perform when they run the page inside the application. We have the same page-and table-based business logic, which also gets executed and published.

 For example, if you consume a customer list or a customer page as a SOAP web service, then when you try to change information, the system will execute all of the triggers you have defined in the `Customer` table, such as `OnValidate`, `OnInsert`, `OnModify`, and so on.

Standard set of page operations

You can use a standard set of functions, as pointed here. You cannot use the function that refers to the page that is pointing to any virtual table or a table where insert and delete operations are not allowed, and those type of functions are not provided. You can also see the available functions in the XML link, which can be seen by entering the SOAP URI in the browser.

The `Create` function can be used for creating a single record:

```
void Create(ref Entity entity)
```

The `CreateMultiple` function can be used for creating a set of records:

```
void CreateMultiple(ref Entity[] entity)
```

The `Delete` function can be used to delete a single record:

```
bool Delete(string key)
```

The `Delete_<part>` function is used to delete a subpage of the current page:

```
bool Delete_<part>(string key)
```

The `GetRecIdFromKey` function is used to convert a key, which is always part of the page result, to a record ID:

```
string GetRecIdFromKey(string key)
```

The `IsUpdated` function is used to check whether an object has been updated since the key was obtained:

```
bool IsUpdated(string key)
```

The `Read` function is used to read a single record:

```
Entity Read(string no)
```

The `ReadbyRecId` function is used to read the record that is identified by `RedId`:

```
Entity ReadByRecId(string formattedRedId)
```

The `ReadMultiple` function is used to read a filtered set of records, paged:

```
Entity[] ReadMultiple(Entity_Filter[] filterArray, string  bookmarkKey, int
setSize)
```

The `Update` function is used to update a single record:

```
Void Update(ref Entity entity)
```

The `UpdateMultiple` function is used to update a set of records:

```
Void UpdateMultiple(ref Entity[] entity)
```

Basic codeunit operations

When you publish codeunits as web services, then you get a different set of functions. Basically, when you expose a codeunit as a web service, all of the functions that have been defined in our codeunits get exposed as operations. You can use these functions to run business logic that is contained in C/AL codes, so you can expose this business logic to the outside world.

For example, you can create a codeunit that allows you to create new sales orders, post a sales order, or release a sales order, and then publish it to the web service, and by acceding it, you can perform the same logic from outside the system, harvesting the published codeunit.

Hiding the function from being published

In order to hide your function from being published, all you need to do is define it as a local function. This will prohibit direct access to this function even if the codeunit containing it is published.

ODATA web services

We can make use of these OData web services to link the Dynamics NAV data to any external application, such as Microsoft Excel. For this example, I am going to select the ODATA service published for the Item list in our web service page of RTC:

1. Open Microsoft Excel, go to the **Data** tab, select the **From Other Sources** option, and select **From OData Data Feed**:

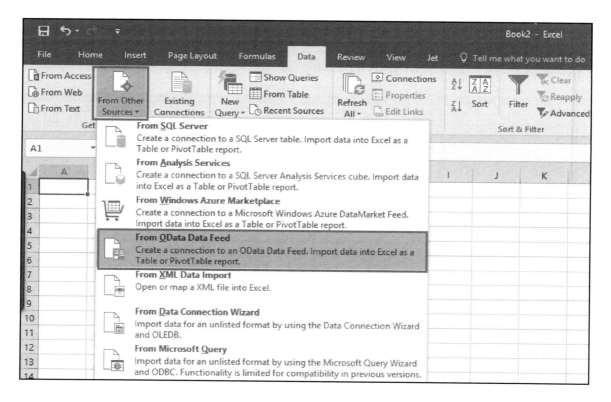

2. You will be prompted with a window called **Data Connection Wizard**, where you need to paste the ODATA link that you copied from the web service page of RTC. Always make sure the service is published in the Dynamics NAV.

Then, you will get the option to select the dataset; just select it and then finally close the wizard by clicking the **Finish** button:

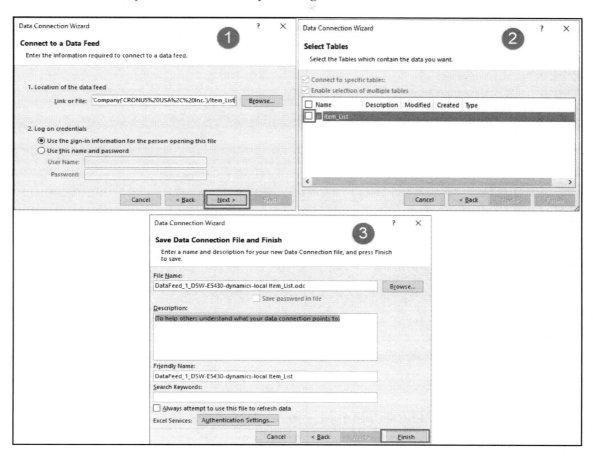

3. After closing the wizard, you will be prompted with the template in which you want to show the data; you can simply select the table view and then select the tabular form of the report containing the list of all items directly fetched from the Dynamics NAV system:

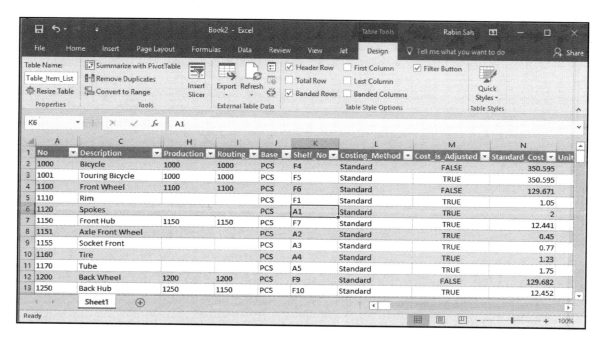

 You might be asked for authentication in this process; just make sure you enter the Windows authentication user ID and password to complete the process.

Combining multiple datasets

It is also possible to combine multiple datasets using the ODATA web service. You just need to link it again, and it will open on a different sheet. Follow the relationship operation to link it. For this you can carry out the operation all over again for the second data item.

Using ODATA for APIs

Like SOAP web services, ODATA web services can be used to connect Dynamics NAV to external APIs. It can sometimes perform better when you just need to perform the data passing from and to the external system. Unlike the SOAP web service, it does not provide the business logic access to the external system.

When you expose an editable page to an external API using the ODATA web service, it is possible to modify the data using that page. Basic operations that can be used with ODATA services are as follows:

Function	Operation	Triggers
POST	Creates a new entity	OnNewRecord and OnInsert
PUT and MERGE	Modifies the specified existing entity	OnModify
DELETE	Deletes the specified existing entity	OnDelete

Always make sure you have relevant permission before accessing the ODATA web service because all calls will fail if you do not have permission.

Handling UI interaction for web services

Whenever you are using web services, especially SOAP web services, you need to be careful with user interface interaction because it might cause your web service to throw an exception at runtime if we are going to consume it. We must ensure the following point when using UI interaction for web services:

- Exceptions and dialog boxes must be handled carefully
- Exceptions must be handled to prevent the system from ending the web service client execution

So, any exceptions and dialog boxes that your web services display must be handled correctly. You need to handle these exceptions; otherwise, the client that is making use of our web services might crash or have an exception or an error that's displayed.

For example, if you are running or executing a dialogue datatype to show a progress bar to a user in the codeunits that you have published as a SOAP web service, this type of datatype will cause an exception callback from not allowing to happen when an external application makes use of our web service.

> Basically, the only function that is not going to throw an exception or an error is the message function.

Functions not to use

The functions or keywords you should not use if you are going to publish business logic as a web service are as follows:

- The `Page.run` or `Runmodal` functions
- Activate
- Running a report
- The hyperlink function
- Uploading or downloading a file, and so on

Using external web services in NAV

It is also possible to use an external web service in the NAV. Microsoft provided this functionality using the inbuilt codeunit **1290: SOAP Web Service Request Mgt.**. Here, you can write your own codeunits and call codeunit 1290 to send a request and get a response.

> I would recommend that you take a look at `https://community.dynamics.com/nav/b/moxie4nav/archive/2015/09/10/call-external-web-service-using-new-cu-1290`, which is an interesting way to harvest this functionality.

DotNet interoperability

Microsoft Dynamics NAV 2016 has added the interoperability feature with the DotNet Programming language. Support for DotNet was first introduced in the previous version of NAV in exchange for automation control. Now in Dynamics NAV 2016, it is possible to use a wider range of .NET objects directly in C/AL programming by creating the .NET type variable, as shown in the following screenshot:

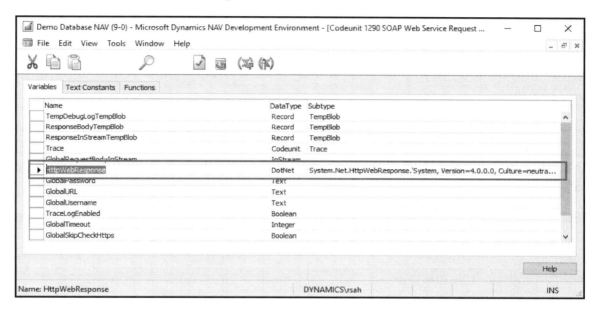

In the preceding screenshot, you can see that, in codeunit 1290, there is a variable of type **DotNet** with **System.Net.HttpWebResponse.'System, Version=4.0.0.0, Culture=neutral, PublicKeyToken=b77a5c561934e089'** as **Subtype**, which cannot be directly implemented in C/AL code.

The DotNet objects can be implemented on both the server side and the client side. There are limitations to using .NET in Microsoft Dynamics NAV 2016, which are typically solved by creating **Wrapper DLL** objects in C#. The Excel interface is also an example of this.

I would recommend that you take a look at www.vjeko.com to start learning about .NET in C/AL.

Open Database Connectivity

Open Database Connectivity (ODBC) allows all types of databases to exchange data in a unified way. ADO is the successor of ODBC.

ADO and ODBC for Microsoft Dynamics NAV 2016 allow both reading and writing in the application database as well as reading and writing to other databases. In the following figure, you can see that using open data connectivity protocol, the system can access different kinds of database and thus it can be useful while performing the data exchange or integrating some section of the solution with other system:

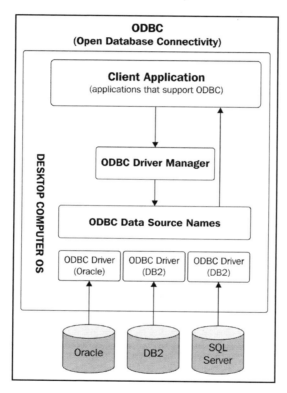

Summary

In this chapter, we understood the most important concept of integration with external systems. An interface is like a trade route through which the outside world can help your system grow. The best software has a most secure and powerful integration system so that it can be extended as per the requirement. Here, we learned about the concepts that can be used in Microsoft Dynamics NAV to make it an even better and stronger solution.

In the next chapter, we will discuss the extension possibility of the Microsoft Dynamics NAV system with other Microsoft products. Many other tools that are developed parallel to Dynamics NAV that can be often used to fill the gaps, which allows the user to get the best experience. We are going to take a good look at all of these features and possibilities in the next chapter.

11
Extending Dynamics NAV 2016

In the previous chapter, we looked at different extension possibilities in the Dynamics NAV system. We also visualized how this functionality fortified the dynamism of the Dynamics NAV product solution. We perceived the knowledge of ODATA and the SOAP web service and also understood their architecture and functions that can be used to harvest the system in and out.

In this chapter, we will be circumscribing our conversation to the integration of the Dynamics NAV system with other Microsoft and related technologies. Actually, most of the related Microsoft technologies have been made to assist the operations of the Microsoft Dynamics NAV system. They have been made outside the Dynamics NAV in order to utilize the power of other languages and technologies that can be integrated into NAV to provide out-of-the-box functionalities and solve the problem of the end user. It has been proved over hundreds of NAV implementations that-integrating the Dynamics NAV system with other Microsoft solutions such as the Office package, reporting tools, and some NAV-based extensions-has reduced the cost and time of the overall implementation. We will be discussing all of these concepts in this chapter.

By the end of this chapter, you should be able to integrate your Dynamics NAV system with PowerBI, the Jet Express reporting tool, and also understand how to integrate your NAV extension with your current NAV system.

This chapter will cover the following topics:

- Integrating with PowerBI and its background
- Implementing Jet Express
- Working with NAV Extension

Integration with Power BI

Power BI is a business analytical tool that can take your reports and dashboards to the next level. It not only gives a better angle to play with your data, but it can also present the result in the way you can better understand it. It's a free tool suite that you can use to create very rich visualizations, but you can also do very deep analysis of your data with it. You can have the power of visualization and analysis at your fingertips using PowerBI:

You can easily download the desktop application from https://powerbi.microsoft.com/, or you can also use the online application to harvest the awesome functionality of PowerBI.

You can perform the following steps to connect the Microsoft Dynamics NAV with Power BI and totally play with your Dynamics NAV data in PowerBI:

1. Load the desktop application of PowerBI or sign in to `https://powerbi.microso` `ft.com`:

2. You will get a page where you will be able to connect to the data or services and other integrations. I would highly recommend that you try other integration features, such as Excel, CSV files, and Azure SQL connections. It is an awesome tool that can be linked to almost all your applications and can provide you with a great interface to play around with.

3. If you are using a PowerBI Desktop app, then click on the **Get Data** icon in the top bar and then click on **OData Feed**:

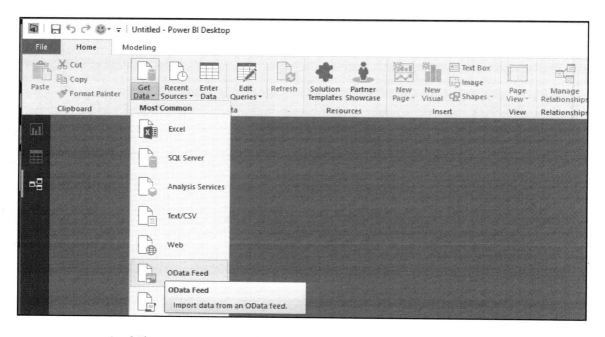

And if you are using web login, then click on the **Get** button in the **Services** box:

For the desktop app, you just need to provide the ODATA link that you can copy from the **Web Services** page of Microsoft Dynamics NAV RTC:

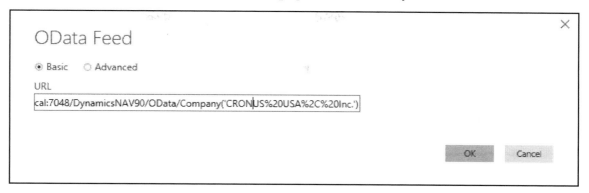

 Always make sure the ODATA service is enabled in the Microsoft Dynamics NAV Server and the service is published in the Web Services page of RTC.

4. After you connect to the OData service, you will be able to design different reports and eventually set up up a dashboard. You have now connected to the Microsoft Dynamics NAV.

Power BI is a suite of business analytical tools that can be used to analyze data and share insights. It can also be used to monitor the business and get answers quickly. It has been released with a rich dashboard and is available on every device (laptop, phone, and tablet).

Using PowerBI, you can transform and clean your data quite easily from data sources such as Microsoft Dynamics NAV, which you know can be quite messy and hard to analyze from time to time. It can also allow you to perform a complete analytical lifecycle. Another very interesting feature of PowerBI is that you just need to design it once, and you will be able to view it anywhere:

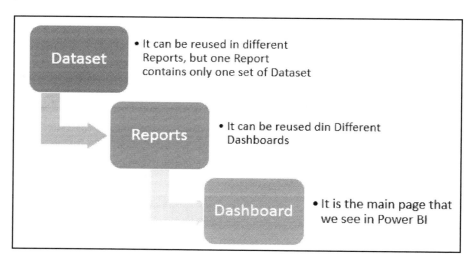

Power BI consists of the main section, which is a dashboard. In order to create a dashboard, you first need to create several reports. The combination of the different reports will make up the dashboards. Now, to be able to create a report, you require a dataset. And the dataset is the set of data, the information that comes from our data source, Microsoft Dynamics NAV, that will feed your report; the report is then used to build the dashboards.

PowerBI is also built so that you can reuse the same datasets in multiple reports, and you can also reuse reports in two different dashboards. So, a dataset is the information that you will use as a basis for your reports.

Understanding datasets

A dataset is something that you import or connect to. It's the data that you will use in your reports. PowerBI allows us to use all sorts of data sets and bring them all together in one place, which means that not only can you use the data from Dynamics NAV, you can use it from multiple companies in Dynamics NAV or multiple databases, or you can also combine your ERP Dynamics NAV data with the data from other systems:

One dataset in PowerBI can be used over and over. It can be used in many different reports. And it can be used in different dashboards.

Understanding reports

Reports are basically visuals of the dataset that is imported from a data source such as Microsoft Dynamics NAV. The visuals can be in the form of charts and graphs, such as line charts, pie charts, tree maps, and many more. All of the visualizations in a report come from a single dataset:

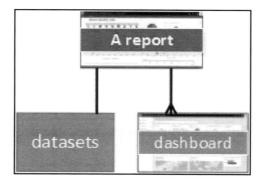

One report can have just one dataset, and one report can be used in different dashboards.

 For more information on how to work around with PowerBI, you can always use the online resource that can be found at
https://powerbi.microsoft.com/en-us/documentation.

Integration with Jet Express

Jet Express is a report building solution that can be used alongside Microsoft Dynamics NAV for some specific report design solutions. Sometimes, it is also known as a complete business intelligence Excel-based Dynamics NAV reporting tool. There are some instances where designing reports using a Dynamics NAV system might not be a feasible solution. It's predefined or preconfigured in Dynamics NAV. It is very easy to link, and you can use it to create reports in Excel. Let's perform the following steps to configure the Jet Express with the Dynamics NAV system:

1. Go to `https://www.jetreports.com/` and download Jet Express for Excel with the Dynamics NAV software:

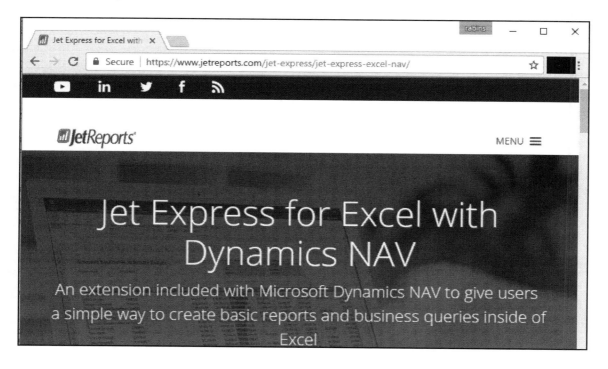

2. After you download the product, just follow the installation instruction as with any other software on Windows:

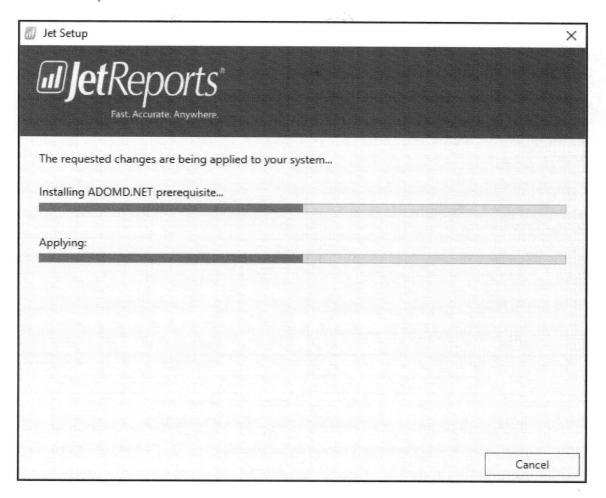

 If you are using the previous version, then in the last step, do not forget to select the option to put the Jet add-ons for Excel. It is not required for the newer version.

Now you can see a new tab in your Excel named **Jet**; in this tab's ribbon bar, you can find many functionalities that you can use in the process of generating Jet reports. The most useful features that we are going to use are **Table Builder**, **Application Setting**, **Data Source Setting**, and **Refresh**:

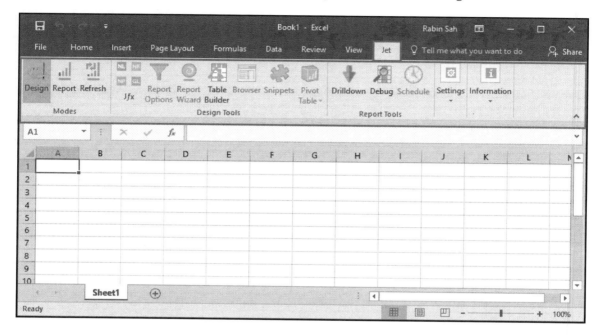

3. Download the FOB file from the Jet report website and import it into the Dynamics NAV system:

	Type	No.	Name	New Object	New Obj...	Existing ...	W..
▶	Table	14125600	Jet Cancellation				
	Codeunit	14125500	Jet Data Source				
	Codeunit	14125501	Jet Query Iterator				
	Codeunit	14125502	Jet Link Filter Iterator				
	Codeunit	14125503	Jet Safe Action				
	Codeunit	14125504	Jet Link Field				

This FOB can be found under **Quick Start Training Section: Jet Report Business Object**.

4. Publish the Jet web service so that the web service can be used to link to the Excel sheet containing the Jet service:

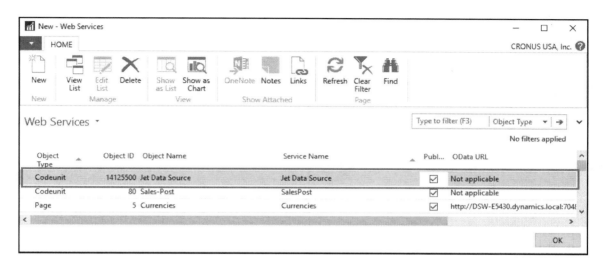

Configuring the data source from Excel

You can continue following the steps, which will now guide you through the configurations of data source in Excel:

1. Open the Excel application and then click on the **Jet** tab. The, click on the **Data Source Settings** button:

Fill in the options properly. The setting should be tested by the **Test Connection** icon.

2. After the settings are successful, move forward to create a report.
3. Click on the **Table Builder** icon in the **Jet** ribbon bar:

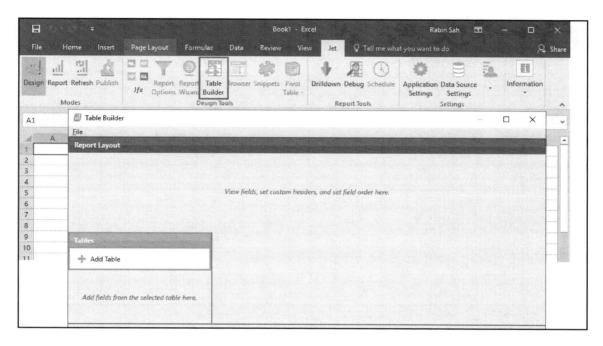

4. From the **Add Table** option, add as many tables as you want to add to this report. You just need to click on the icon, and you will get options to select the tables. You can also select the relevant columns from a specific table:

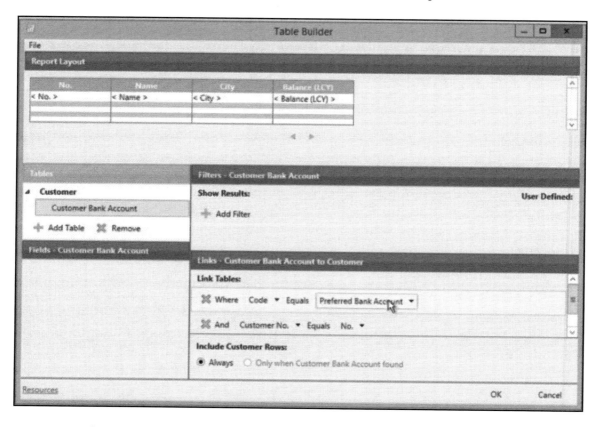

5. After you are done with setting fields and relationships (if you choose to select multiple tables), click on the **OK** button to close the **Table Builder** window.

This will result in the generation of the structure of the report you just configured in the previous window. Now you just need to click on the **Refresh** button, and you will get a table view of your report, as show in the following screenshot:

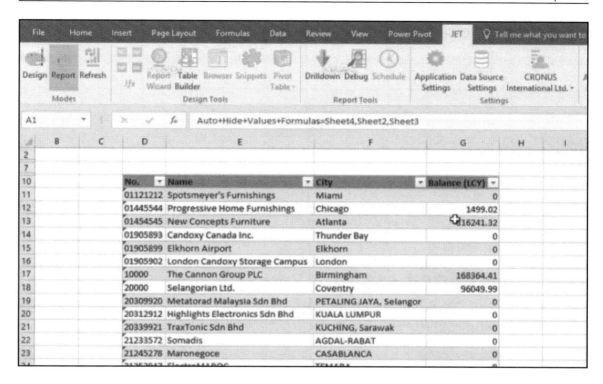

Even after generation, you will be able to modify the relationship or add or remove the fields as per your need. It is a really flexible add-on that gives you the power to generate some really dynamic reports.

Here are some of the benefits of Jet Express:

- It provides the ability to work in Microsoft Excel's friendly and familiar environment, and it provides the safety feature of Dynamics NAV to protect your valuable data.
- You can simply click on the **Drilldown** button, and Jet will open Dynamics NAV and show you the data behind the number to view the summary number.
- Jet allows you to automatically send reports by E-mail, with a summary of the key data shown in the E-mail subject or body.

NAV extensions

In this section, we will discuss the most basic way to develop NAV extensions. For this, we are going to use the cmdlets to achieve our goal of creating an NAV extension. Let's take a look at some of the prerequisites.

Prerequisites

I will not get into details on the creation of an isolated environment for working on NAV extensions. For more information on how to build your own development environment to start developing Microsoft Dynamics NAV extensions, refer to
`https://msdn.microsoft.com/en-us/library/mt574395(v=nav.90).aspx`.

Customization in Dynamics NAV

For the purpose of this example, we are going to introduce some changes to the Development Environment in Microsoft Dynamics NAV:

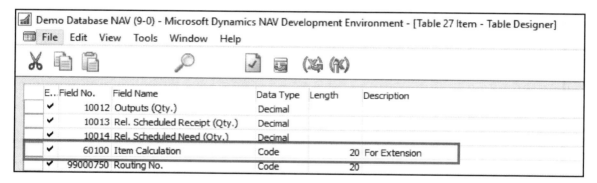

I have created a menu in the item list that will basically calculate some things in the item table, which will then be shown on the item list page. For the sake of simplicity, I am not going to explain what this function is actually going to do. You can assume any functionality, and we are trying to implement it as the extension here:

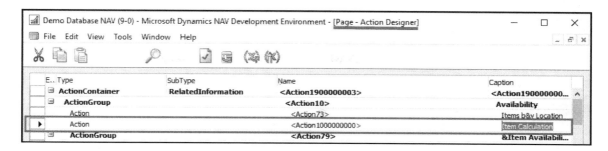

 Just keep in mind that I am playing with my own isolated development environment, which will be connected to the main server using the deltas.

In the following screenshot, you can clearly see that I am using a new a new codeunit called **Item Calculation codeunit** and creating a new **Table Item Calculation** codeunit. A function will be called from the **Item List** page, and it will generate values in the **Item** table:

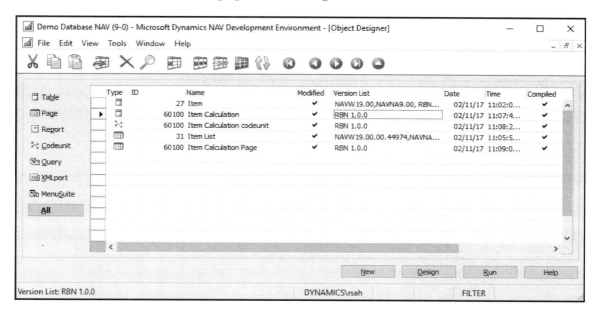

 Keep in mind that, when you are done with the extension, you will see that the object in the main production environment will not copy all these modified objects as it is, but it will have a linked extension that performs the same purpose here. It helps keep the main live system clean while achieving new functionalities.

It is recommended that you keep the versioning of one extension unique. This will allow you to identity the object that reflects the specific extension and easily modify the extension if needed.

Creating the NAVX file

Now the next major step, after you have modified objects and worked around with the changes in the isolated Dynamics NAV environment, is creating the NAVX file. To make it simple, we are going to follow the PowerShell cmdlets. Even in cmdlets, you can see the pattern in which the process flows:

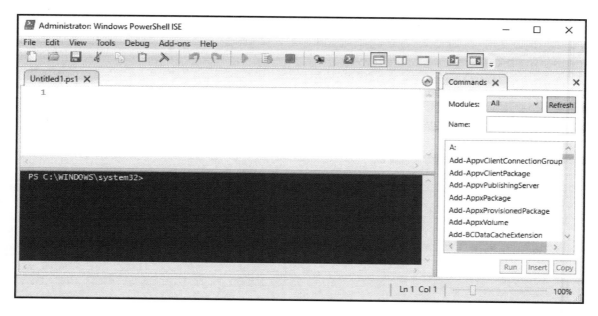

It is recommended that you run the Windows PowerShell ISE in the administrative mode before you actually start running cmdlets.

The following are the basic steps that we use in order to create the NAVX file. Follow the step flow; that is, do not try to run the command in a different order. Always follow the steps:

1. **Load modules**: In this cmdlet, we are going to load different modules that will help us access different admin and model tools. Just type this cmdlet and press *F8* or click on the **Run Selection** button:

```
#Load Modules
Import-Module 'C:\Program File\Microsoft Dynamics NAV
   \90\Service\NavAdminTool.ps1'
Import-Module "${env:ProgramFiles(x86)}\Microsoft Dynamics
NAV\90\RoleTailored Client\
   Microsoft.Dynamics.Nav.Model.Tools.ps1"
Import-Module 'C:\Program files (x86)\Microsoft Dynamics
   NAV\90\RoleTailored Client\
   Microsoft.Dynamics.Nav.Model.Tools.ps1'
```

If you have many other types of code, then do not forget to select only the code that you are going to run.

2. **Create a working file**: In this step, we are going to create a working folder where we can place all our files and folders for this purpose. You can also choose any other drive; here, I have selected the C drive as the root:

```
#Create workingfolder
if(!(Test-Path 'C:\WorkingFolder\ItemCalculation'))
   {New-Item -ItemType directory
   'C:\WorkingFolder\ItemCalculation\}
```

3. **Export original files**: Generally, it is recommended that you keep the original file as a backup. In this command, we are going to export the original file and keep it as Original.txt in the folder we created in Step 2:

```
#Export Original
Export-NAVApplicationObject
-DatabaseName 'ItemCalculation_ORIG'
-DatabaseServer '.\NAVDEMO'
-ExportTxtSkipUnlicensed
-Path 'C:\WorkingFolder\ItemCalculation\Original.txt'
-Verbose
```

4. **Export modified files**: We are now going to export the modified file. The modified file means the file that we modified in customization in the Dynamics NAV section:

```
#Export Modified
Export-NAVApplicationObject
-DatabaseName 'ItemCalculation_DEV'
-DatabaseServer '.\NAVDEMO'
-ExportTxtSkipUnlicensed
-Path 'C:\WorkingFolder\ItemCalculation\Modification.txt'
-Force
-Verbose
```

5. **Create deltas**: Creating deltas is very important since it provides a link between the original and modified files. Also, make sure that, in the previous processes, the text files are created successfully. For this purpose, you can check the folder that you created in Step 2:

```
#Create deltas
if(!(Test-path 'C:\WorkingFolder\ItemCalculation\Deltas')){
   New-Item -ItemType directory -Path
   'C:\WorkingFolder\ItemCalculation\Deltas'
}
Compare-NAVApplicationObject
-OriginalPath
   'C:\WorkingFolder\ItemCalculation\Original.txt'-Modification
   'C:\WorkingFolder\ItemCalculation\Modified.txt'
-DeltaPath 'C:\Workingfolder\ItemCalculation\Deltas'
-Force
-Verbose
```

6. **Create a manifest**: A manifest is a file that contains the metadata of processes that you carried out in previous steps that are part of a set or a coherent unit; here, the coherent unit is the extension file:

```
#Create Manifest
if (!(Test-Path
   'C:\WorkingFolder\ItemCalculation\Manifest.xml))
{
   $Manifest - New-NAVAppManifest
   -Name 'ItemCladdification'
   -Publisher 'Cloud Ready Softare GmgH'
   -Description 'Item Calculation'
   -Version '1.0.0.0'
}
```

This screenshot shows how different files are created while performing the previous operations:

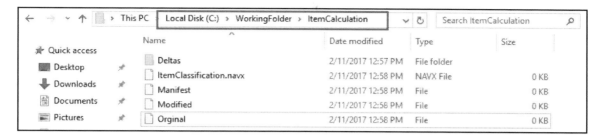

The final step is to create a package.

7. **Create a package**: The final step in this section is to create a package file. It uses the delta we created in Step 5. It also utilizes the metadata contained in the manifest file:

```
#Create Package
New-NAVAppPackage
  -Path 'C:\WorkingFolder\ItemCalculation.navx'
  -Manifest (Get-NAVAppManifest -Path
    'C:\WorkingFolder\ItemCalculation\Manifest.xml')
  -SourcePath 'C:\Workingfolder\ItemCalculation\Deltas'
  -Verbose
  -Force
Start 'C:\WorkingFolder\ItemCalculation'
```

Publishing and testing the extension

After we have successfully created the extension package, it is the time to first publish and then test the extension. This can be achieved in the following three steps.

1. **Publish NAVX**: Here, we are going to publish the NAVX file, and it can be done with the help of the same PowerShell application:

```
#Publish The NAVX
Publish-NAVApp
  -Path
    'C:\WorkingFolder\ItemCalculation\ItemCalculation.navx'
  -ServerInstance 'ItemCalculation_TEST'
  -Verbose
```

2. **Install the extension to the default tenant**: After the NAVX file is published, we install the extension into the default tenant. Make sure you understand the concept of a tenant properly and that you identify your default tenant:

```
#Install the Extension to the default tenant
Get-NAVAppInfo -ServerInstance 'ItemCalculation_TEST' -Name
'ItemCalculation'
   Install-NAVApp
   -ServerInstance 'ItemCalculation_TEST'
```

3. **Start Windows RTC to perform a test**: The final step in the extension test is to open the Windows RTC and go to the **Item List** page. Here, you should see a field called **Item Calculation** and a menu called **Item Calculation** in the ribbon bar:

```
#Start Windows Client to test the Extension
start 'DynamicsNAV://localhost:7046/ItemCalculation_TEST/CRONUS
   USA, Inc./?tenant=default'
```

You can see the final result in the following screenshot:

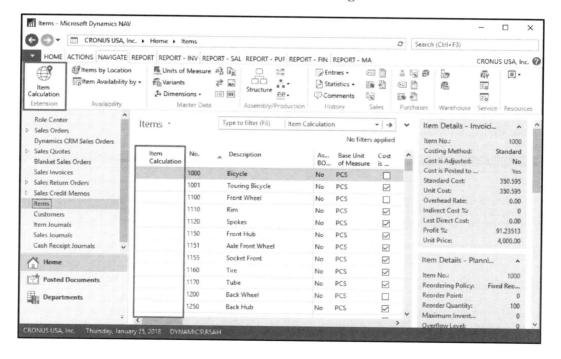

You can also click on the button and see whether it is performing the same task that you intended it to do it by writing code in the **Item Calculation Codeunit** codeunit. This brings us to the end of this chapter.

Summary

In this chapter, we looked at the important concept of integration with an external system in the form of extensions. Our focus was on how to utilize the parallel Microsoft systems in order to increase the productivity of the NAV system. An interface is like a trade route through which the outside world can help your system grow. We learned about the concepts of PowerBI, Jet Express, and NAV add-ons, which can surely make the NAV system more dynamic if used together. We explored how these tools can help change Dynamics NAV to solve some issues with ease.

In the next chapter, we will discuss the future aspects of the Dynamics NAV system. In the chapter, we will discuss the major products that will shape the future of the system and also how the NAV system itself will be upgraded in the new release. This is crucial for all NAV professionals since, in recent years, there have been many rumors about the future changes that might happen.

12
The Future of NAV

In the previous chapter, we discussed how other Microsoft and non-Microsoft solutions can be integrated to a Dynamics NAV system as an extension and can be used to solve some of the problems that are either hard to solve or are not possible to be solved with the standard NAV system. We also understood how Microsoft has built different, closely related systems keeping the connectivity in mind so that they can be used together to meet different kinds of real-life problems.

In this chapter, we will be discussing the technologies that will follow the Microsoft Dynamics NAV 2016 release. Some of the technologies are already present in the market either in the form of a beta or alpha release, while some others are just announced to be released sooner to solve a particular type of mainstream problem. We will also be discussing the basics of some of the successors of the ERP system that should be watched closely.

By the end of this chapter, you should be able to understand the trend for Microsoft customization and development in the coming years. It is obvious that nothing stays the same, but the next couple of years can be considered important years in terms of a major technical redesign of new technologies that are either evolving out of the existing system or are the existing system itself. You should get an idea about this from this chapter.

This chapter will cover the following topics:

- Basics of Microsoft Dynamics NAV 2017 and its major functional upgrades
- Dynamics 365 and its classification
- New development tools and extensions

Dynamics NAV 2017 (10.00)

Microsoft Dynamics NAV 2017 is the latest release of Microsoft, which became available on October 24, 2016. The main modification in the Dynamics NAV system that came in this release is mostly focused on finance, jobs, and items. In addition to these sections, there is significant work has been done in the field of the **Open Character Recognition** (**OCR**) functionality, which is the extension of the OCR functionality introduced in Microsoft Dynamics NAV 2016. Another major change in this version is the ability to cancel credit notes and purchase and sales invoices. It also has account reconciliation enhancements and improvements in fixed assets:

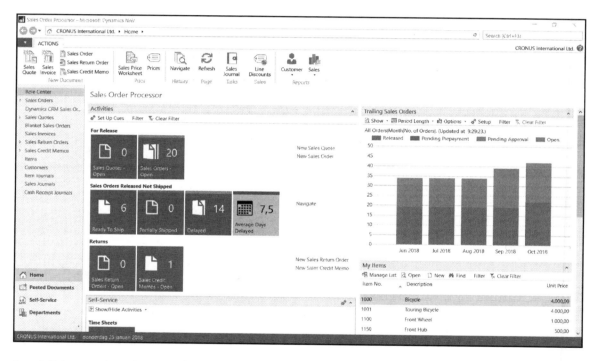

In addition to the afore mentioned major changes, the following are some of the significant modifications that help the latest release cover most of the challenges faced by previous releases:

- Better notification technique for the web client experience
- Dynamics CRM integration in the sales order process, allowing better customer interaction in the orders placed
- The possibility to develop vertical solutions and extensions

Microsoft Dynamics 365

Madeira is the codename for Microsoft Dynamics 365. Microsoft Dynamics 365 is a cloud-based service provided by Microsoft that provides an ERP solution that combines Microsoft's best technologies into a single solution. With the release of Microsoft Dynamics 365, Microsoft has tried to integrate the traditional trend of ERP and CRM and bring the solution together for a variety of solutions.

Dynamics 365 Enterprise

Dynamics 365 Enterprise is designed by keeping large-sized organizations in mind, where the number of users is often large and the complexity of the business processes is high. The Enterprise edition can be implemented for organizations with a user size larger than 250.

The following diagram shows different modules that are present in the Dynamics 365 Enterprise edition. It also presents a comparative view of Dynamics 365 with other similar Microsoft Technologies:

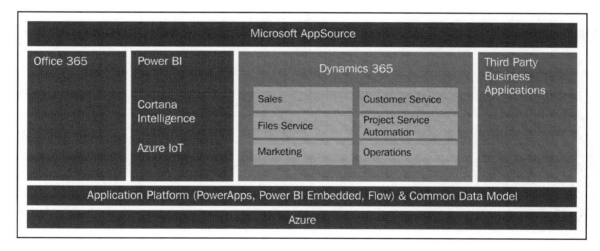

Dynamics 365 Business

Dynamics 365 Business is designed by keeping short- and medium-sized organizations in mind, where the load of concurrent users is generally low. The Business edition can facilitate 10 to 250 users. The following diagram shows the different modules of the Dynamics 365 Business edition:

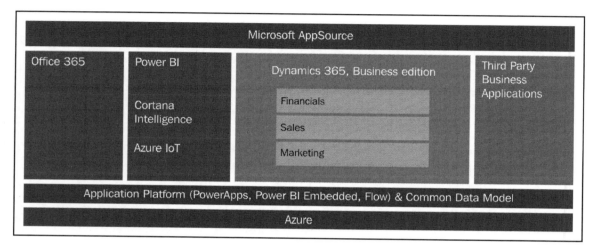

Dynamics 365 for financials

Dynamics 365 for Financials is a comprehensive business management solution. It is designed for small-and-medium-sized businesses that will probably outgrow their existing accounting software. Dynamics 365 for financials is deeply integrated within Microsoft Office 365 so that customers can go all the way from quote to cash in the Outlook experience.

For example, organizations can create **quotes**, **orders**, or **invoices** right within the Outlook environment. Additionally, organizations that like to use Microsoft Word to create their templates can use those templates to create quotes within Dynamics 365 for financials. It also provides solution for other organizations that like to use Microsoft Excel to do things such as data manipulation, reporting, and analysis within a common, accessible environment:

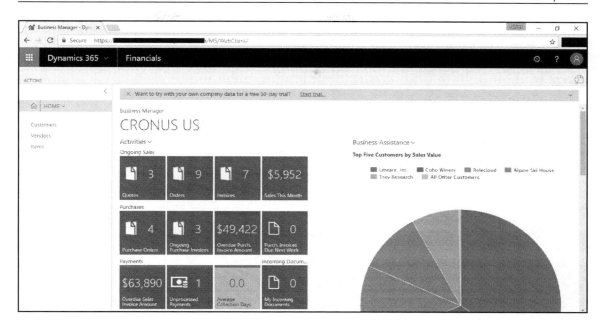

Dynamics 365 for financials is sold exclusively by Microsoft Partners, and financials is also a platform that Microsoft partners can build upon or integrate with other solutions that they have already built. It basically allows customers to get a solution that's tailored for their specific environment or industry or verticals or a particular work problem they are trying to solve with the application. All these apps can be found on the Microsoft App store.

Visual Studio Code (Development Environment)

In order to design the system and extension using the new Development environment, you must install Visual Studio Code first. You can find Visual Studio Code at `https://code.visualstudio.com/`.

You also need Microsoft Dynamics NAV 2017 for this development environment. The following screenshot shows Visual Studio Code:

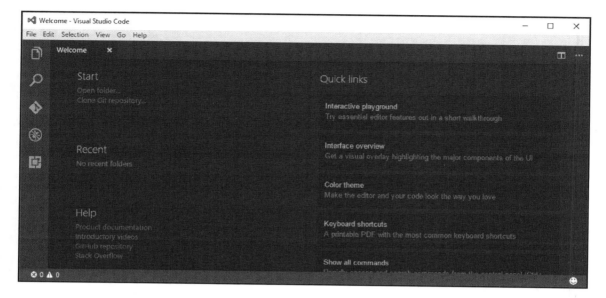

Here, it is easy to create the extensions using this tool effectively. The following are some of the attractive features that you will get with Visual Studio Code:

- Built-in Git command for version control
- Intelligent code completion (IntelliSense)
- Better code navigation and refactoring
- Debug code right from the Editor (streamlined debugging)
- Add extensions to boost your Visual Studio Code experience

After you integrate Dynamics NAV with Visual Studio Code, you can directly open the extension folder in Visual Studio Code by right-clicking on it. The following screenshot shows how close the language is to the C/AL code:

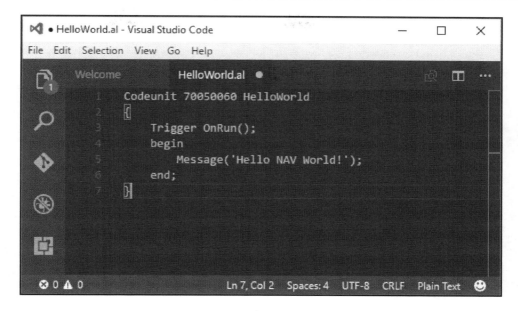

Microsoft has created a project called AL, where you can find the `HelloWorld` code and project, `https://github.com/Microsoft/AL`.

Also, you can submit your bugs and queries regarding any test and failure issues in the project.

Dynamics NAV extensions

Microsoft Dynamics NAV, in future, is going to heavily rely on the development and integration of Dynamics NAV extensions. Microsoft has already released a development environment that is designed to support these activities. We will also take a look at the new development environment in the next section of this chapter.

Extensions in Microsoft Dynamics NAV allow Microsoft Partners and ISVs to extend the functionality of the Microsoft Dynamics NAV product while keeping the source code intact. It is exactly like adding some add-ons to an Internet browser or to your other Microsoft or non-Microsoft products to enhance the experience. This allows you to not only develop all these add-ons in parallel, but it also helps reduce the maintenance cost on the main system.

The extensions package file is most often small in size, but it can also be large depending on the nature of the requirements. It can be easily installed and uninstalled, which gives the customer the complete control over the features that are provided by the add-ons they want to integrate.

 In order to make it easy to install and work with, Microsoft has also released a full suite of new cmdlets using Administrative Shell.

They also can be upgraded very easily without disturbing the core NAV functionality and without affecting the clients working on other modules:

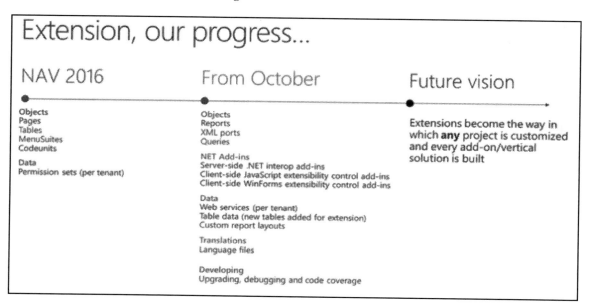

The following are some of the major benefits of extensions:

- Easy to integrate
- Easy to upgrade
- Easy to distribute
- Easy to maintain

Extensions are most often self-managed and self-contained, which eliminates import and merge conflicts. In addition, multiple extensions can also be integrated and run on the same system, allowing the distribution of your functionality in a modular fashion.

You can read more about NAV extensions at
`https://mbs.microsoft.com/Files/partner/All_Products/Readiness_Training/Readine`
`ssTrainingNews/Learning_Plan_Extensions.pdf`.

I have also explained how to get going with Dynamics NAV Extension with PowerShell in
`Chapter 11`, *Extending Dynamics NAV 2016*.

Summary

In this chapter, we had an overview of major future products from the perspective of Microsoft Dynamics NAV 2016. At the time of writing, Microsoft Dynamics NAV 2017 is already in the market, but 2016 is still the most recent and stable release of the Microsoft Dynamics NAV technology. In addition to the future release of Microsoft Dynamics NAC, we also discussed closely related technologies such as Dynamics 365, which is one of the most talked about and most confusing technologies (in terms of figures) of the Dynamics technology. We also took a look at the new development environment, which can be used to develop vertical solutions, such as extensions with a simple interface.

This concludes all the chapters that were selected to be a part of the book compilation. In previous chapters of the book, we studied different techniques to enhance the Dynamics NAV experience, optimize its processes, and make the system secure and efficient. We also discussed different new techniques that are closely related and can be integrated into the system to make it more productive. In some of the previous chapters, we also discussed how to improve our coding experience with C/AL programming and test our code for better output; we also discussed the version control aspects of our code to keep track of our progress and help our roll back changes in any hazardous situation. We tried to cover all the aspects that can help you better understand the system and better harvest its capabilities.

Index